HARROW
TWICE TOLD
COUNTY

HARROW
◆ TWICE TOLD ◆
COUNTY ™

Script
CULLEN BUNN

Art and Lettering
TYLER CROOK

DARK HORSE BOOKS

President and Publisher
MIKE RICHARDSON

Editor
DANIEL CHABON

Assistant Editors
IAN TUCKER and
CARDNER CLARK

Designer
KEITH WOOD

Digital Art Technician
CHRISTIANNE GOUDREAU

NEIL HANKERSON *Executive Vice President* · **TOM WEDDLE** *Chief Financial Officer*
RANDY STRADLEY *Vice President of Publishing* · **MICHAEL MARTENS** *Vice President of Book Trade Sales*
MATT PARKINSON *Vice President of Marketing* · **DAVID SCROGGY** *Vice President of Product Development*
DALE LaFOUNTAIN *Vice President of Information Technology* · **CARA NIECE** *Vice President of Production and Scheduling*
KEN LIZZI *General Counsel* · **DAVEY ESTRADA** *Editorial Director* · **DAVE MARSHALL** *Editor in Chief*
SCOTT ALLIE *Executive Senior Editor* · **CHRIS WARNER** *Senior Books Editor*
CARY GRAZZINI *Director of Print and Development* · **LIA RIBACCHI** *Art Director*
MARK BERNARDI *Director of Digital Publishing*

Published by Dark Horse Books
A division of Dark Horse Comics, Inc.
10956 SE Main Street
Milwaukie, OR 97222

First edition: April 2016
ISBN 978-1-61655-900-7

International Licensing: (503) 905-2377
Comic Shop Locator Service: (888) 266-4226

Harrow County Volume 2: Twice Told

This volume collects *Harrow County* #5–#8.

1 3 5 7 9 10 8 6 4 2

T 112304

DarkHorse.com

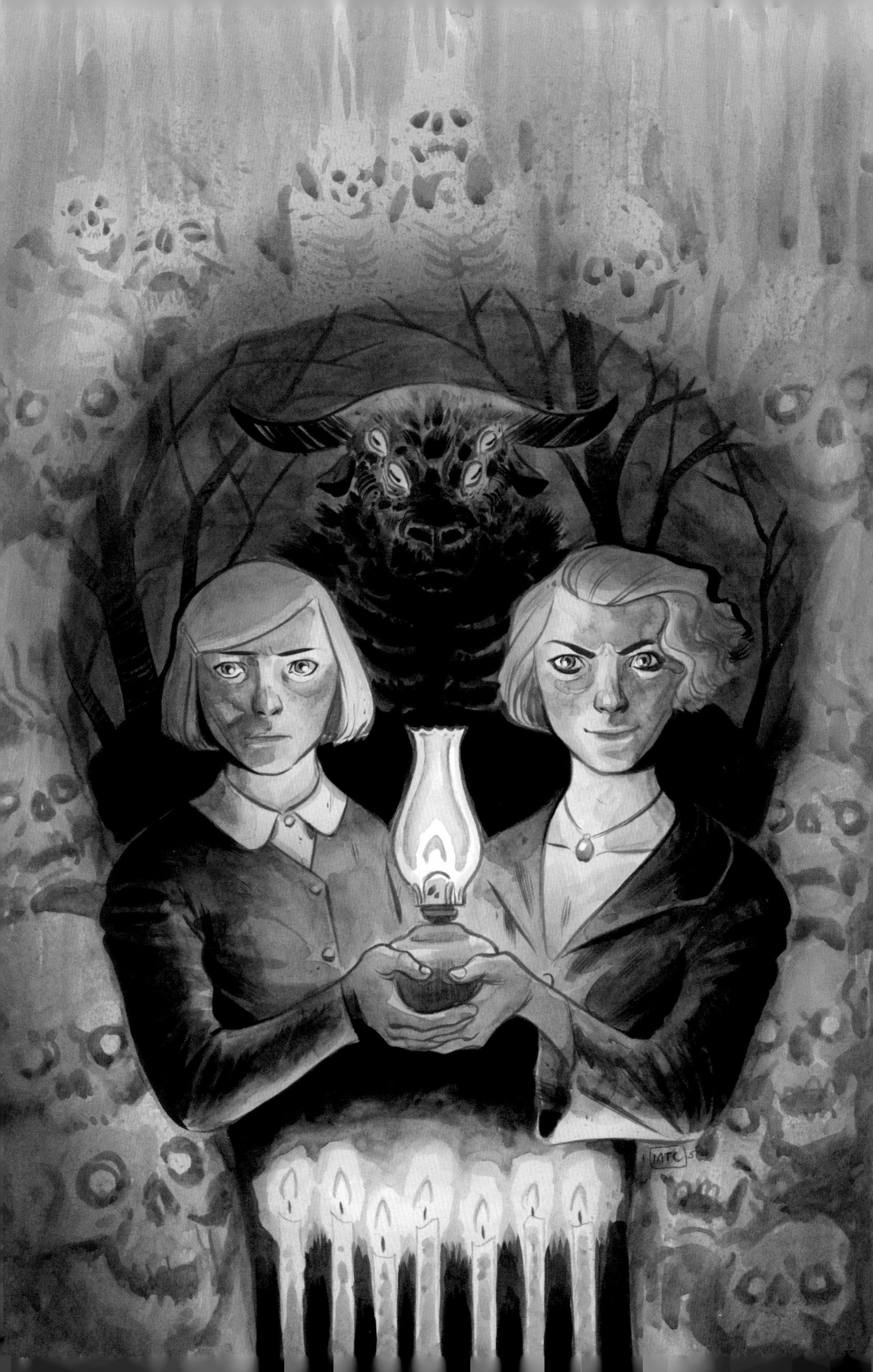

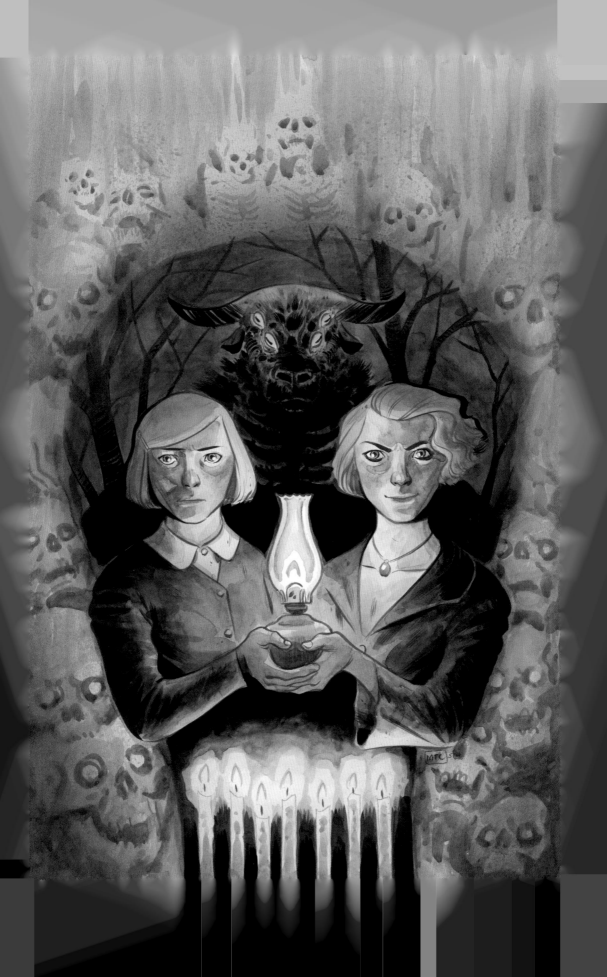

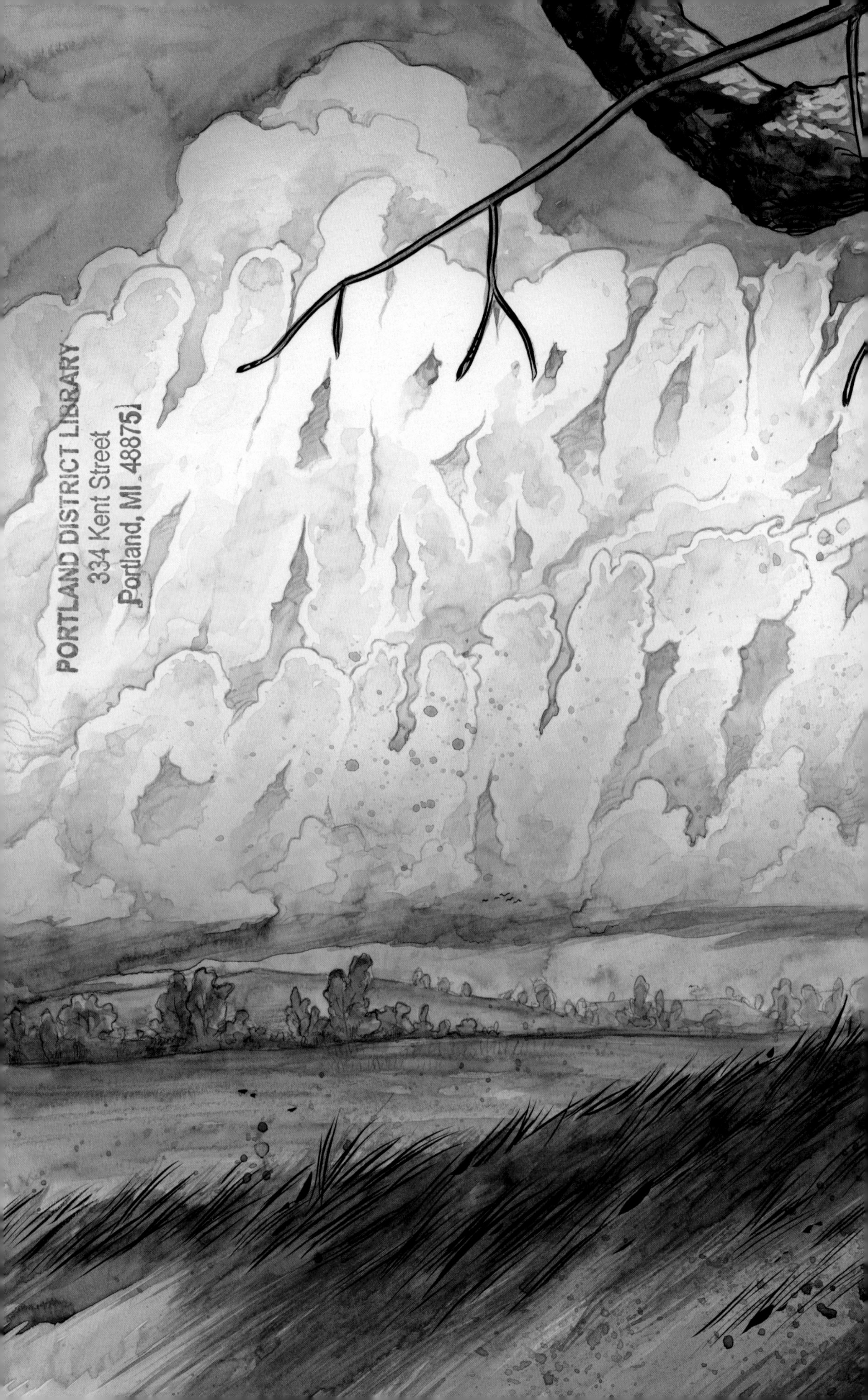

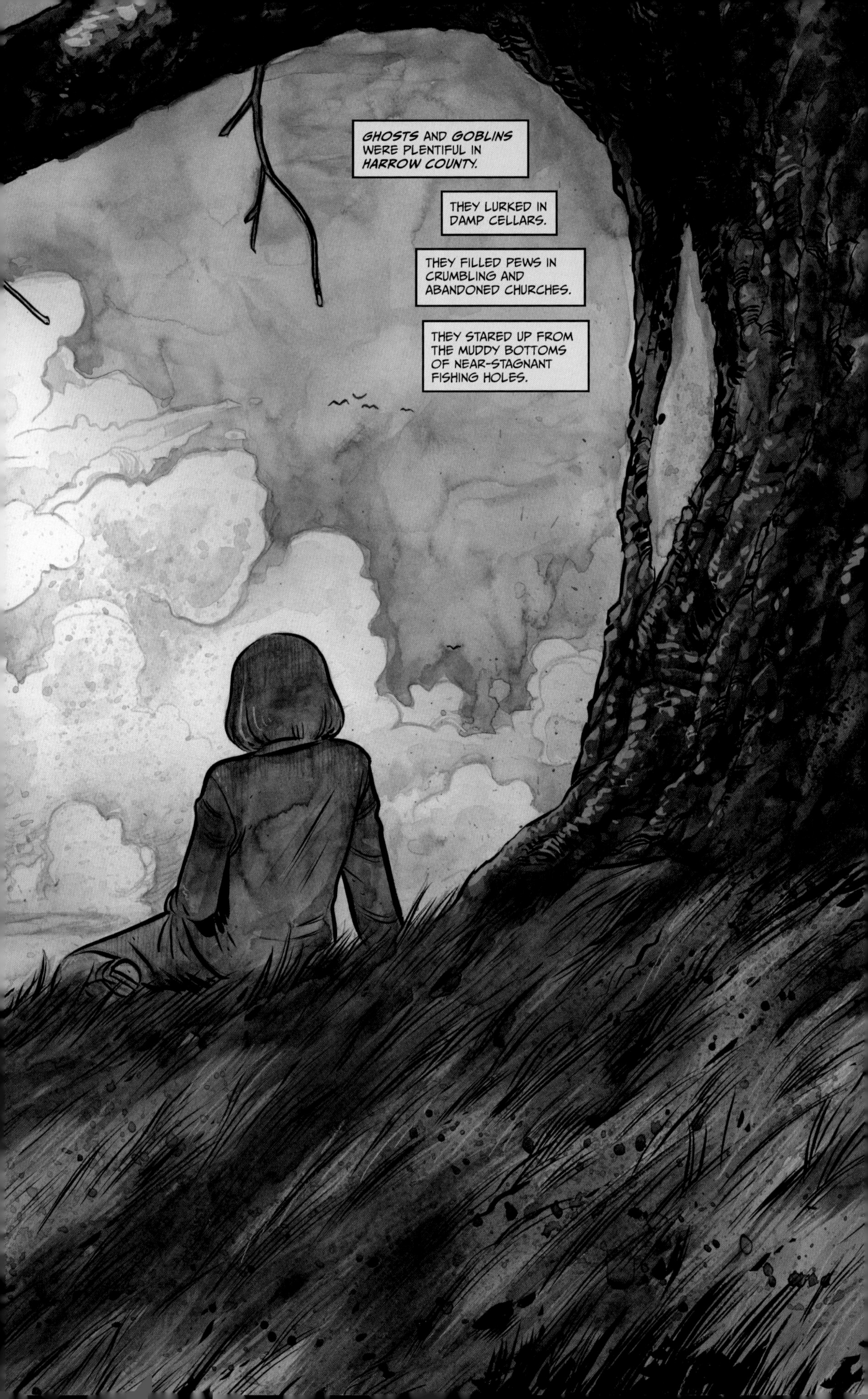
GHOSTS AND GOBLINS WERE PLENTIFUL IN HARROW COUNTY.
THEY LURKED IN DAMP CELLARS.
THEY FILLED PEWS IN CRUMBLING AND ABANDONED CHURCHES.
THEY STARED UP FROM THE MUDDY BOTTOMS OF NEAR-STAGNANT FISHING HOLES.

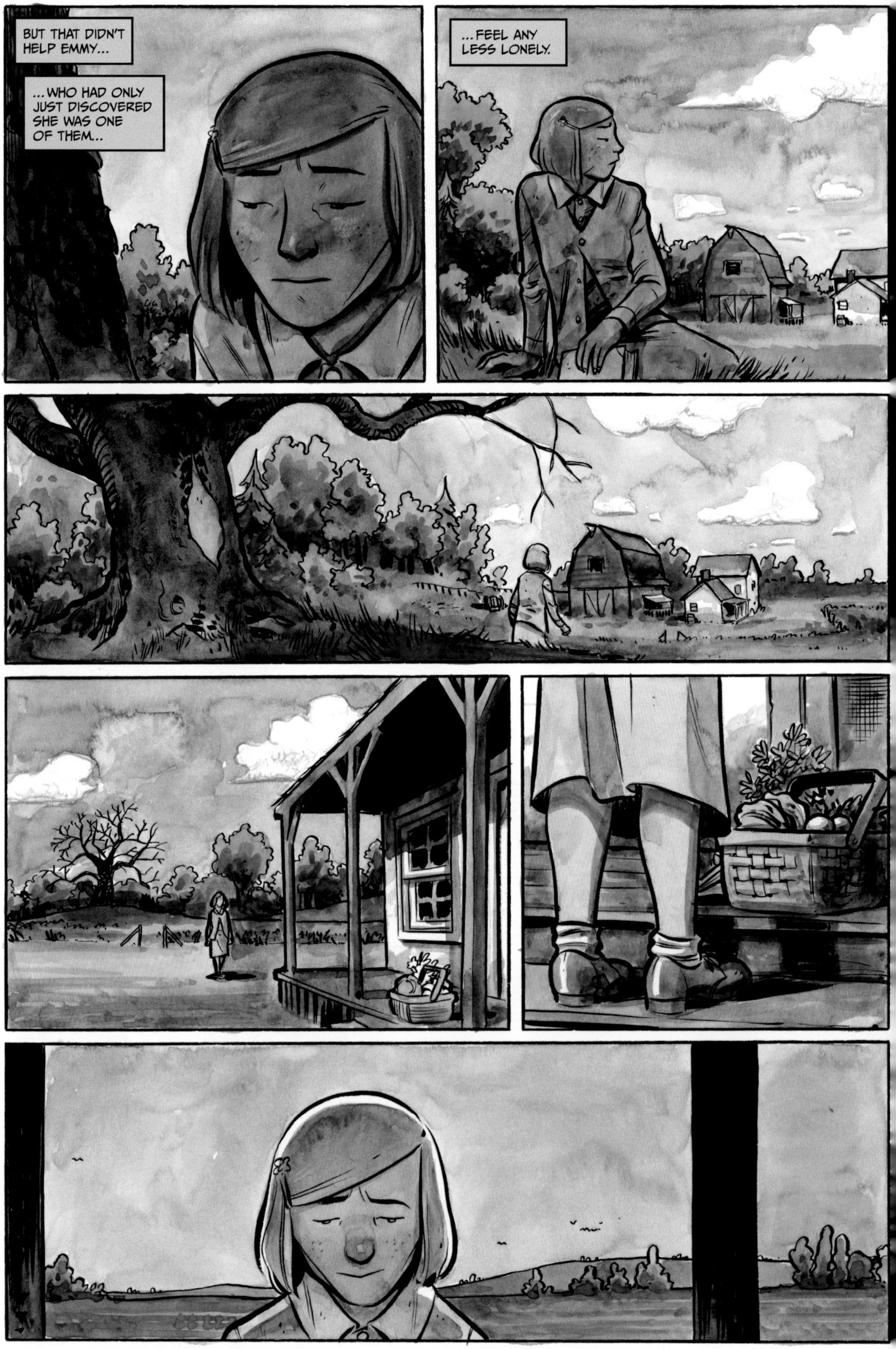
BUT THAT DIDN'T HELP EMMY...
...WHO HAD ONLY JUST DISCOVERED SHE WAS ONE OF THEM...
...FEEL ANY LESS LONELY.

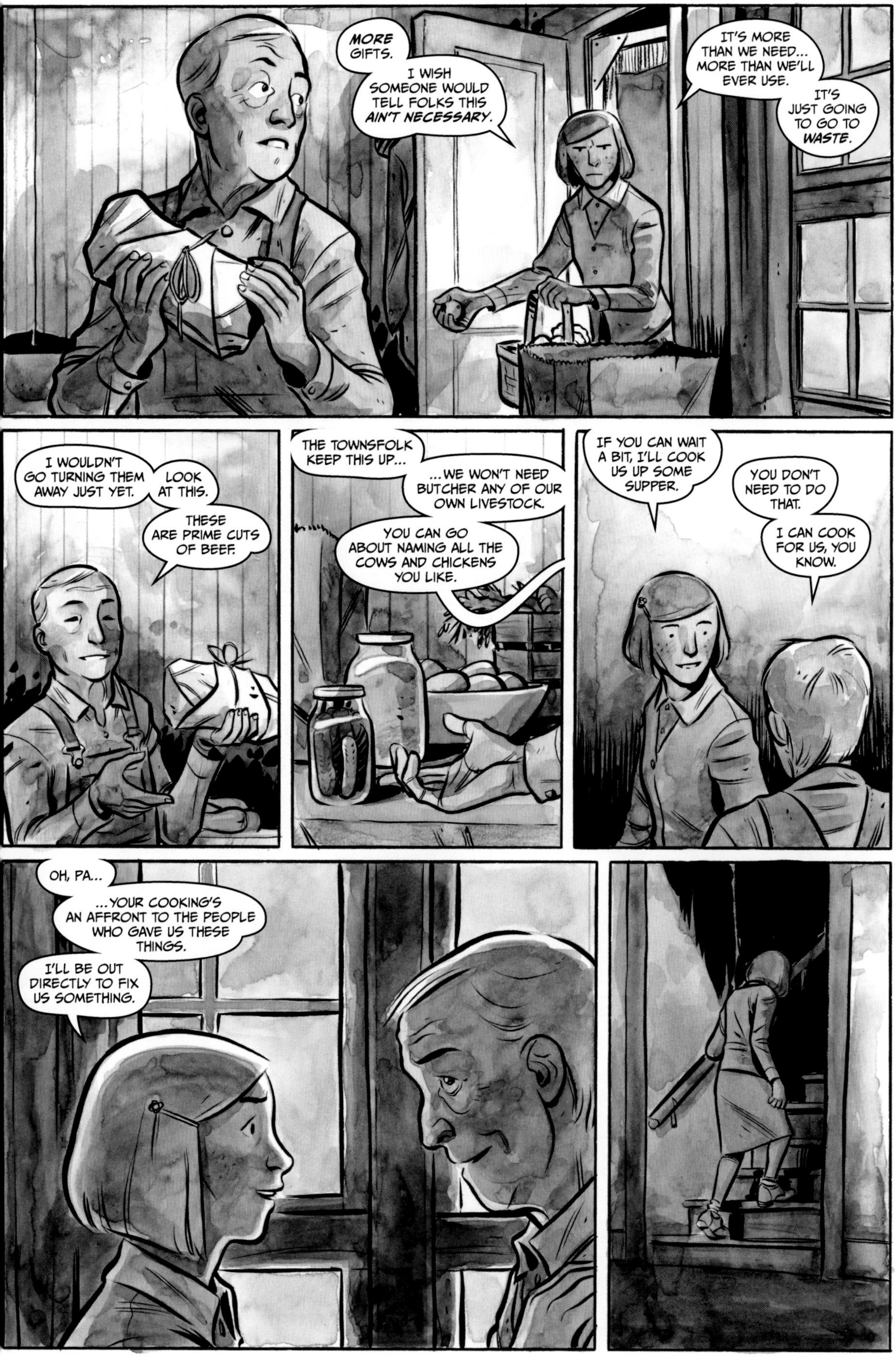
MORE GIFTS.
I WISH SOMEONE WOULD TELL FOLKS THIS AIN'T NECESSARY.
IT'S MORE THAN WE NEED... MORE THAN WE'LL EVER USE.
IT'S JUST GOING TO GO TO WASTE.
I WOULDN'T GO TURNING THEM AWAY JUST YET.
LOOK AT THIS.
THESE ARE PRIME CUTS OF BEEF.
THE TOWNSFOLK KEEP THIS UP...
...WE WON'T NEED BUTCHER ANY OF OUR OWN LIVESTOCK.
YOU CAN GO ABOUT NAMING ALL THE COWS AND CHICKENS YOU LIKE.
IF YOU CAN WAIT A BIT, I'LL COOK US UP SOME SUPPER.
YOU DON'T NEED TO DO THAT.
I CAN COOK FOR US, YOU KNOW.
OH, PA...
...YOUR COOKING'S AN AFFRONT TO THE PEOPLE WHO GAVE US THESE THINGS.
I'LL BE OUT DIRECTLY TO FIX US SOMETHING.

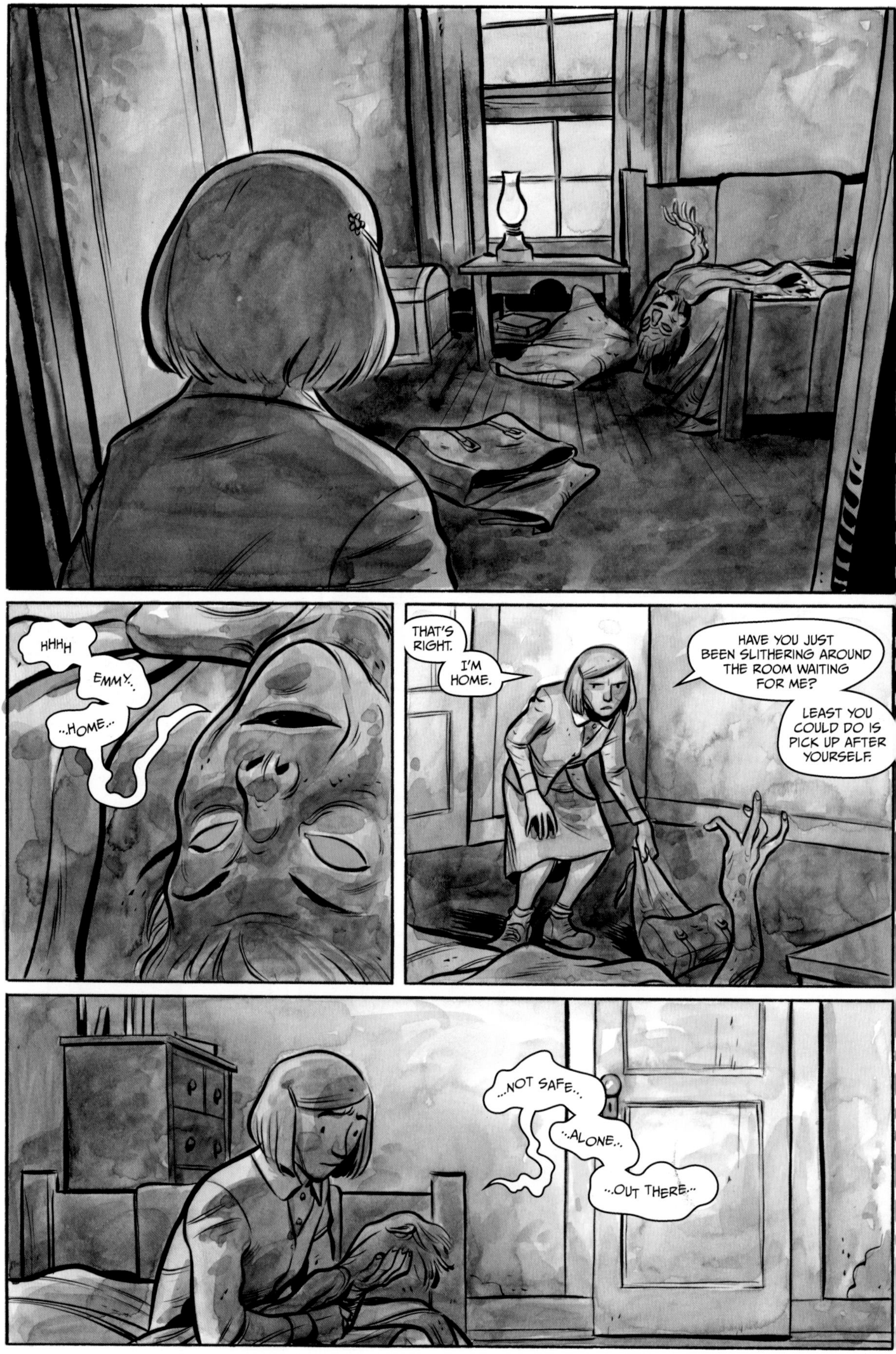
HHHH
EMMY...
...HOME...
THAT'S RIGHT.
I'M HOME.
HAVE YOU JUST BEEN SLITHERING AROUND THE ROOM WAITING FOR ME?
LEAST YOU COULD DO IS PICK UP AFTER YOURSELF.
...NOT SAFE...
...ALONE...
...OUT THERE...

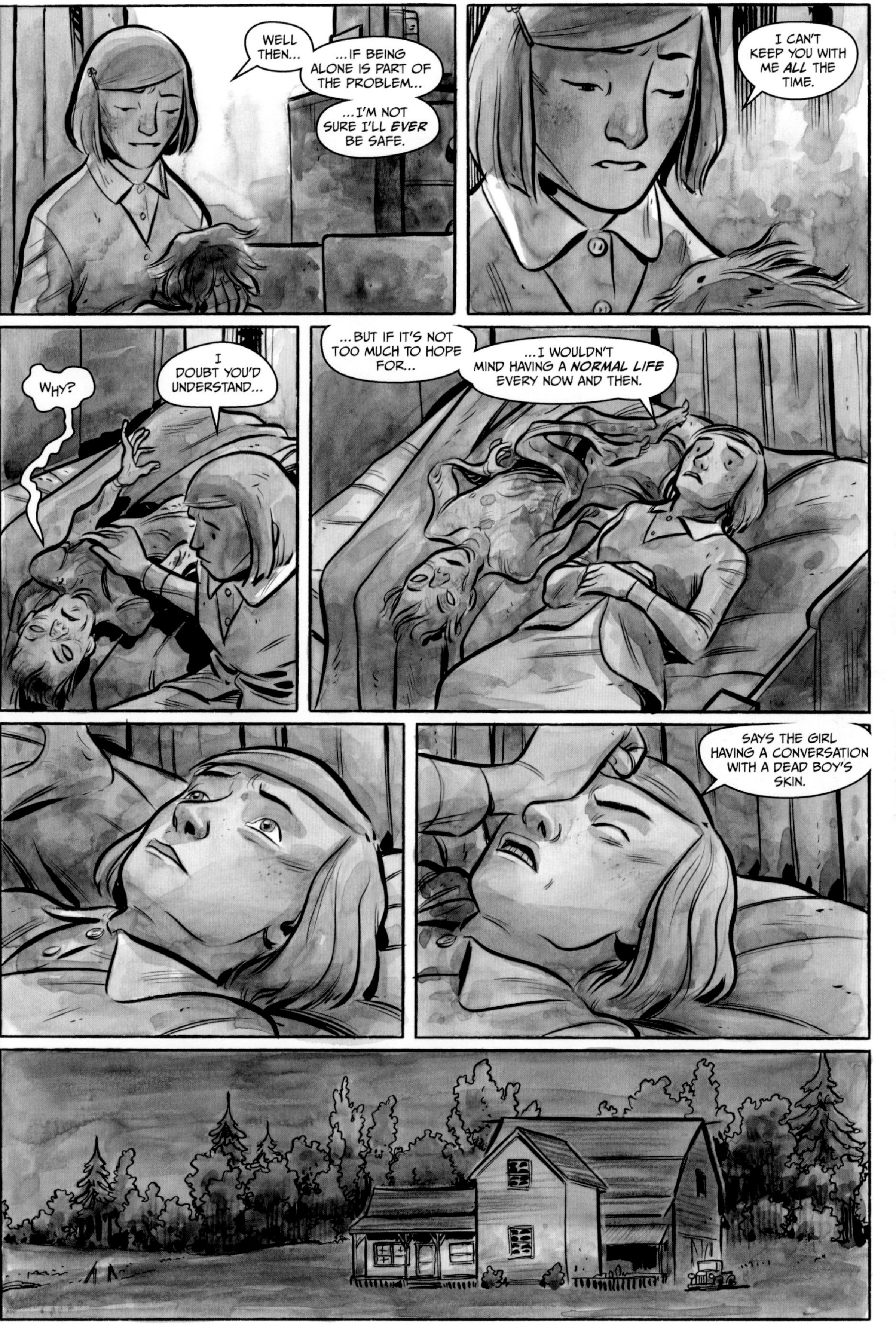
WELL THEN...
...IF BEING ALONE IS PART OF THE PROBLEM...
...I'M NOT SURE I'LL EVER BE SAFE.
I CAN'T KEEP YOU WITH ME ALL THE TIME.
WHY?
I DOUBT YOU'D UNDERSTAND...
...BUT IF IT'S NOT TOO MUCH TO HOPE FOR...
...I WOULDN'T MIND HAVING A NORMAL LIFE EVERY NOW AND THEN.
SAYS THE GIRL HAVING A CONVERSATION WITH A DEAD BOY'S SKIN.

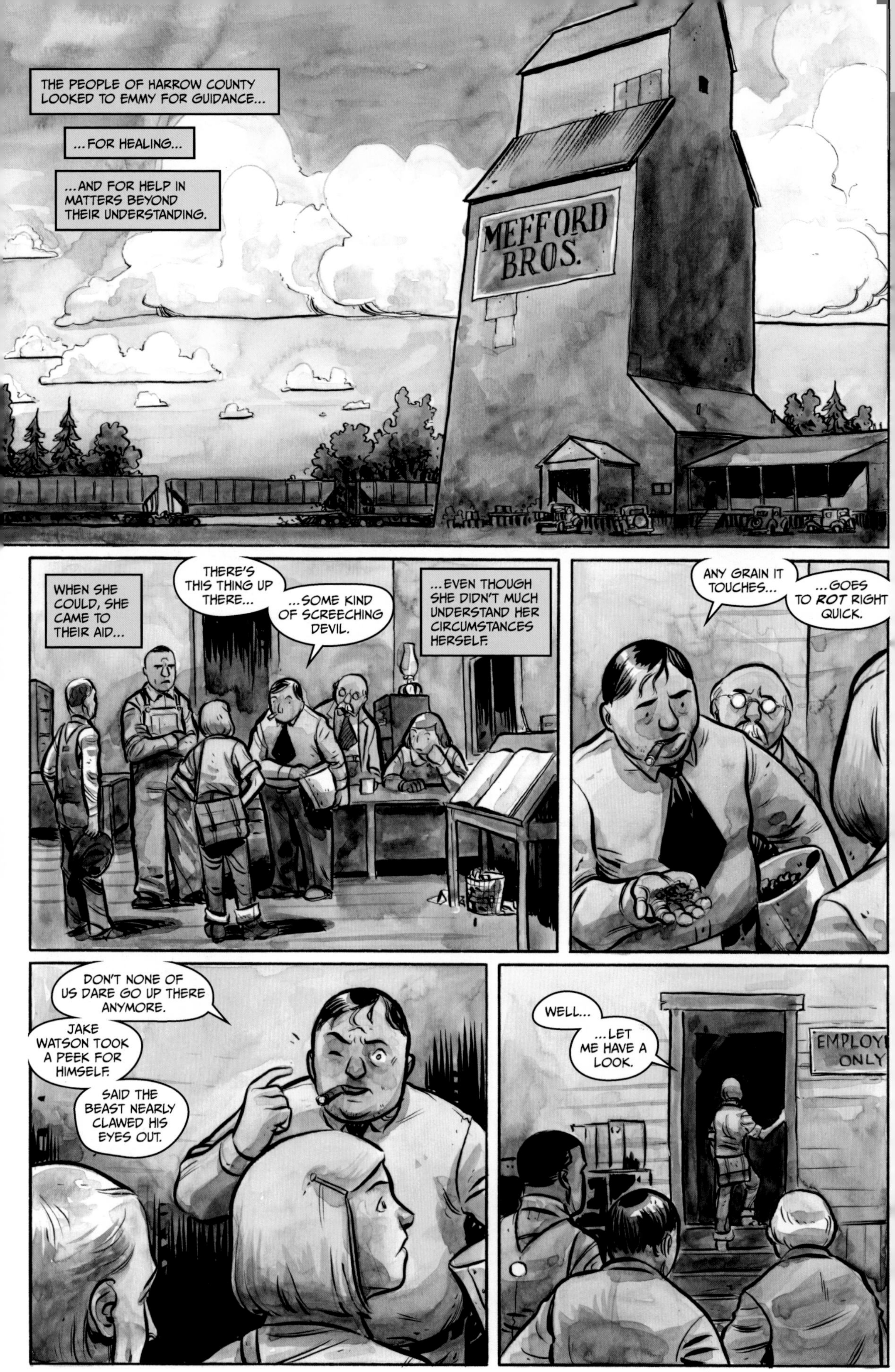

THE PEOPLE OF HARROW COUNTY LOOKED TO EMMY FOR GUIDANCE...
...FOR HEALING...
...AND FOR HELP IN MATTERS BEYOND THEIR UNDERSTANDING.
MEFFORD BROS.
WHEN SHE COULD, SHE CAME TO THEIR AID...
THERE'S THIS THING UP THERE...
...SOME KIND OF SCREECHING DEVIL.
...EVEN THOUGH SHE DIDN'T MUCH UNDERSTAND HER CIRCUMSTANCES HERSELF.
ANY GRAIN IT TOUCHES...
...GOES TO ROT RIGHT QUICK.
DON'T NONE OF US DARE GO UP THERE ANYMORE.
JAKE WATSON TOOK A PEEK FOR HIMSELF.
SAID THE BEAST NEARLY CLAWED HIS EYES OUT.
WELL...
...LET ME HAVE A LOOK.

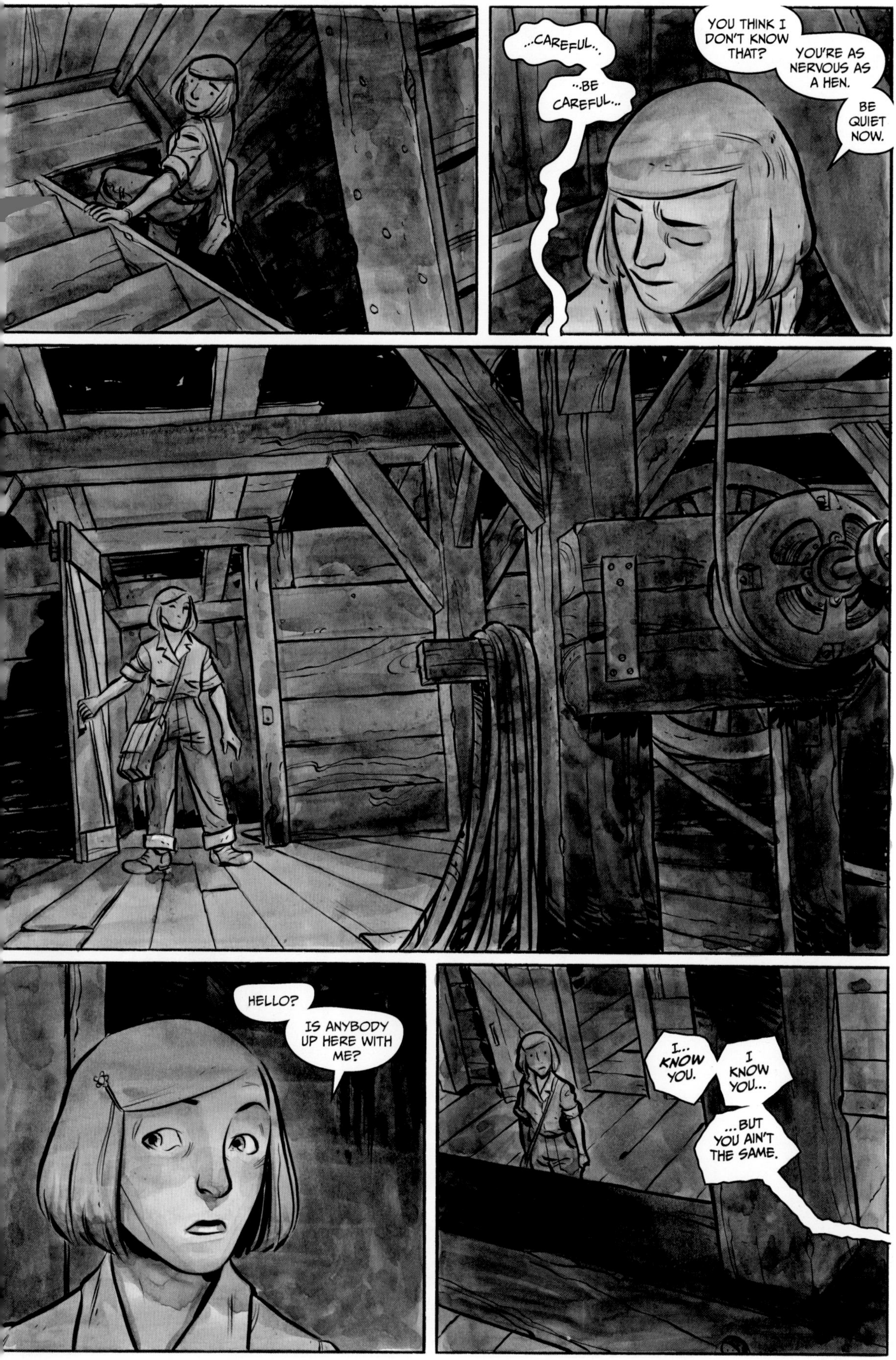
...CAREFUL...
...BE CAREFUL...
YOU THINK I DON'T KNOW THAT?
YOU'RE AS NERVOUS AS A HEN.
BE QUIET NOW.
HELLO?
IS ANYBODY UP HERE WITH ME?
I... KNOW YOU.
I KNOW YOU...
...BUT YOU AIN'T THE SAME.

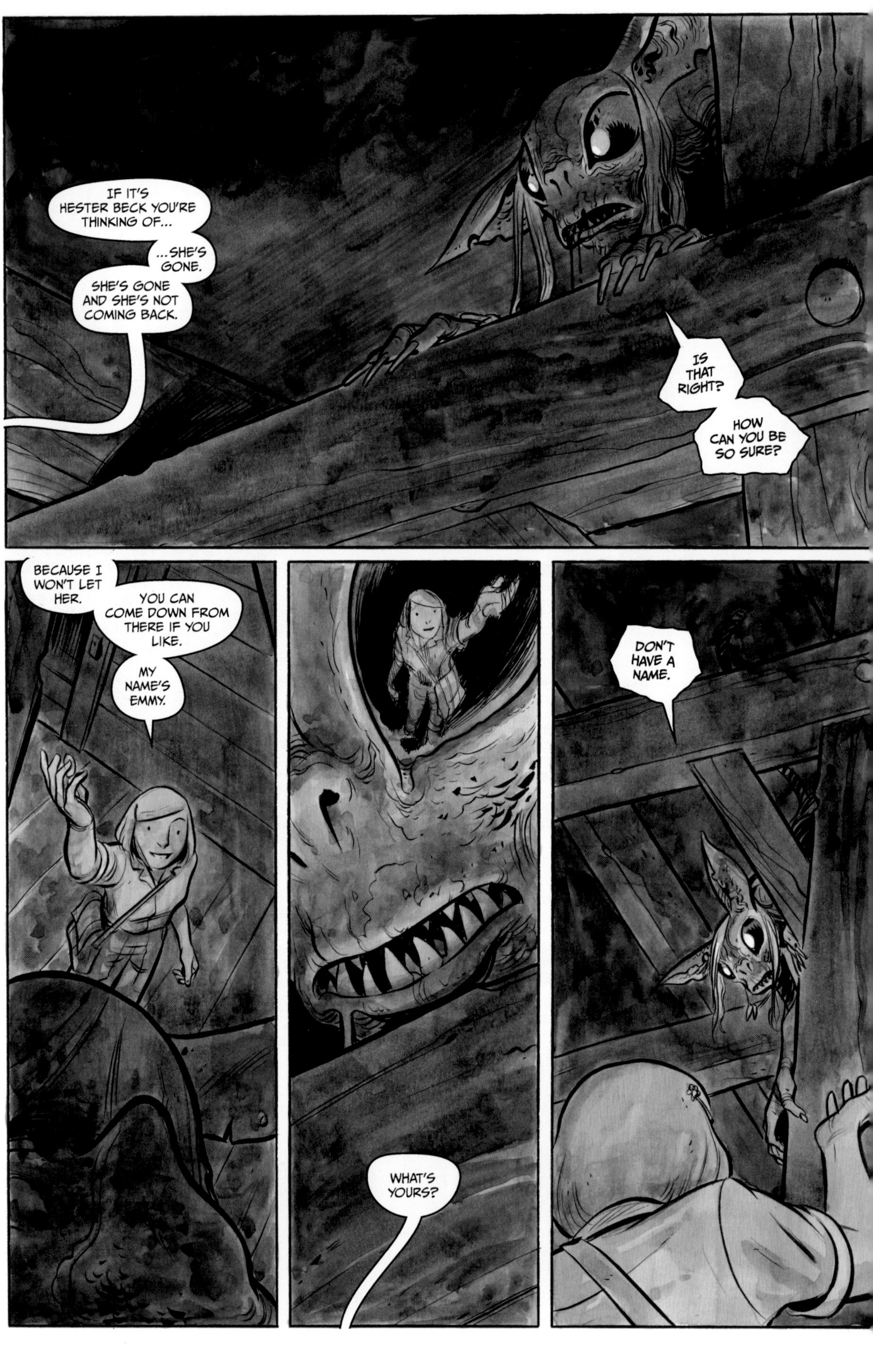
IF IT'S HESTER BECK YOU'RE THINKING OF...
...SHE'S GONE.
SHE'S GONE AND SHE'S NOT COMING BACK.
IS THAT RIGHT?
HOW CAN YOU BE SO SURE?
BECAUSE I WON'T LET HER.
YOU CAN COME DOWN FROM THERE IF YOU LIKE.
MY NAME'S EMMY.
WHAT'S YOURS?
DON'T HAVE A NAME.

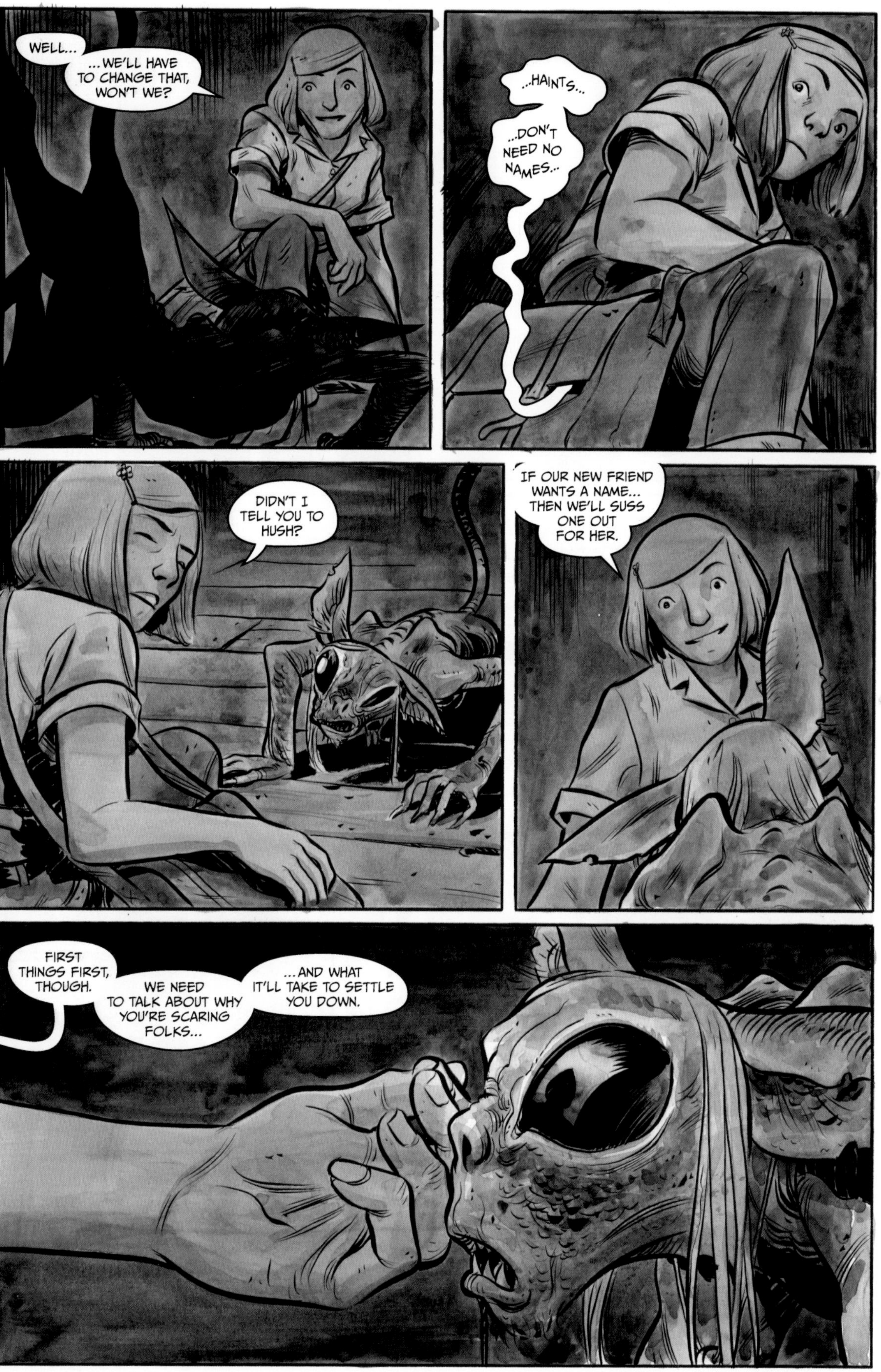
WELL...
...WE'LL HAVE TO CHANGE THAT, WON'T WE?
...HAINTS...
...DON'T NEED NO NAMES...
DIDN'T I TELL YOU TO HUSH?
IF OUR NEW FRIEND WANTS A NAME... THEN WE'LL SUSS ONE OUT FOR HER.
FIRST THINGS FIRST, THOUGH.
WE NEED TO TALK ABOUT WHY YOU'RE SCARING FOLKS...
...AND WHAT IT'LL TAKE TO SETTLE YOU DOWN.

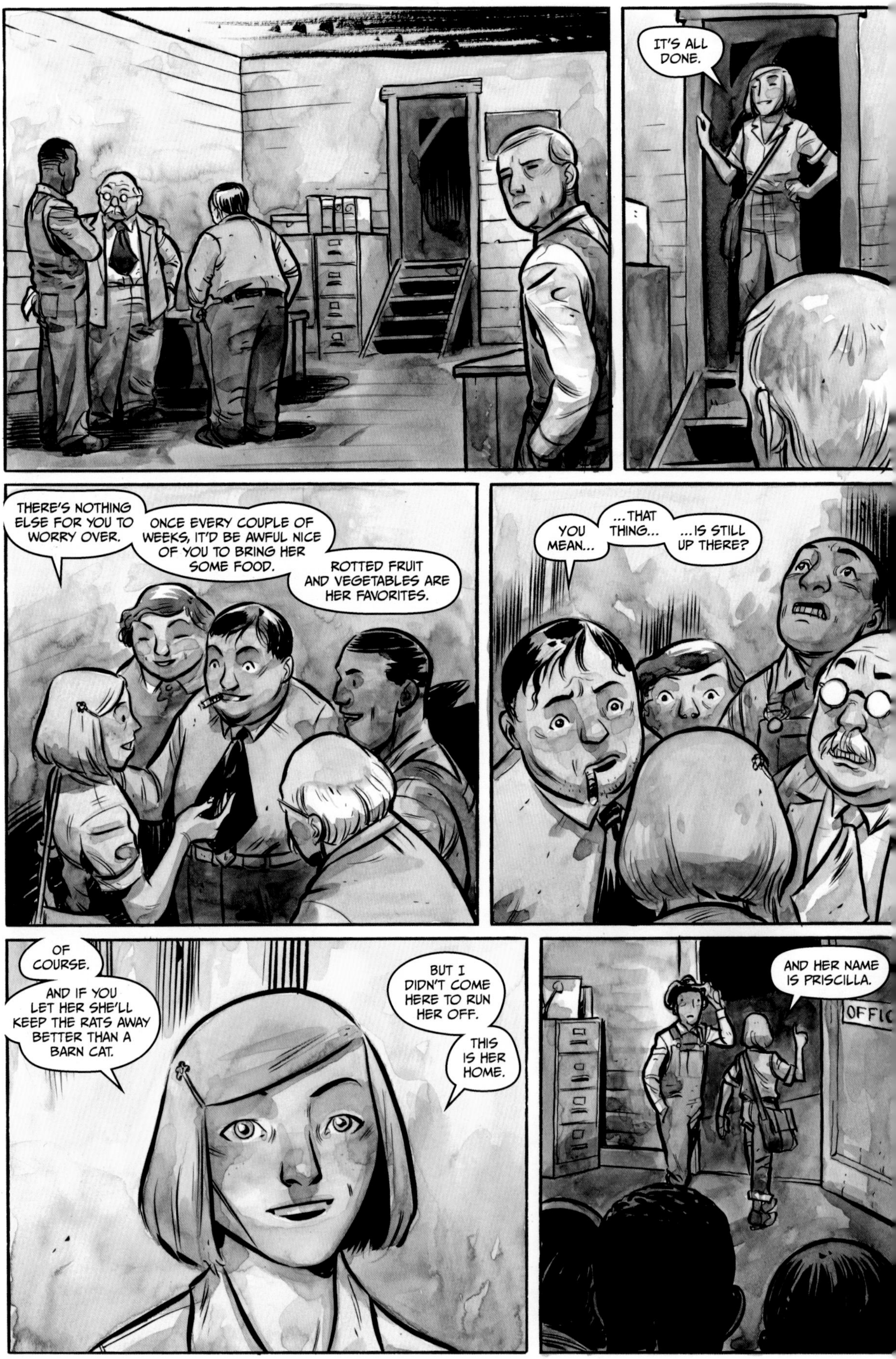
IT'S ALL DONE.
THERE'S NOTHING ELSE FOR YOU TO WORRY OVER.
ONCE EVERY COUPLE OF WEEKS, IT'D BE AWFUL NICE OF YOU TO BRING HER SOME FOOD.
ROTTED FRUIT AND VEGETABLES ARE HER FAVORITES.
YOU MEAN...
...THAT THING...
...IS STILL UP THERE?
OF COURSE.
AND IF YOU LET HER SHE'LL KEEP THE RATS AWAY BETTER THAN A BARN CAT.
BUT I DIDN'T COME HERE TO RUN HER OFF.
THIS IS HER HOME.
AND HER NAME IS PRISCILLA.
OFFIC

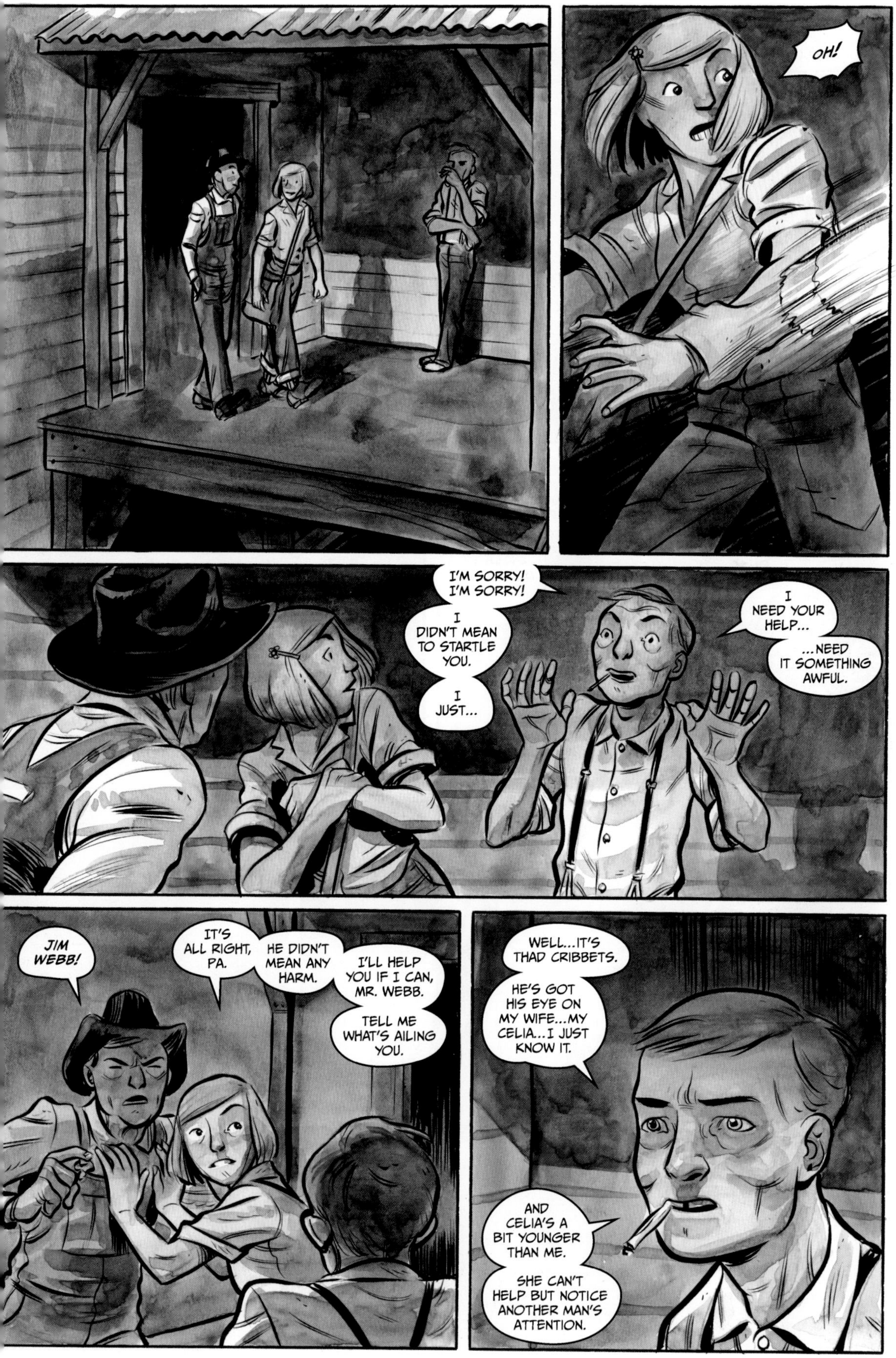
OH!
I'M SORRY! I'M SORRY!
I DIDN'T MEAN TO STARTLE YOU.
I JUST...
I NEED YOUR HELP...
...NEED IT SOMETHING AWFUL.
JIM WEBB!
IT'S ALL RIGHT, PA.
HE DIDN'T MEAN ANY HARM.
I'LL HELP YOU IF I CAN, MR. WEBB.
TELL ME WHAT'S AILING YOU.
WELL...IT'S THAD CRIBBETS.
HE'S GOT HIS EYE ON MY WIFE...MY CELIA...I JUST KNOW IT.
AND CELIA'S A BIT YOUNGER THAN ME.
SHE CAN'T HELP BUT NOTICE ANOTHER MAN'S ATTENTION.

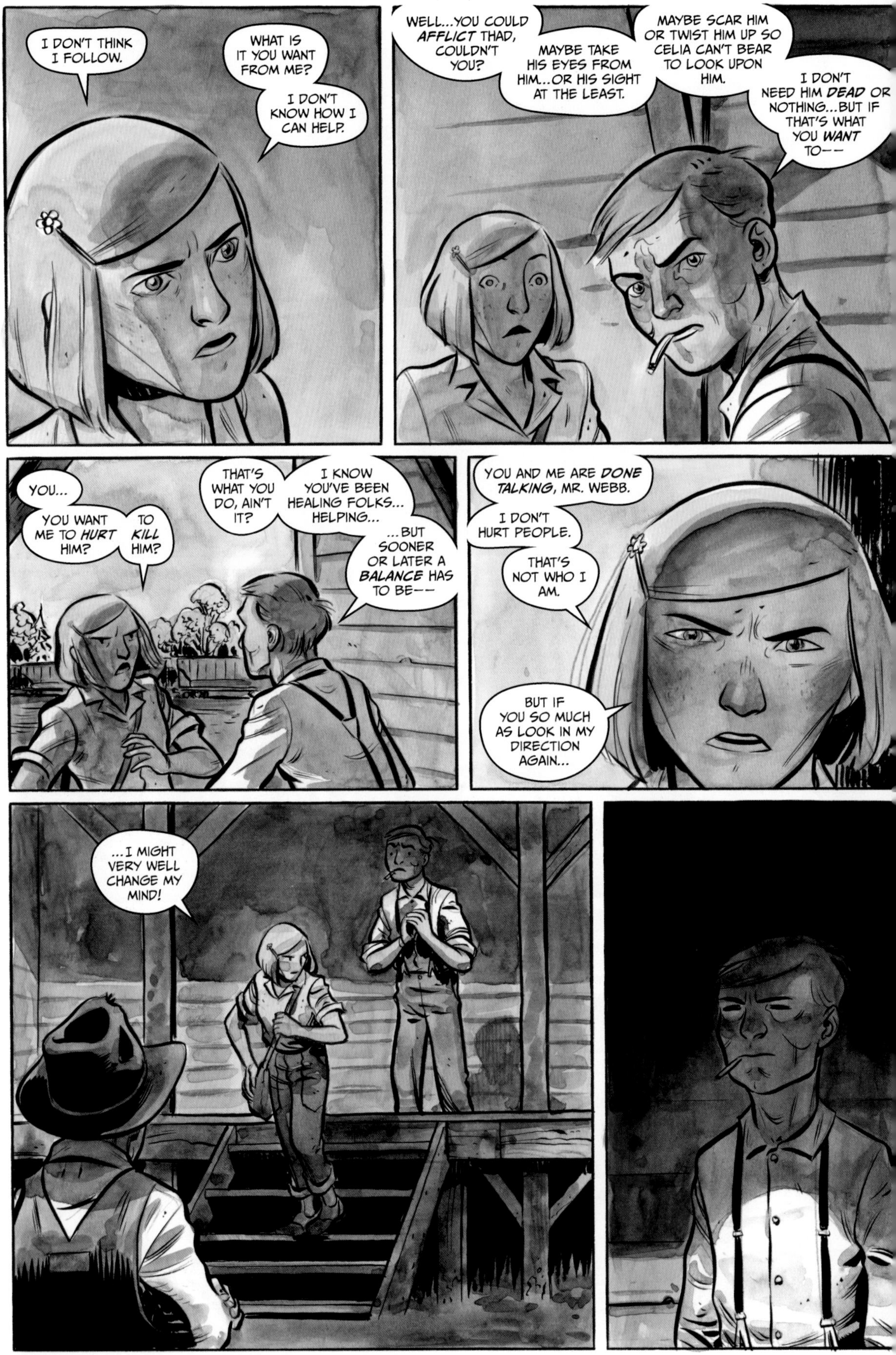

I DON'T THINK I FOLLOW.
WHAT IS IT YOU WANT FROM ME?
I DON'T KNOW HOW I CAN HELP.
WELL...YOU COULD *AFFLICT* THAD, COULDN'T YOU?
MAYBE TAKE HIS EYES FROM HIM...OR HIS SIGHT AT THE LEAST.
MAYBE SCAR HIM OR TWIST HIM UP SO CELIA CAN'T BEAR TO LOOK UPON HIM.
I DON'T NEED HIM *DEAD* OR NOTHING...BUT IF THAT'S WHAT YOU *WANT* TO--
YOU...
YOU WANT ME TO *HURT* HIM?
TO *KILL* HIM?
THAT'S WHAT YOU DO, AIN'T IT?
I KNOW YOU'VE BEEN HEALING FOLKS... HELPING...
...BUT SOONER OR LATER A *BALANCE* HAS TO BE--
YOU AND ME ARE *DONE TALKING*, MR. WEBB.
I DON'T HURT PEOPLE.
THAT'S NOT WHO I AM.
BUT IF YOU SO MUCH AS LOOK IN MY DIRECTION AGAIN...
...I MIGHT VERY WELL CHANGE MY MIND!

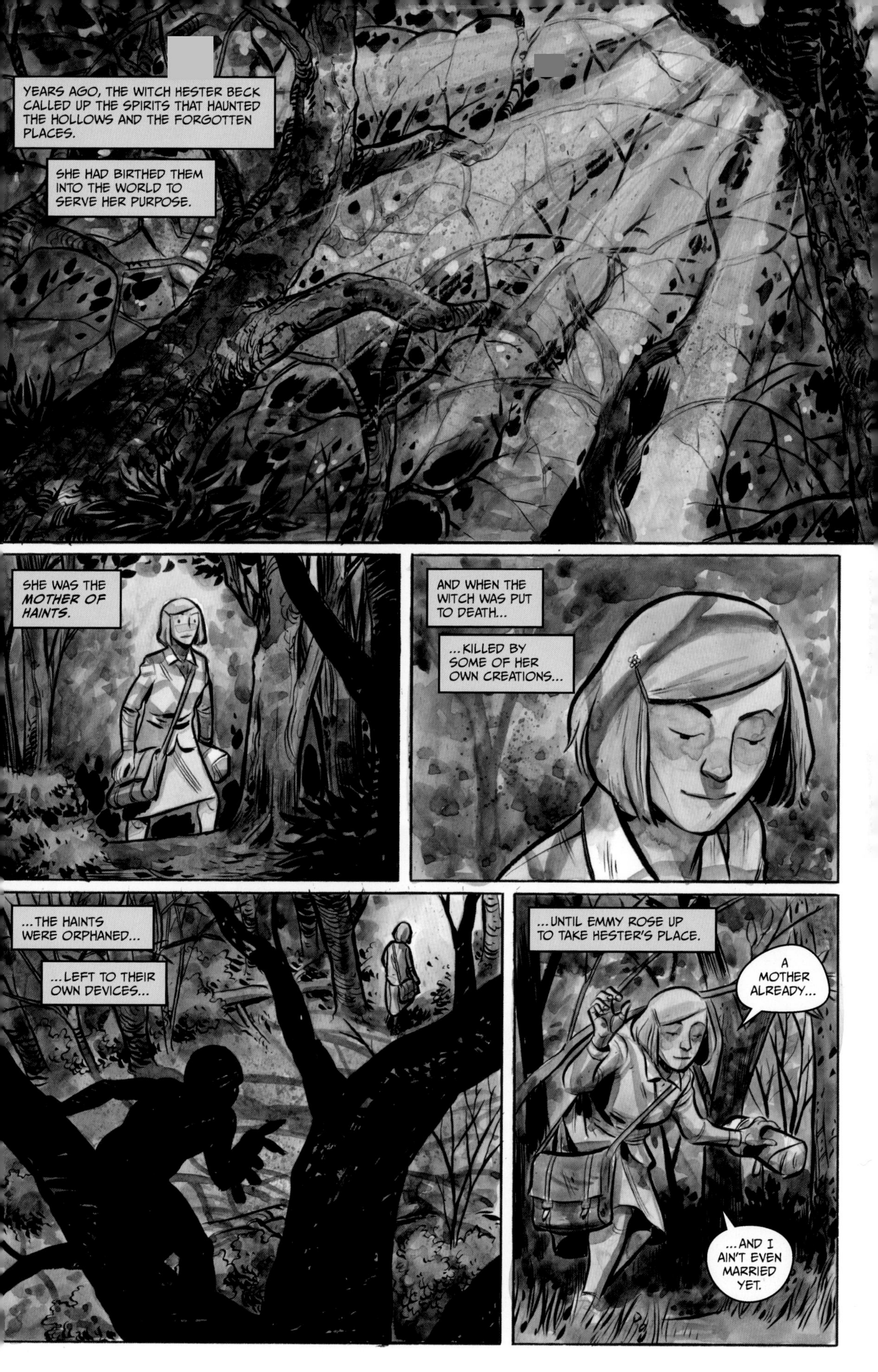
YEARS AGO, THE WITCH HESTER BECK CALLED UP THE SPIRITS THAT HAUNTED THE HOLLOWS AND THE FORGOTTEN PLACES.
SHE HAD BIRTHED THEM INTO THE WORLD TO SERVE HER PURPOSE.
SHE WAS THE *MOTHER OF HAINTS.*
AND WHEN THE WITCH WAS PUT TO DEATH...
...KILLED BY SOME OF HER OWN CREATIONS...
...THE HAINTS WERE ORPHANED...
...LEFT TO THEIR OWN DEVICES...
...UNTIL EMMY ROSE UP TO TAKE HESTER'S PLACE.
A MOTHER ALREADY...
...AND I AIN'T EVEN MARRIED YET.

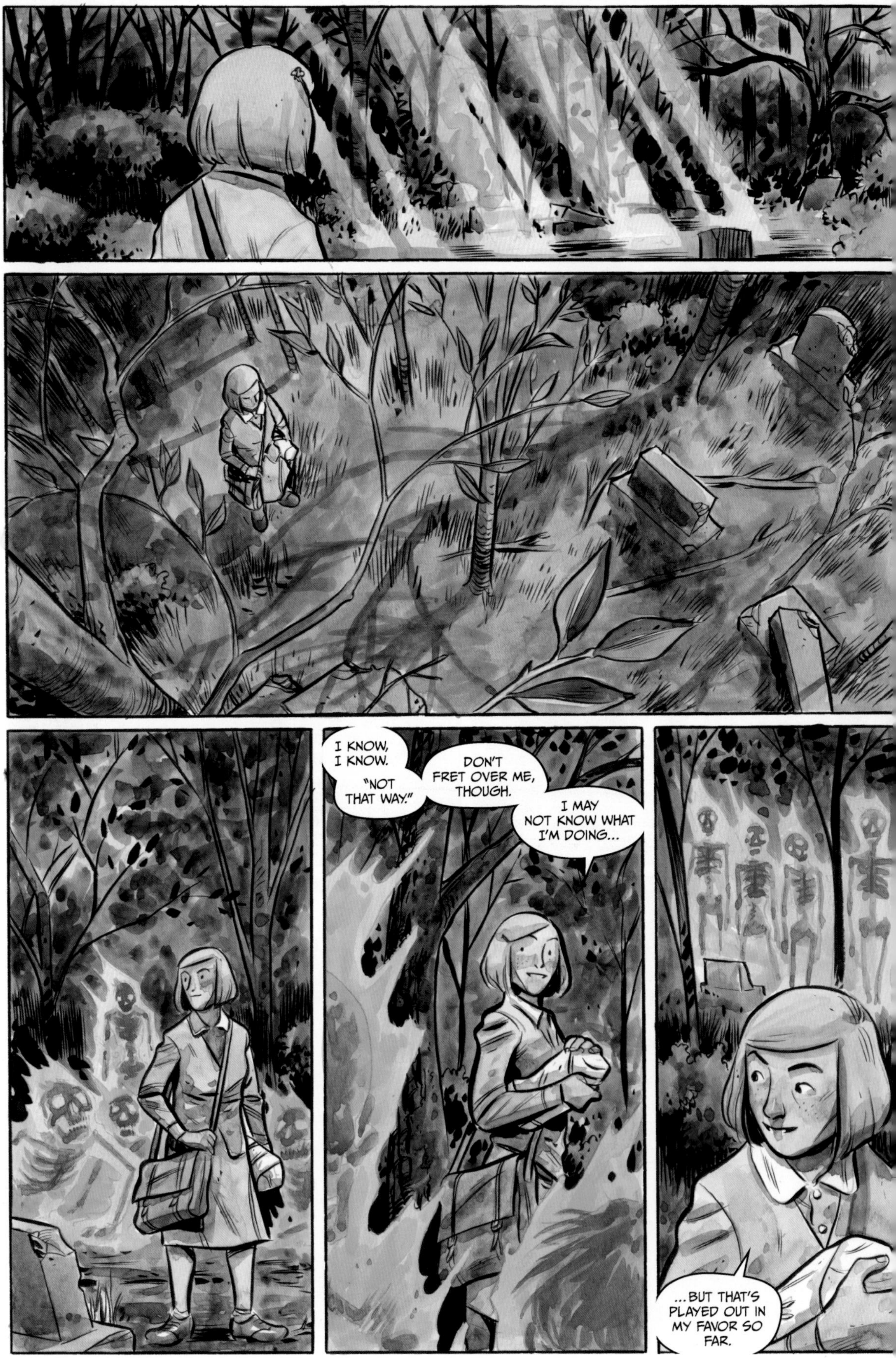
I KNOW, I KNOW.
"NOT THAT WAY."
DON'T FRET OVER ME, THOUGH.
I MAY NOT KNOW WHAT I'M DOING...
...BUT THAT'S PLAYED OUT IN MY FAVOR SO FAR.

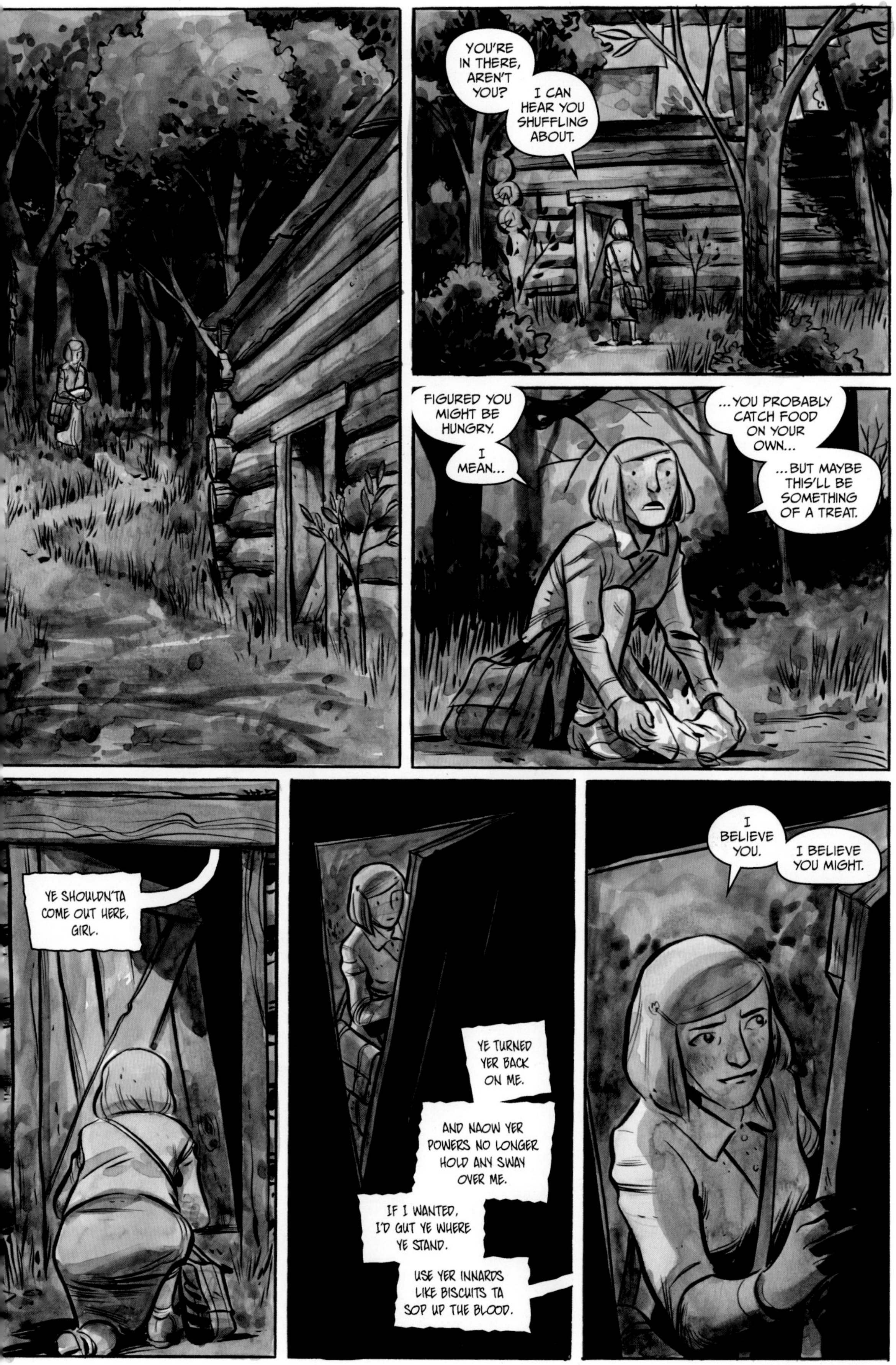
YOU'RE IN THERE, AREN'T YOU?
I CAN HEAR YOU SHUFFLING ABOUT.
FIGURED YOU MIGHT BE HUNGRY.
I MEAN...
...YOU PROBABLY CATCH FOOD ON YOUR OWN...
...BUT MAYBE THIS'LL BE SOMETHING OF A TREAT.
YE SHOULDN'TA COME OUT HERE, GIRL.
YE TURNED YER BACK ON ME.
AND NAOW YER POWERS NO LONGER HOLD ANY SWAY OVER ME.
IF I WANTED, I'D GUT YE WHERE YE STAND.
USE YER INNARDS LIKE BISCUITS TA SOP UP THE BLOOD.
I BELIEVE YOU.
I BELIEVE YOU MIGHT.

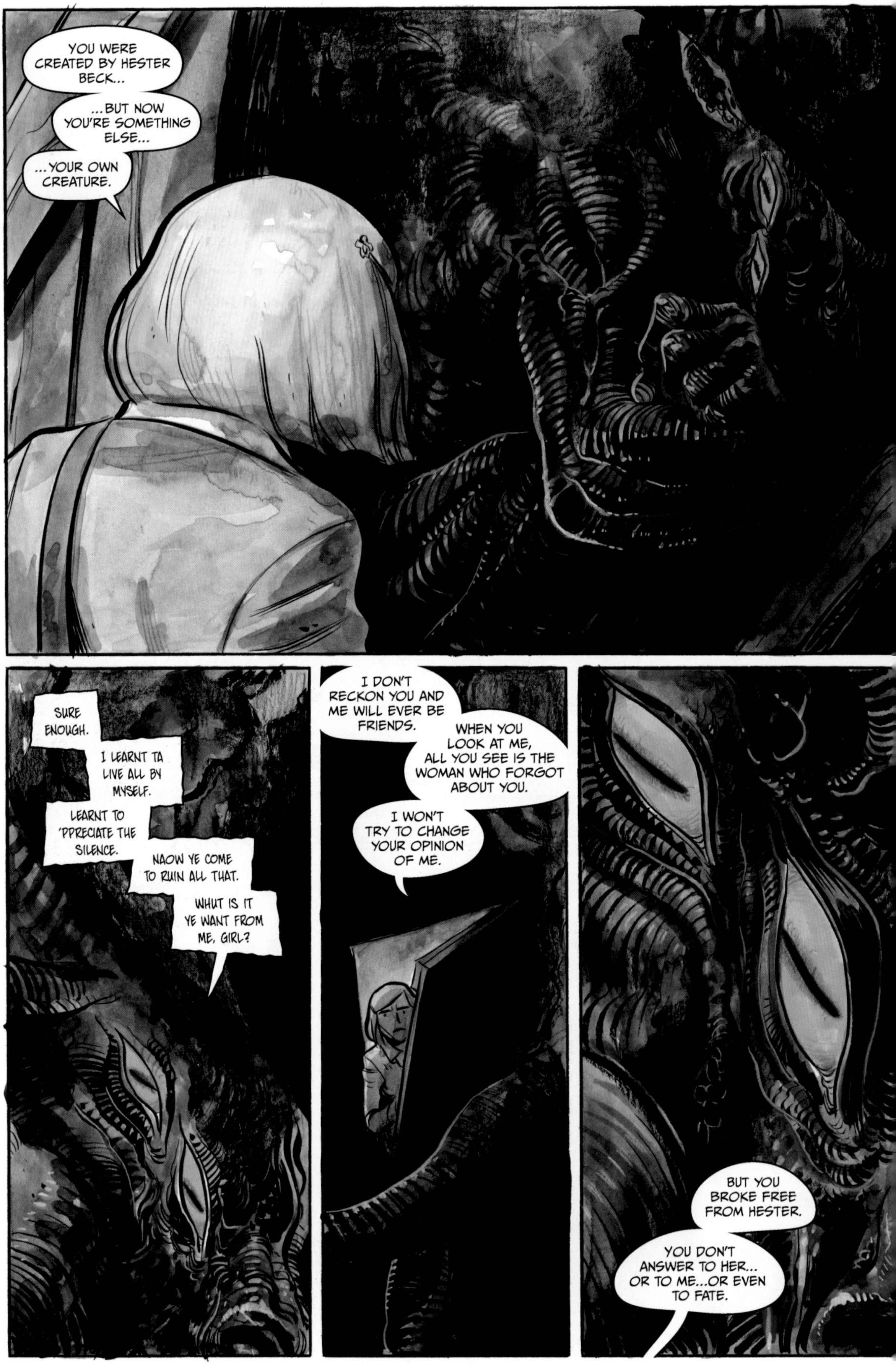
YOU WERE CREATED BY HESTER BECK...
...BUT NOW YOU'RE SOMETHING ELSE...
...YOUR OWN CREATURE.
SURE ENOUGH.
I LEARNT TA LIVE ALL BY MYSELF.
LEARNT TO 'PPRECIATE THE SILENCE.
NAOW YE COME TO RUIN ALL THAT.
WHUT IS IT YE WANT FROM ME, GIRL?
I DON'T RECKON YOU AND ME WILL EVER BE FRIENDS.
WHEN YOU LOOK AT ME, ALL YOU SEE IS THE WOMAN WHO FORGOT ABOUT YOU.
I WON'T TRY TO CHANGE YOUR OPINION OF ME.
BUT YOU BROKE FREE FROM HESTER.
YOU DON'T ANSWER TO HER... OR TO ME...OR EVEN TO FATE.

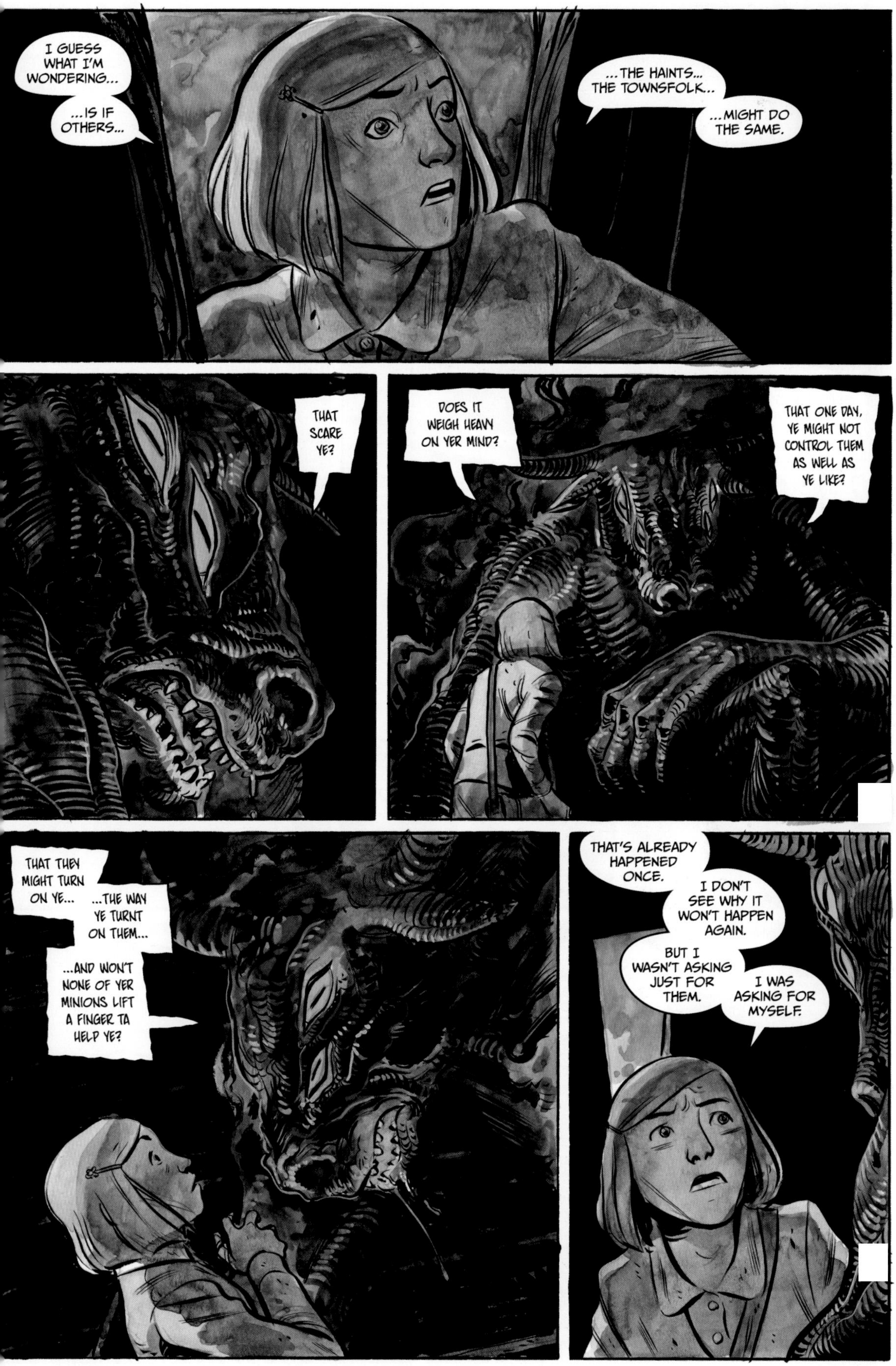
I GUESS WHAT I'M WONDERING...
...IS IF OTHERS...
...THE HAINTS... THE TOWNSFOLK...
...MIGHT DO THE SAME.
THAT SCARE YE?
DOES IT WEIGH HEAVY ON YER MIND?
THAT ONE DAY, YE MIGHT NOT CONTROL THEM AS WELL AS YE LIKE?
THAT THEY MIGHT TURN ON YE...
...THE WAY YE TURNT ON THEM...
...AND WON'T NONE OF YER MINIONS LIFT A FINGER TA HELP YE?
THAT'S ALREADY HAPPENED ONCE.
I DON'T SEE WHY IT WON'T HAPPEN AGAIN.
BUT I WASN'T ASKING JUST FOR THEM.
I WAS ASKING FOR MYSELF.

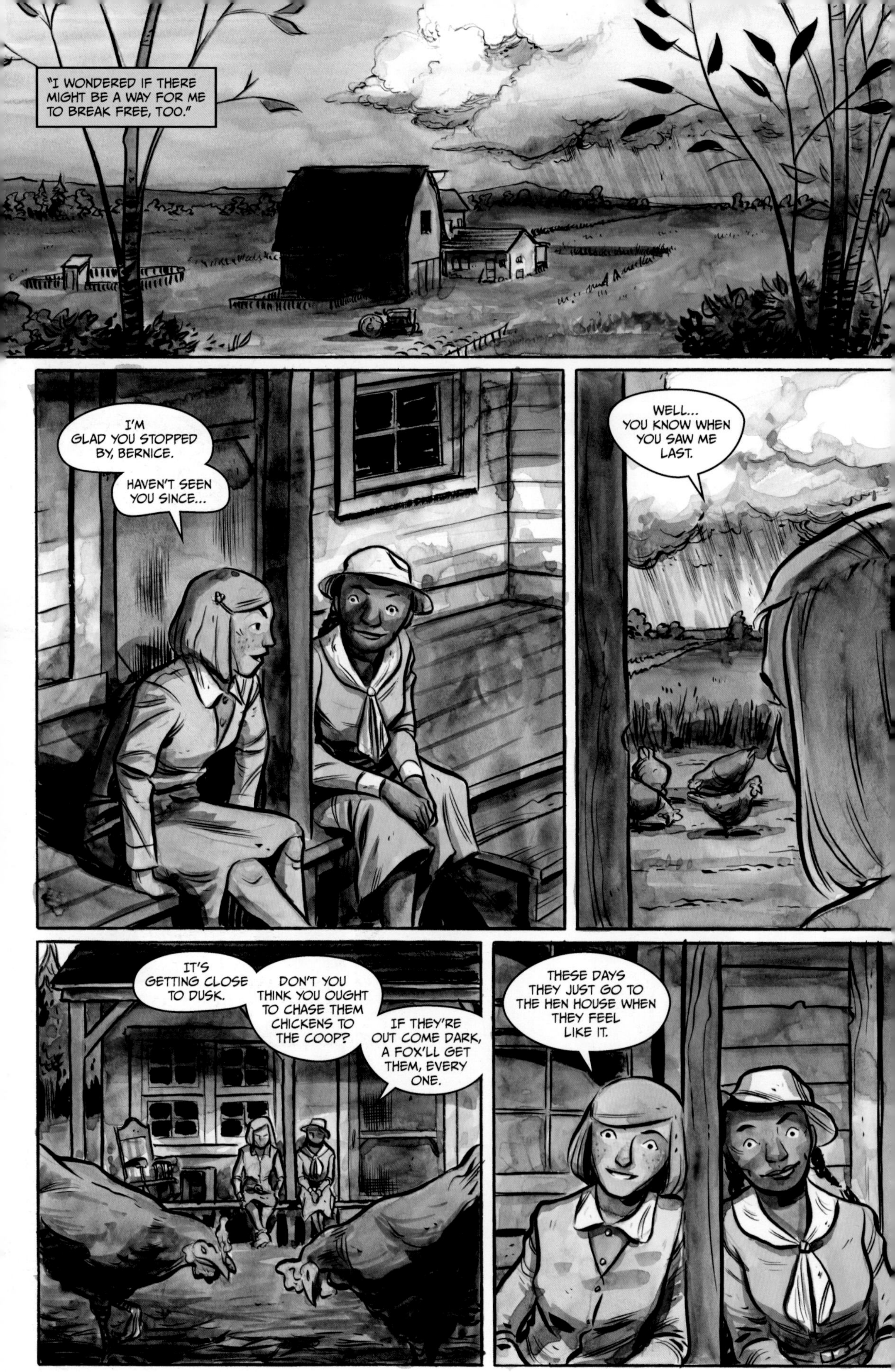
"I WONDERED IF THERE MIGHT BE A WAY FOR ME TO BREAK FREE, TOO."
I'M GLAD YOU STOPPED BY, BERNICE.
HAVEN'T SEEN YOU SINCE...
WELL... YOU KNOW WHEN YOU SAW ME LAST.
IT'S GETTING CLOSE TO DUSK.
DON'T YOU THINK YOU OUGHT TO CHASE THEM CHICKENS TO THE COOP?
IF THEY'RE OUT COME DARK, A FOX'LL GET THEM, EVERY ONE.
THESE DAYS THEY JUST GO TO THE HEN HOUSE WHEN THEY FEEL LIKE IT.

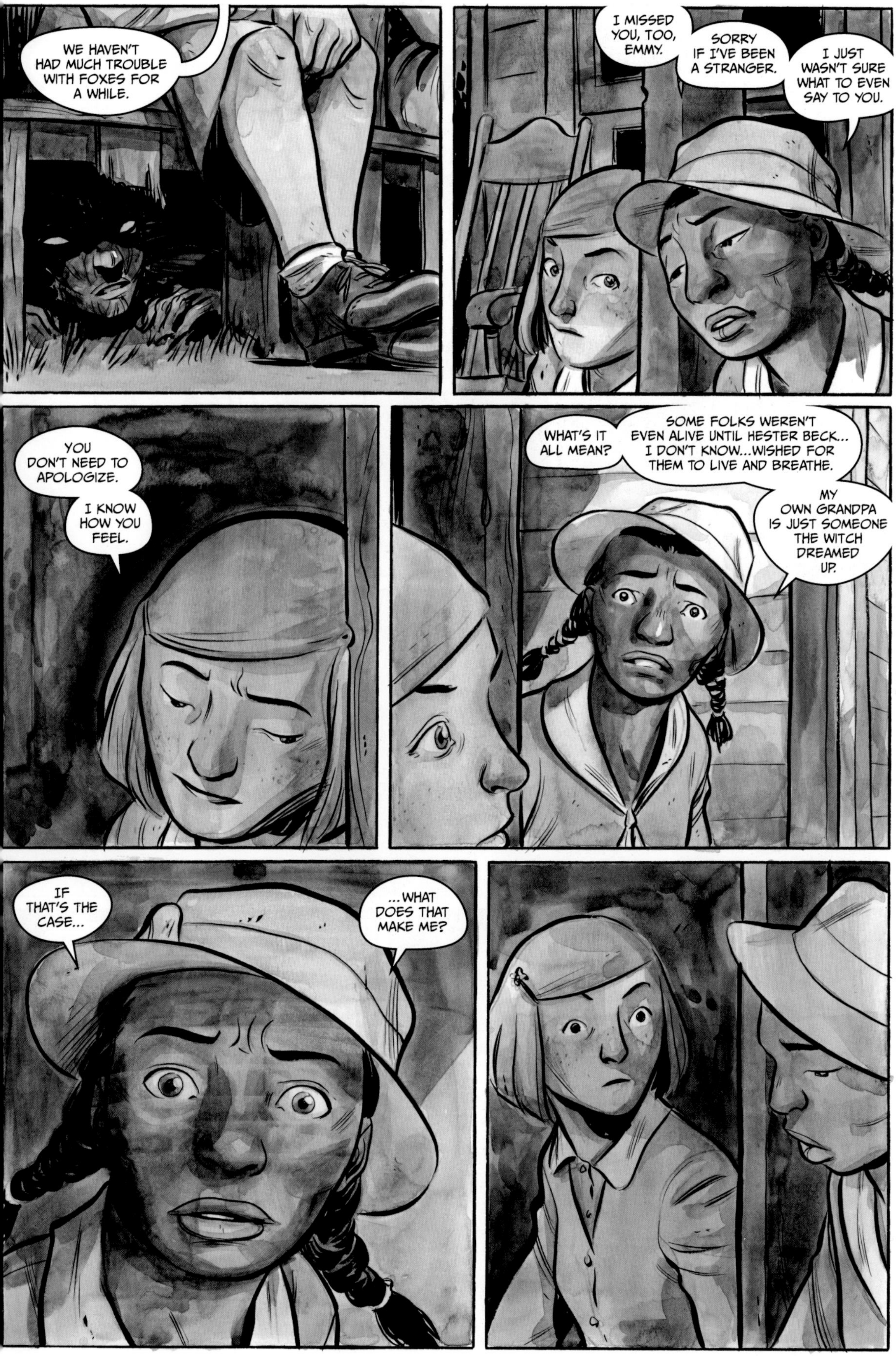
WE HAVEN'T HAD MUCH TROUBLE WITH FOXES FOR A WHILE.
I MISSED YOU, TOO, EMMY.
SORRY IF I'VE BEEN A STRANGER.
I JUST WASN'T SURE WHAT TO EVEN SAY TO YOU.
YOU DON'T NEED TO APOLOGIZE.
I KNOW HOW YOU FEEL.
WHAT'S IT ALL MEAN?
SOME FOLKS WEREN'T EVEN ALIVE UNTIL HESTER BECK... I DON'T KNOW...WISHED FOR THEM TO LIVE AND BREATHE.
MY OWN GRANDPA IS JUST SOMEONE THE WITCH DREAMED UP.
IF THAT'S THE CASE...
...WHAT DOES THAT MAKE ME?

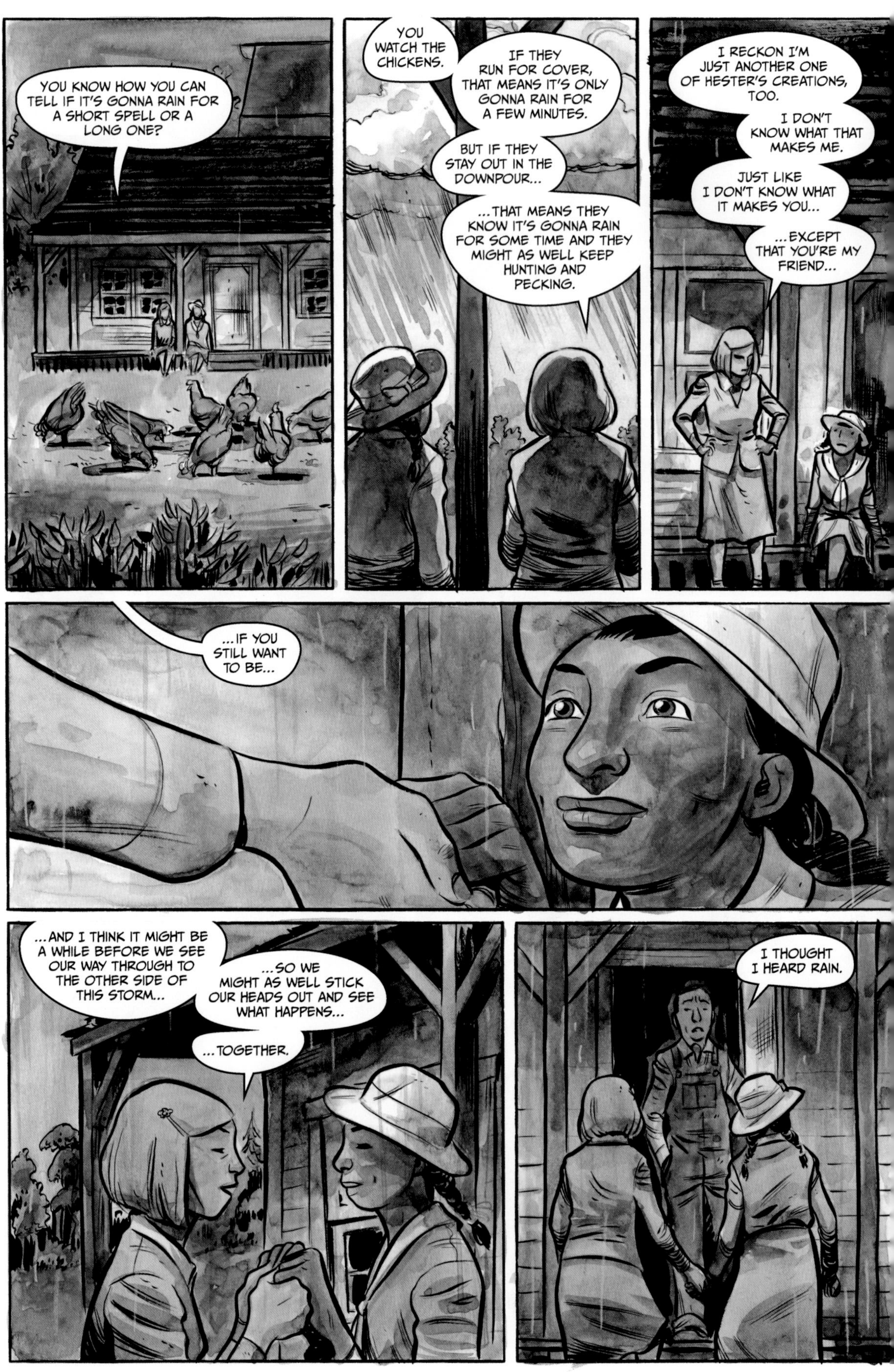
YOU KNOW HOW YOU CAN TELL IF IT'S GONNA RAIN FOR A SHORT SPELL OR A LONG ONE?
YOU WATCH THE CHICKENS.
IF THEY RUN FOR COVER, THAT MEANS IT'S ONLY GONNA RAIN FOR A FEW MINUTES.
BUT IF THEY STAY OUT IN THE DOWNPOUR...
...THAT MEANS THEY KNOW IT'S GONNA RAIN FOR SOME TIME AND THEY MIGHT AS WELL KEEP HUNTING AND PECKING.
I RECKON I'M JUST ANOTHER ONE OF HESTER'S CREATIONS, TOO.
I DON'T KNOW WHAT THAT MAKES ME.
JUST LIKE I DON'T KNOW WHAT IT MAKES YOU...
...EXCEPT THAT YOU'RE MY FRIEND...
...IF YOU STILL WANT TO BE...
...AND I THINK IT MIGHT BE A WHILE BEFORE WE SEE OUR WAY THROUGH TO THE OTHER SIDE OF THIS STORM...
...SO WE MIGHT AS WELL STICK OUR HEADS OUT AND SEE WHAT HAPPENS...
...TOGETHER.
I THOUGHT I HEARD RAIN.

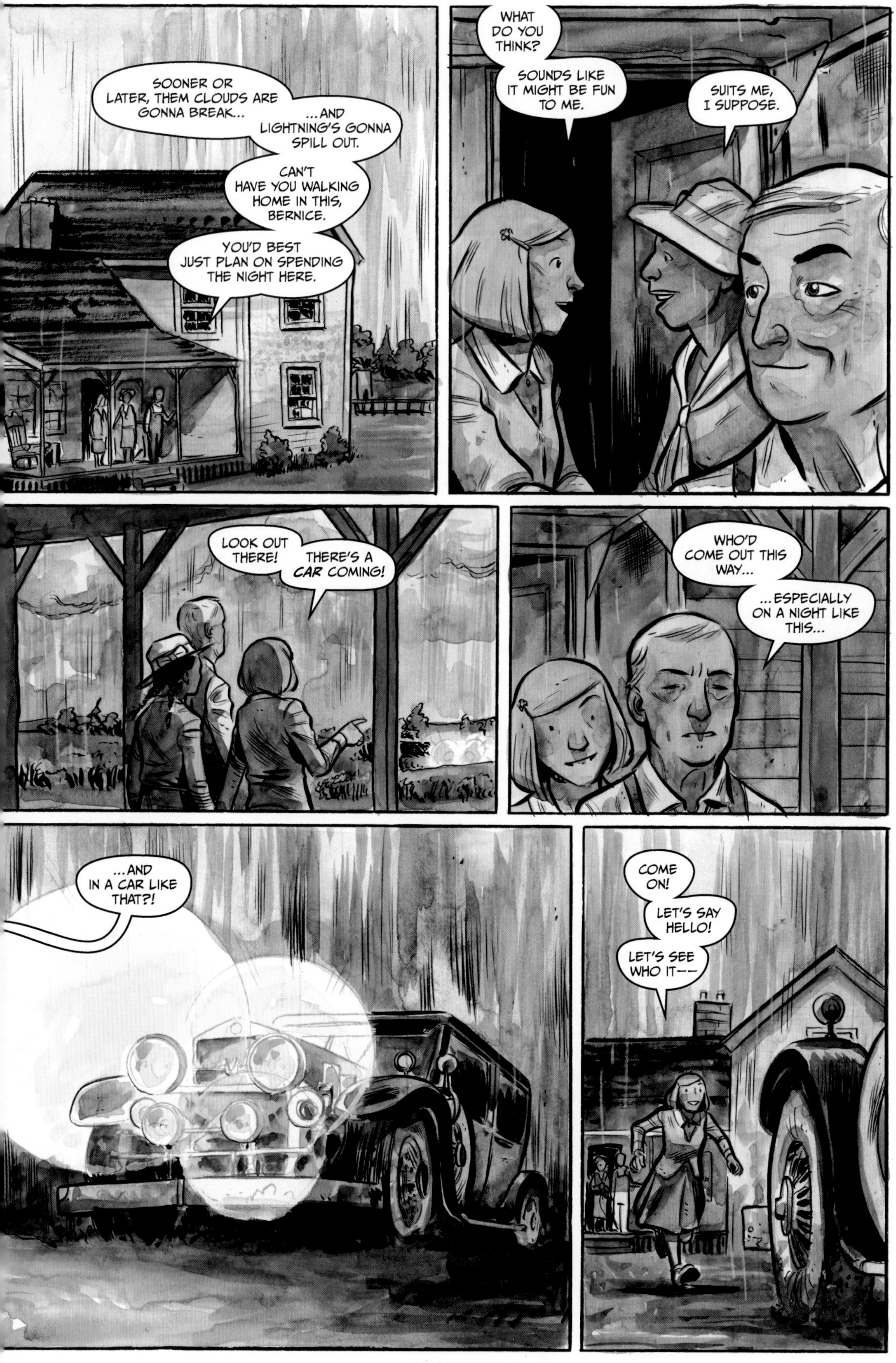
SOONER OR LATER, THEM CLOUDS ARE GONNA BREAK...
...AND LIGHTNING'S GONNA SPILL OUT.
CAN'T HAVE YOU WALKING HOME IN THIS, BERNICE.
YOU'D BEST JUST PLAN ON SPENDING THE NIGHT HERE.
WHAT DO YOU THINK?
SOUNDS LIKE IT MIGHT BE FUN TO ME.
SUITS ME, I SUPPOSE.
LOOK OUT THERE!
THERE'S A CAR COMING!
WHO'D COME OUT THIS WAY...
...ESPECIALLY ON A NIGHT LIKE THIS...
...AND IN A CAR LIKE THAT?!
COME ON!
LET'S SAY HELLO!
LET'S SEE WHO IT--

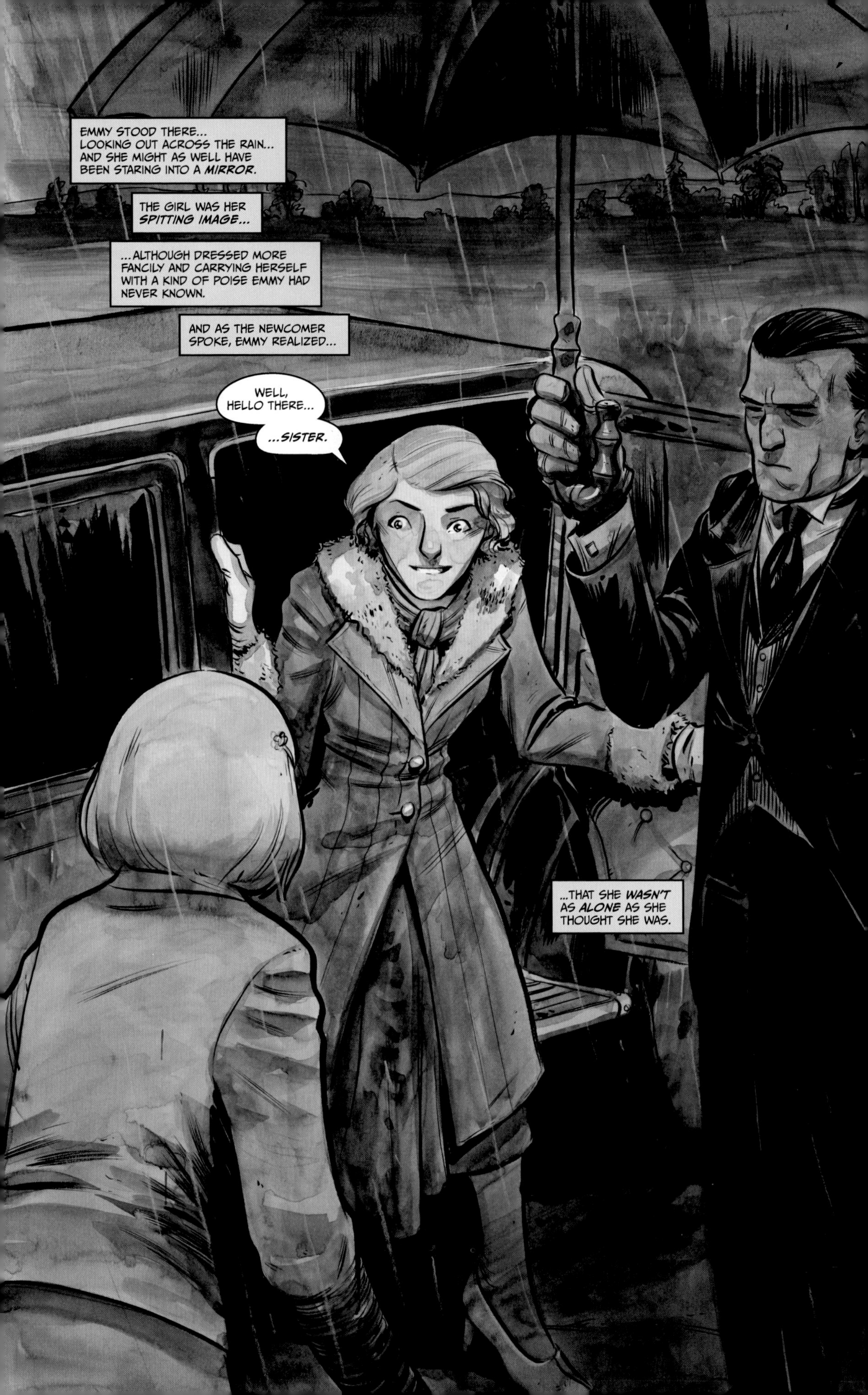
EMMY STOOD THERE... LOOKING OUT ACROSS THE RAIN... AND SHE MIGHT AS WELL HAVE BEEN STARING INTO A *MIRROR*.
THE GIRL WAS HER *SPITTING IMAGE*...
...ALTHOUGH DRESSED MORE FANCILY AND CARRYING HERSELF WITH A KIND OF POISE EMMY HAD NEVER KNOWN.
AND AS THE NEWCOMER SPOKE, EMMY REALIZED...
WELL, HELLO THERE...
...*SISTER*.
...THAT SHE *WASN'T* AS *ALONE* AS SHE THOUGHT SHE WAS.

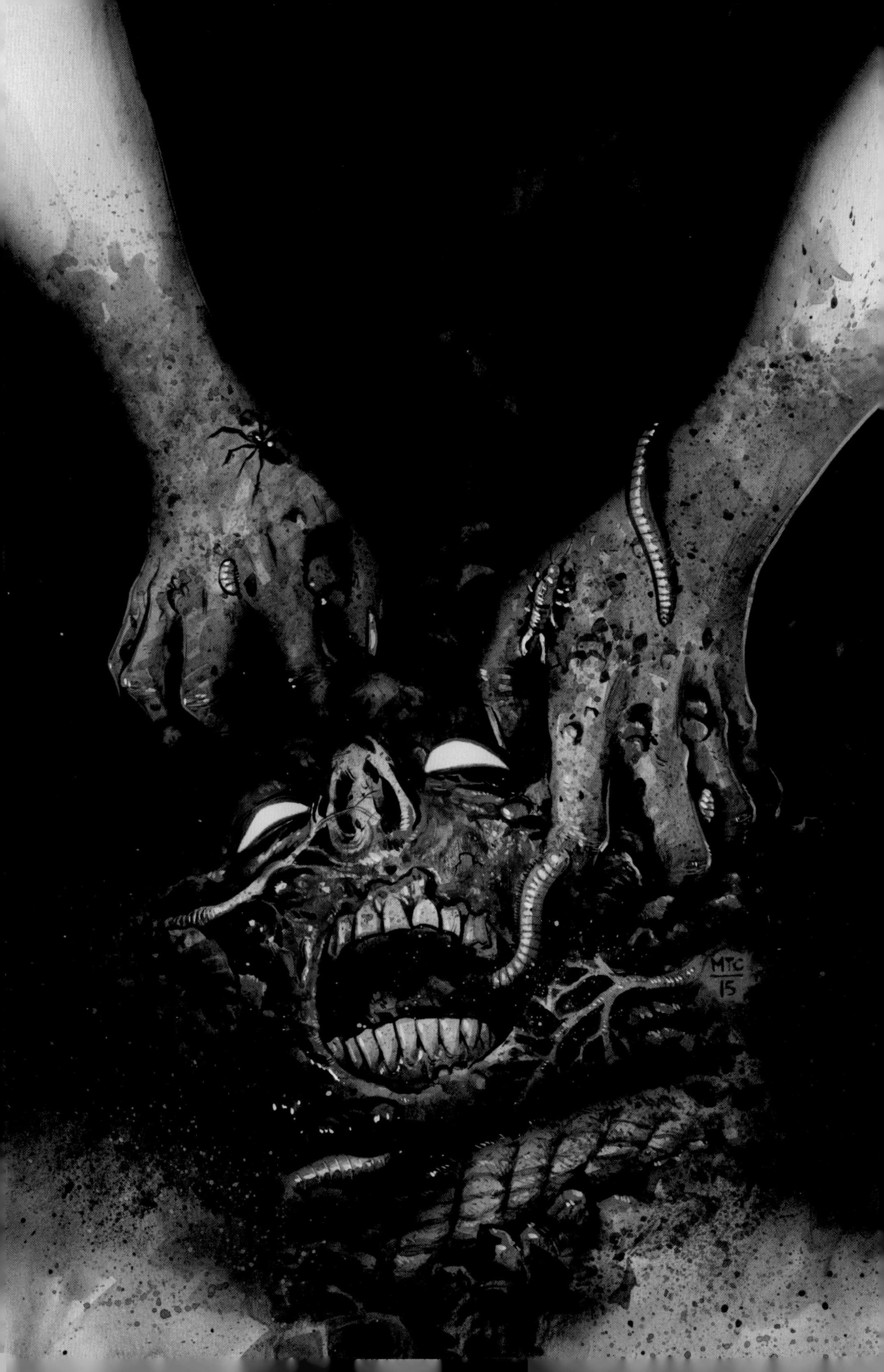
MTC
15

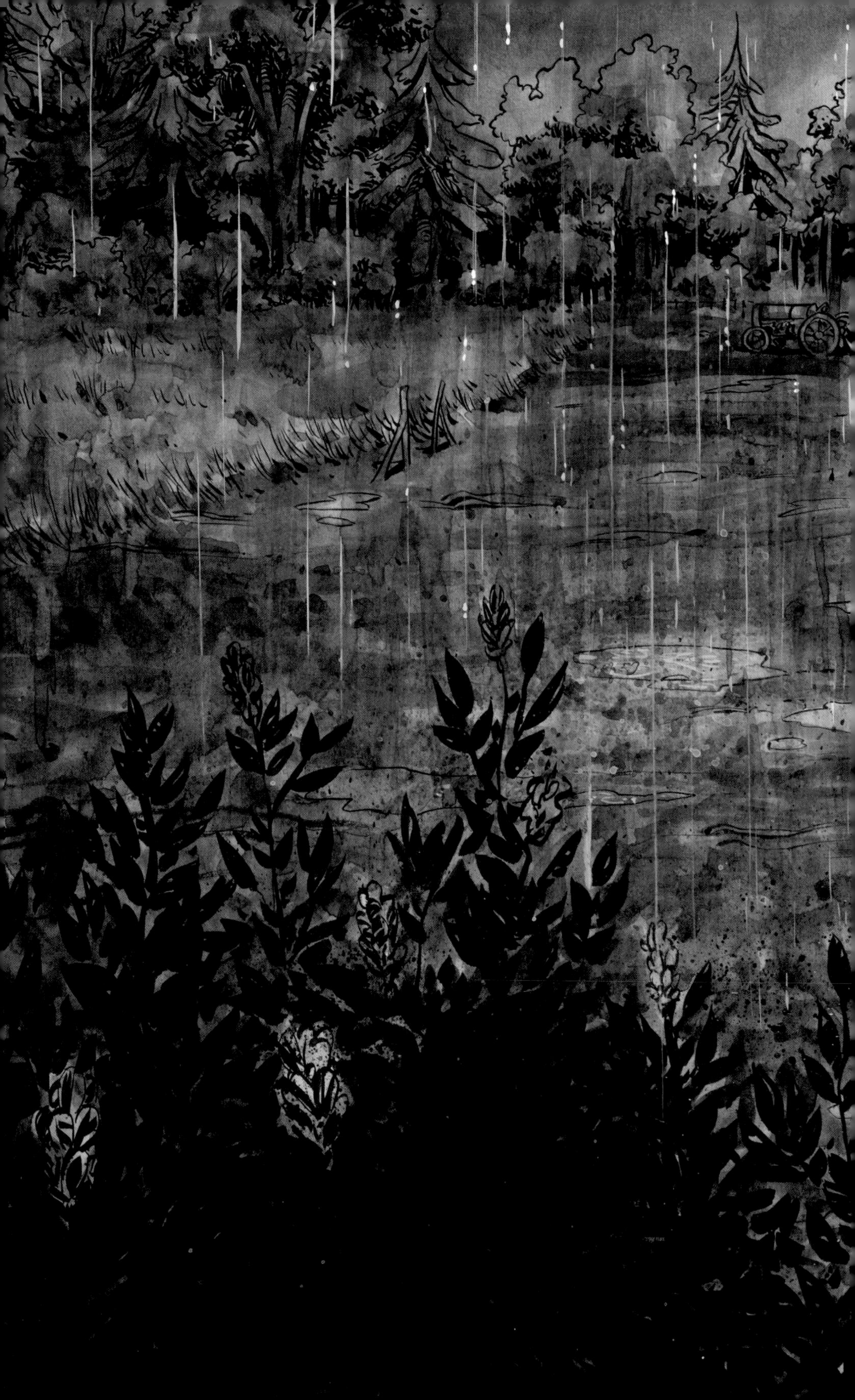

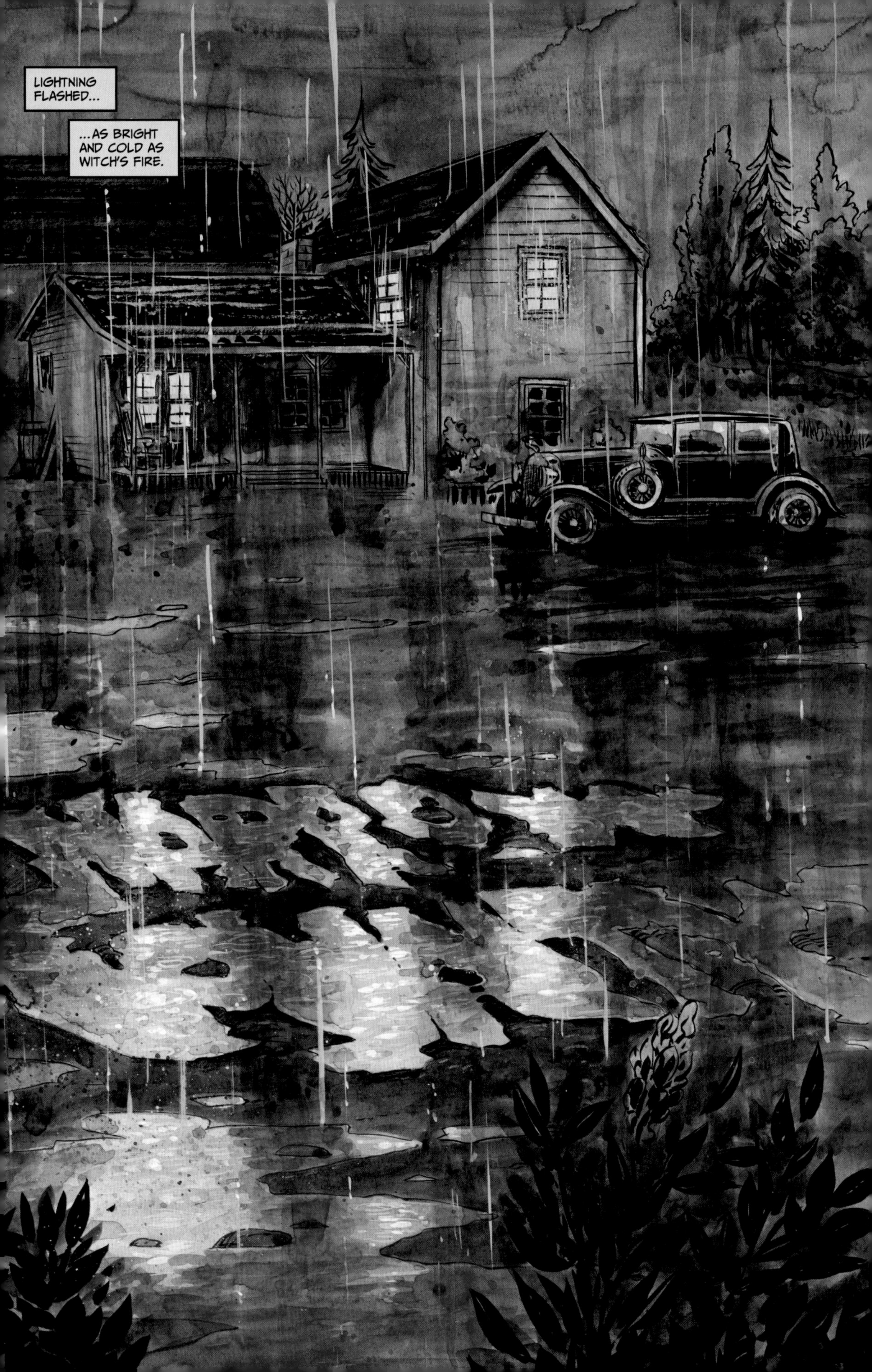
LIGHTNING FLASHED...
...AS BRIGHT AND COLD AS WITCH'S FIRE.

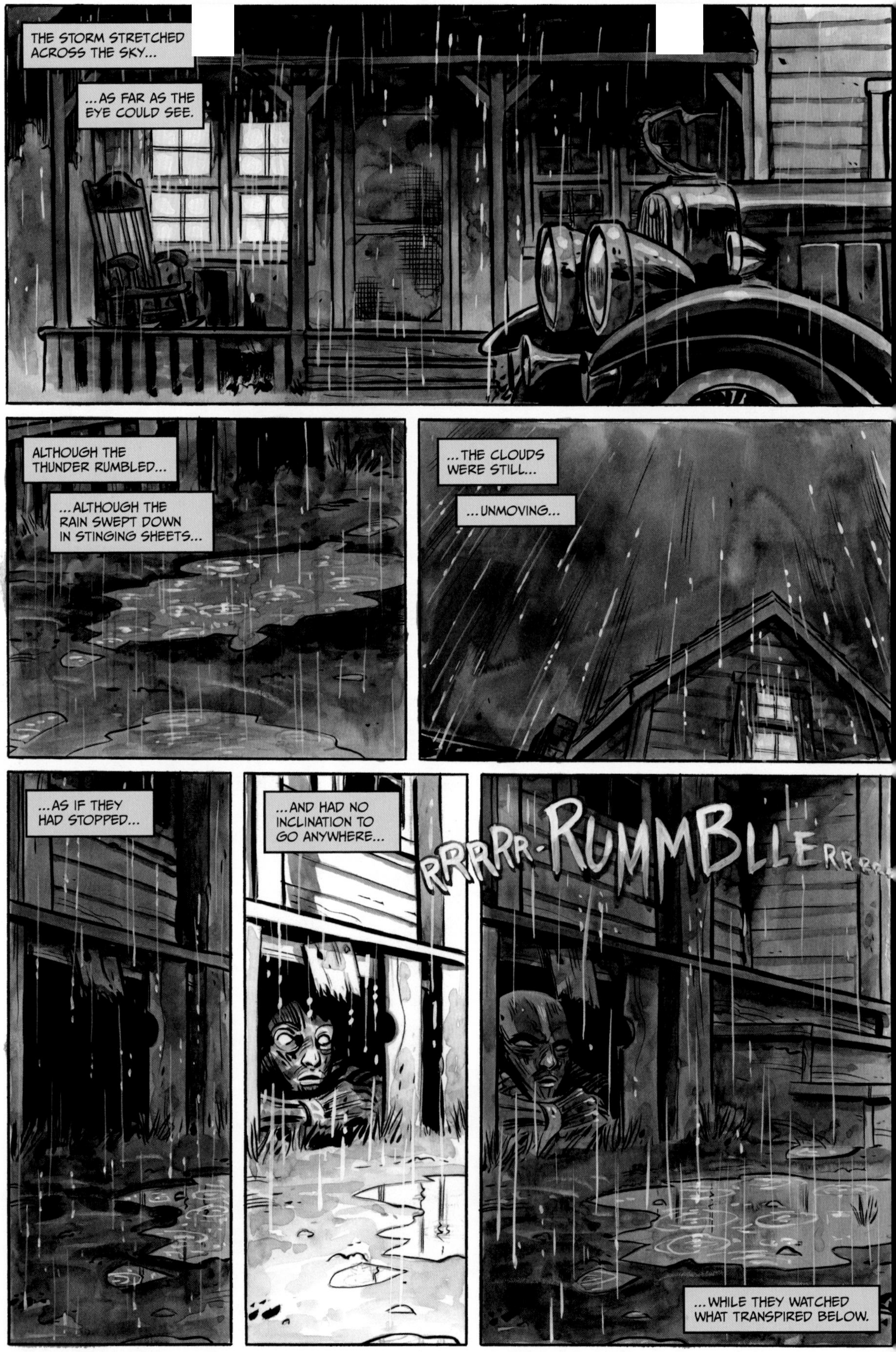
THE STORM STRETCHED ACROSS THE SKY...
...AS FAR AS THE EYE COULD SEE.
ALTHOUGH THE THUNDER RUMBLED...
...ALTHOUGH THE RAIN SWEPT DOWN IN STINGING SHEETS...
...THE CLOUDS WERE STILL...
...UNMOVING...
...AS IF THEY HAD STOPPED...
...AND HAD NO INCLINATION TO GO ANYWHERE...
RRRRR-RUMMBLLERR
...WHILE THEY WATCHED WHAT TRANSPIRED BELOW.

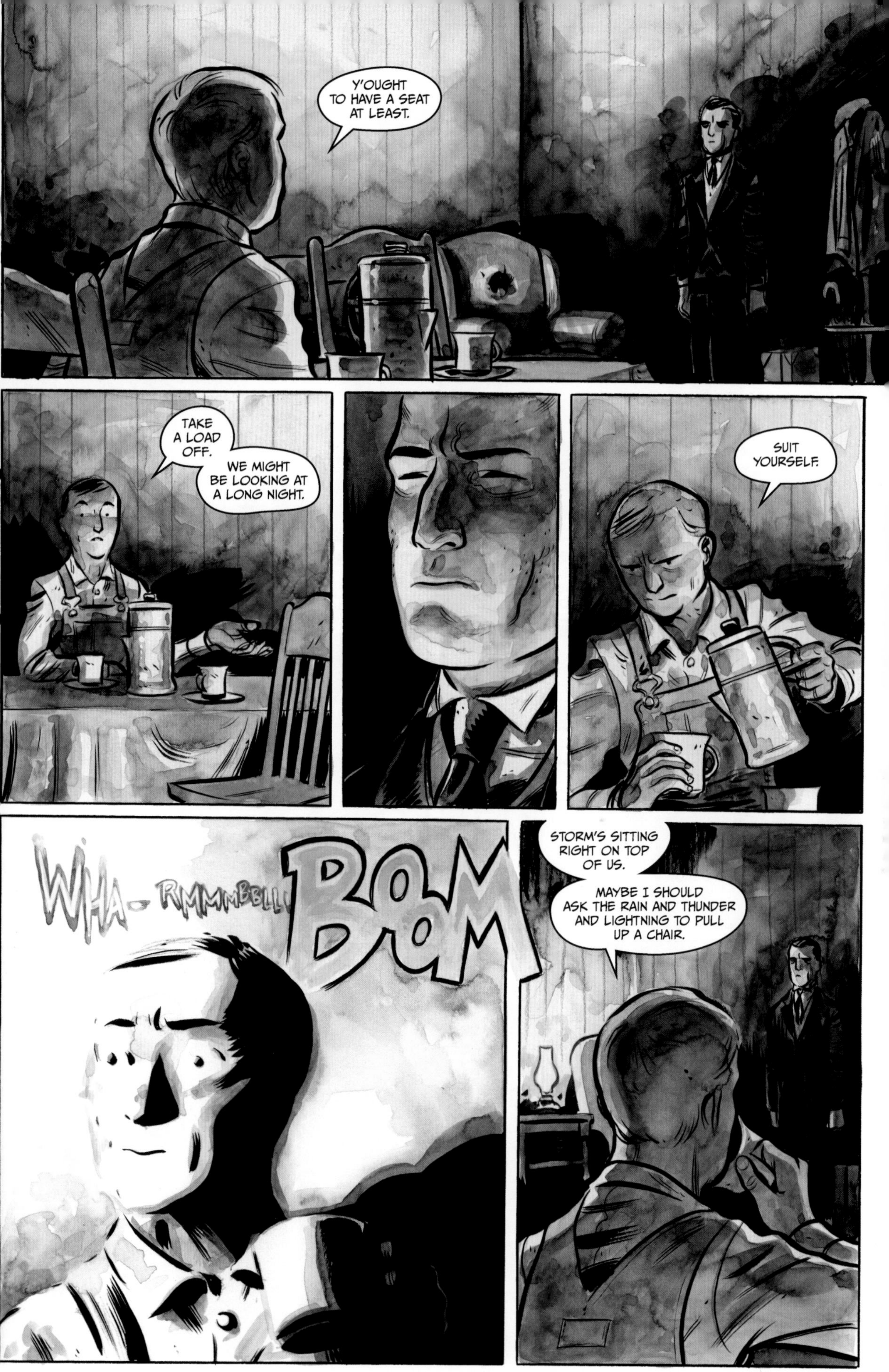
Y'OUGHT TO HAVE A SEAT AT LEAST.
TAKE A LOAD OFF.
WE MIGHT BE LOOKING AT A LONG NIGHT.
SUIT YOURSELF.
WHA- RMMMBBLL BOOM
STORM'S SITTING RIGHT ON TOP OF US.
MAYBE I SHOULD ASK THE RAIN AND THUNDER AND LIGHTNING TO PULL UP A CHAIR.

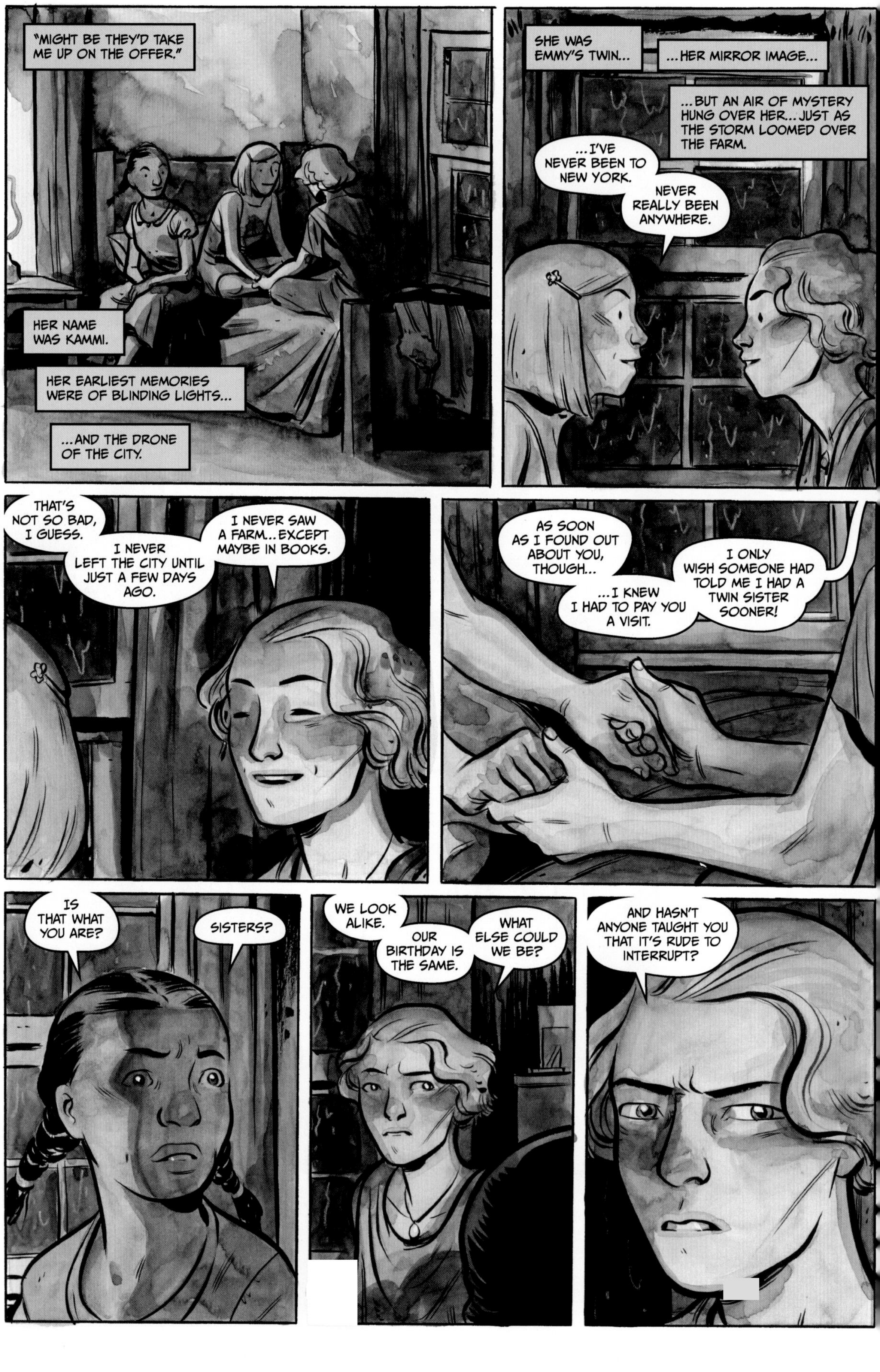
"MIGHT BE THEY'D TAKE ME UP ON THE OFFER."
HER NAME WAS KAMMI.
HER EARLIEST MEMORIES WERE OF BLINDING LIGHTS...
...AND THE DRONE OF THE CITY.
SHE WAS EMMY'S TWIN...
...HER MIRROR IMAGE...
...BUT AN AIR OF MYSTERY HUNG OVER HER... JUST AS THE STORM LOOMED OVER THE FARM.
...I'VE NEVER BEEN TO NEW YORK.
NEVER REALLY BEEN ANYWHERE.
THAT'S NOT SO BAD, I GUESS.
I NEVER LEFT THE CITY UNTIL JUST A FEW DAYS AGO.
I NEVER SAW A FARM... EXCEPT MAYBE IN BOOKS.
AS SOON AS I FOUND OUT ABOUT YOU, THOUGH...
...I KNEW I HAD TO PAY YOU A VISIT.
I ONLY WISH SOMEONE HAD TOLD ME I HAD A TWIN SISTER SOONER!
IS THAT WHAT YOU ARE?
SISTERS?
WE LOOK ALIKE.
OUR BIRTHDAY IS THE SAME.
WHAT ELSE COULD WE BE?
AND HASN'T ANYONE TAUGHT YOU THAT IT'S RUDE TO INTERRUPT?

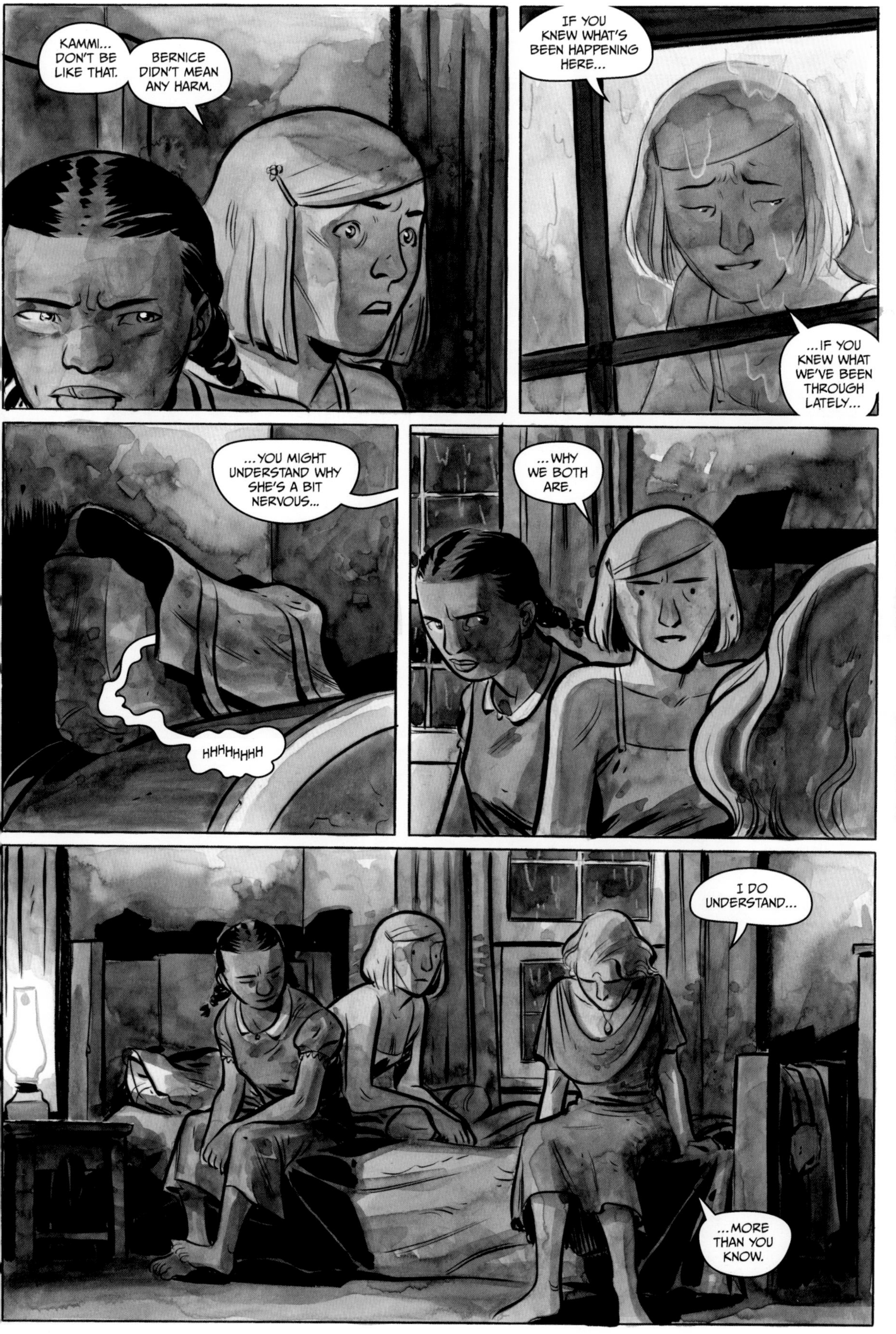
KAMMI... DON'T BE LIKE THAT.
BERNICE DIDN'T MEAN ANY HARM.
IF YOU KNEW WHAT'S BEEN HAPPENING HERE...
...IF YOU KNEW WHAT WE'VE BEEN THROUGH LATELY...
...YOU MIGHT UNDERSTAND WHY SHE'S A BIT NERVOUS...
HHHHHHHH
...WHY WE BOTH ARE.
I DO UNDERSTAND...
...MORE THAN YOU KNOW.

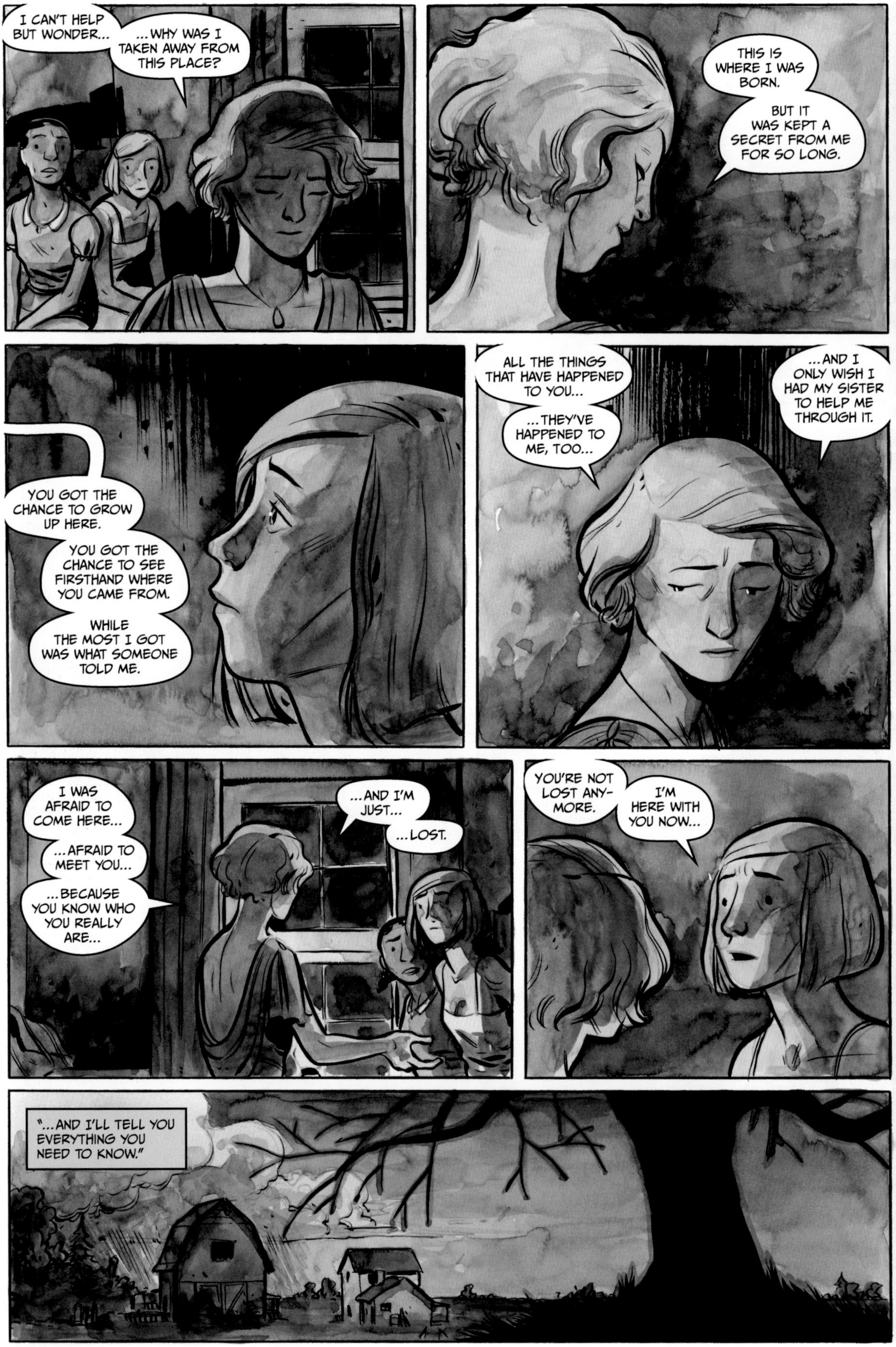
I CAN'T HELP BUT WONDER...
...WHY WAS I TAKEN AWAY FROM THIS PLACE?
THIS IS WHERE I WAS BORN.
BUT IT WAS KEPT A SECRET FROM ME FOR SO LONG.
YOU GOT THE CHANCE TO GROW UP HERE.
YOU GOT THE CHANCE TO SEE FIRSTHAND WHERE YOU CAME FROM.
WHILE THE MOST I GOT WAS WHAT SOMEONE TOLD ME.
ALL THE THINGS THAT HAVE HAPPENED TO YOU...
...THEY'VE HAPPENED TO ME, TOO...
...AND I ONLY WISH I HAD MY SISTER TO HELP ME THROUGH IT.
I WAS AFRAID TO COME HERE...
...AFRAID TO MEET YOU...
...BECAUSE YOU KNOW WHO YOU REALLY ARE...
...AND I'M JUST...
...LOST.
YOU'RE NOT LOST ANY-MORE.
I'M HERE WITH YOU NOW...
"...AND I'LL TELL YOU EVERYTHING YOU NEED TO KNOW."

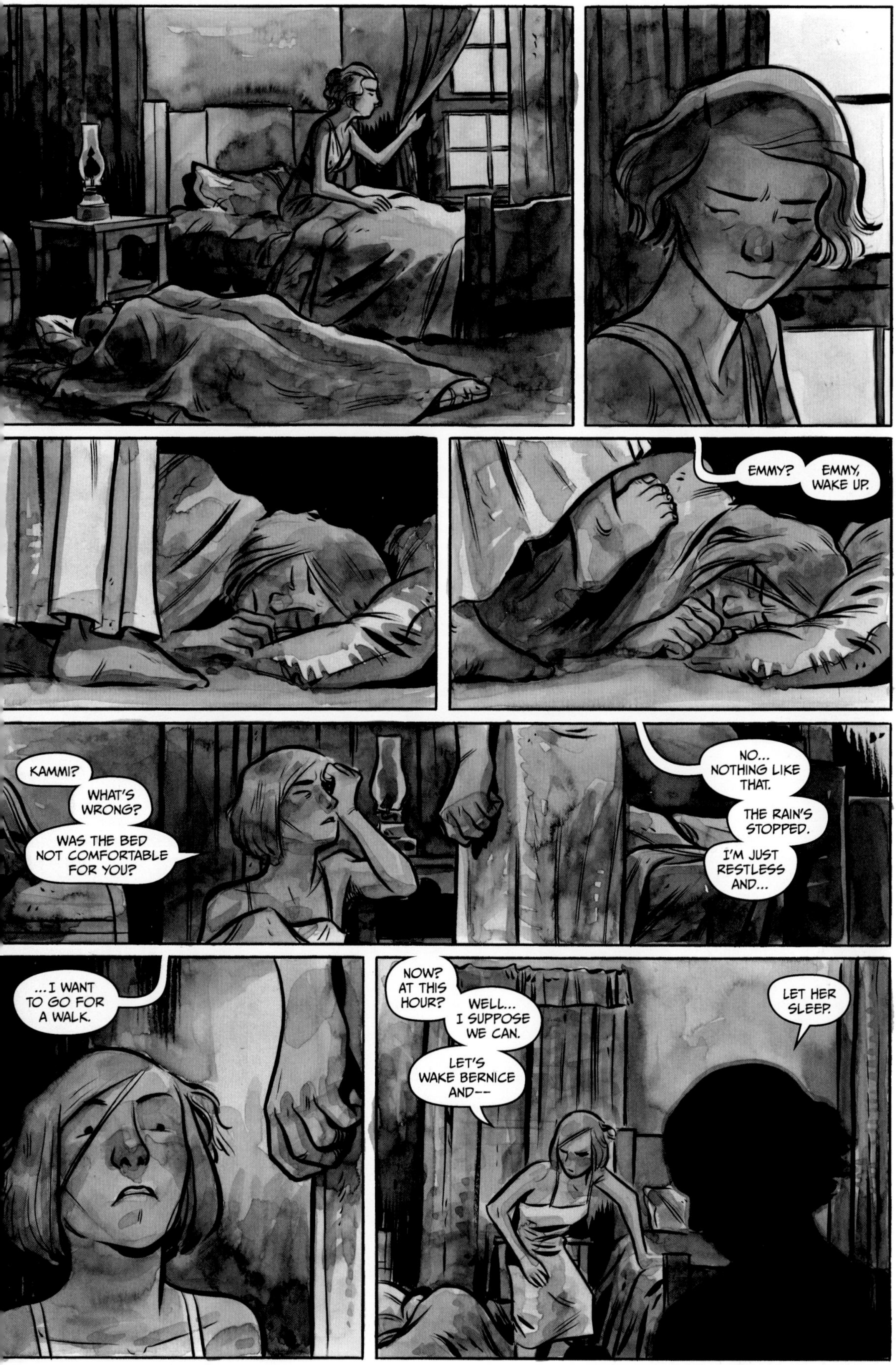
EMMY? EMMY, WAKE UP.
KAMMI?
WHAT'S WRONG?
WAS THE BED NOT COMFORTABLE FOR YOU?
NO... NOTHING LIKE THAT.
THE RAIN'S STOPPED.
I'M JUST RESTLESS AND...
...I WANT TO GO FOR A WALK.
NOW? AT THIS HOUR?
WELL... I SUPPOSE WE CAN.
LET'S WAKE BERNICE AND--
LET HER SLEEP.

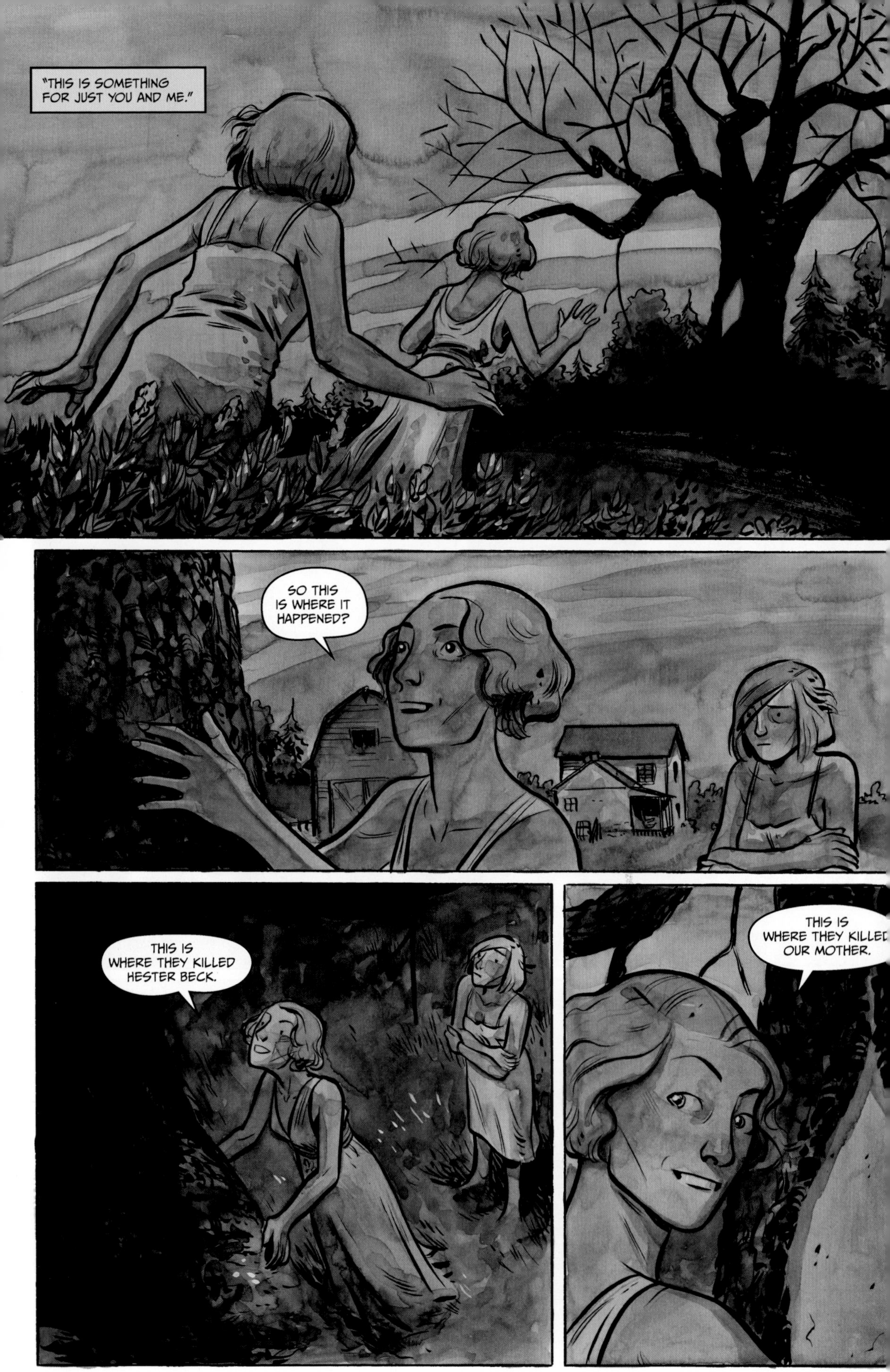
"THIS IS SOMETHING FOR JUST YOU AND ME."
SO THIS IS WHERE IT HAPPENED?
THIS IS WHERE THEY KILLED HESTER BECK.
THIS IS WHERE THEY KILLED OUR MOTHER.

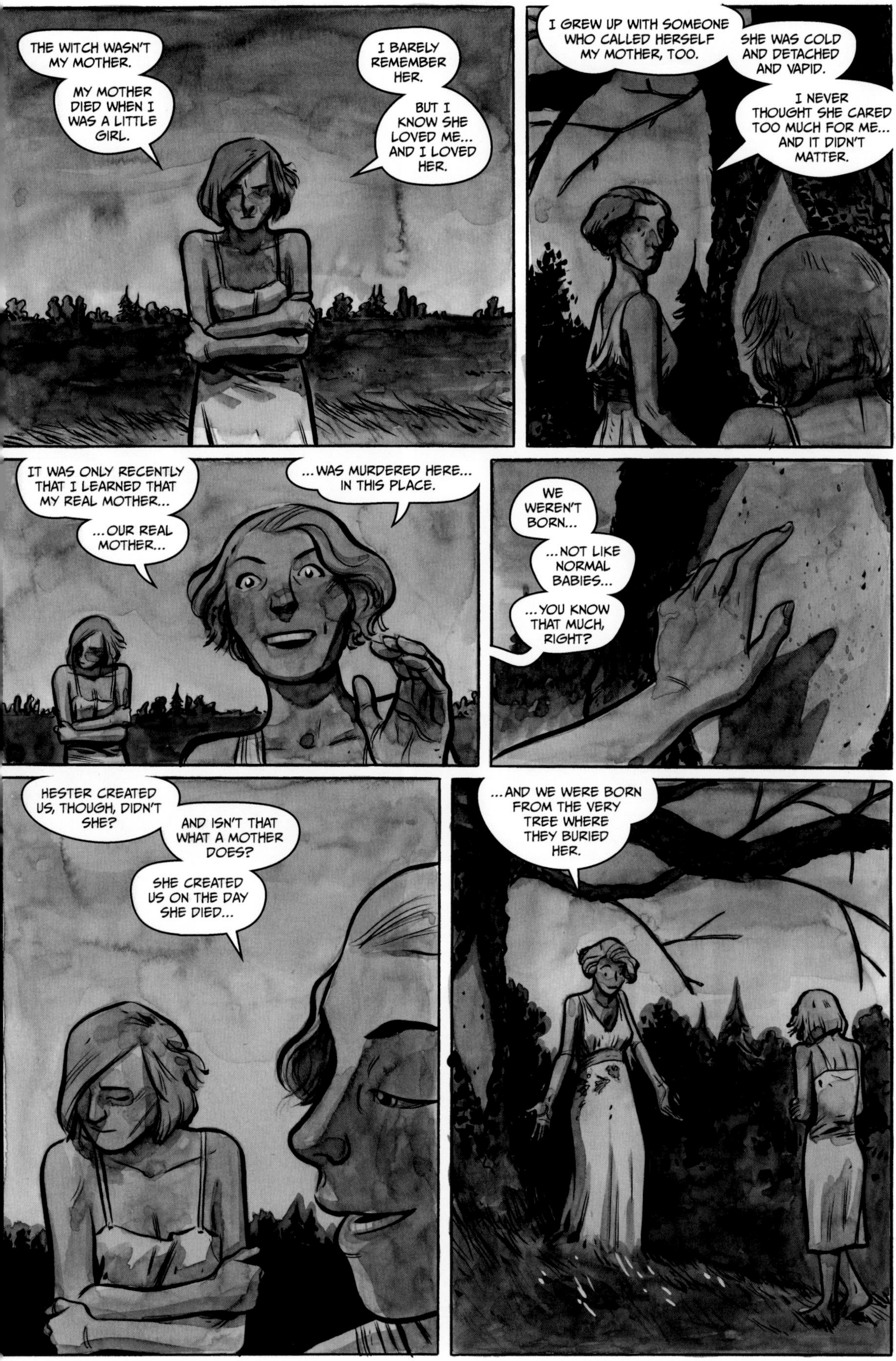
THE WITCH WASN'T MY MOTHER.
MY MOTHER DIED WHEN I WAS A LITTLE GIRL.
I BARELY REMEMBER HER.
BUT I KNOW SHE LOVED ME... AND I LOVED HER.
I GREW UP WITH SOMEONE WHO CALLED HERSELF MY MOTHER, TOO.
SHE WAS COLD AND DETACHED AND VAPID.
I NEVER THOUGHT SHE CARED TOO MUCH FOR ME... AND IT DIDN'T MATTER.
IT WAS ONLY RECENTLY THAT I LEARNED THAT MY REAL MOTHER...
...OUR REAL MOTHER...
...WAS MURDERED HERE... IN THIS PLACE.
WE WEREN'T BORN...
...NOT LIKE NORMAL BABIES...
...YOU KNOW THAT MUCH, RIGHT?
HESTER CREATED US, THOUGH, DIDN'T SHE?
AND ISN'T THAT WHAT A MOTHER DOES?
SHE CREATED US ON THE DAY SHE DIED...
...AND WE WERE BORN FROM THE VERY TREE WHERE THEY BURIED HER.

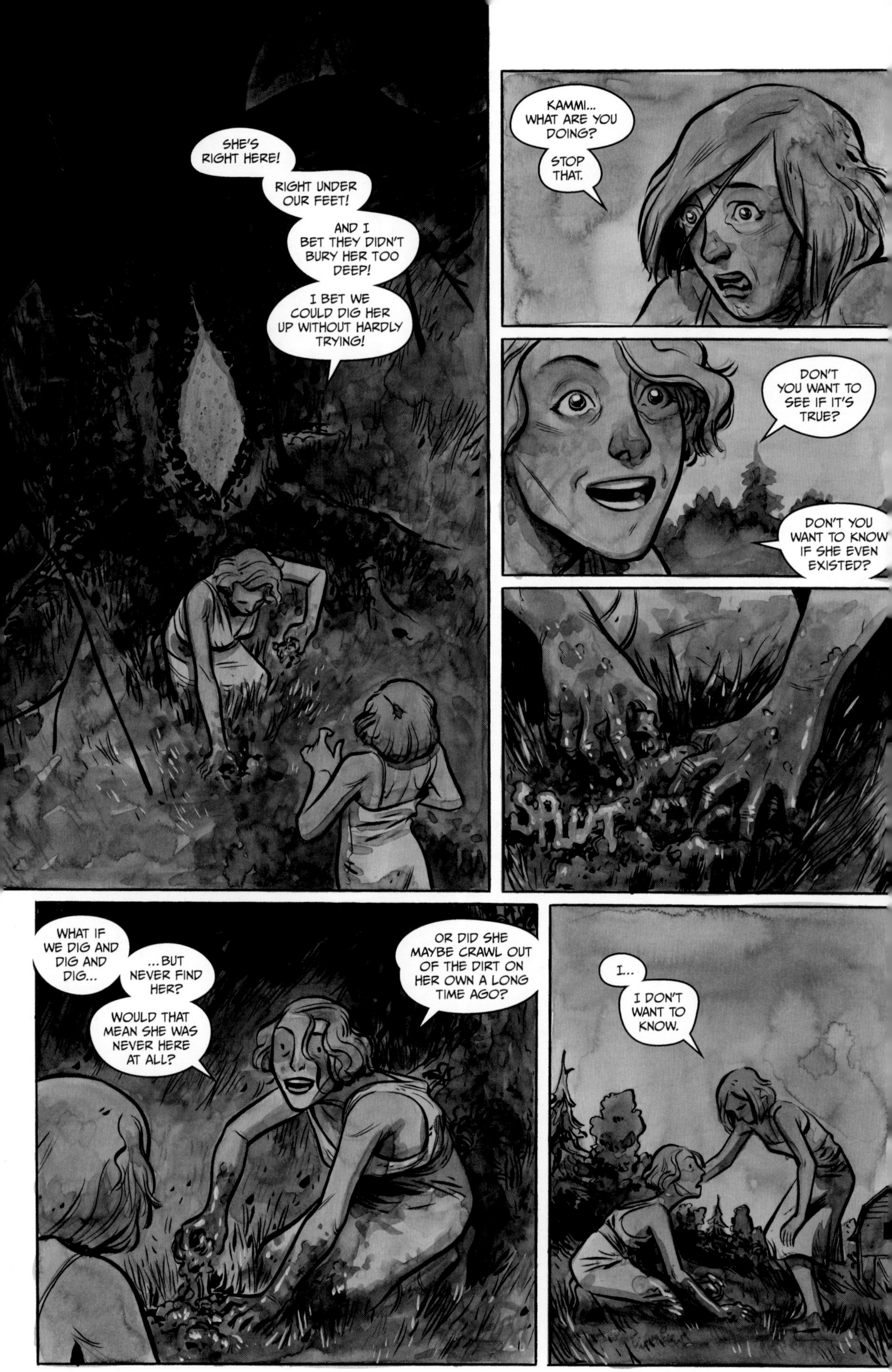
SHE'S RIGHT HERE!
RIGHT UNDER OUR FEET!
AND I BET THEY DIDN'T BURY HER TOO DEEP!
I BET WE COULD DIG HER UP WITHOUT HARDLY TRYING!
KAMMI... WHAT ARE YOU DOING?
STOP THAT.
DON'T YOU WANT TO SEE IF IT'S TRUE?
DON'T YOU WANT TO KNOW IF SHE EVEN EXISTED?
SPLUT
WHAT IF WE DIG AND DIG AND DIG...
...BUT NEVER FIND HER?
WOULD THAT MEAN SHE WAS NEVER HERE AT ALL?
OR DID SHE MAYBE CRAWL OUT OF THE DIRT ON HER OWN A LONG TIME AGO?
I...
I DON'T WANT TO KNOW.

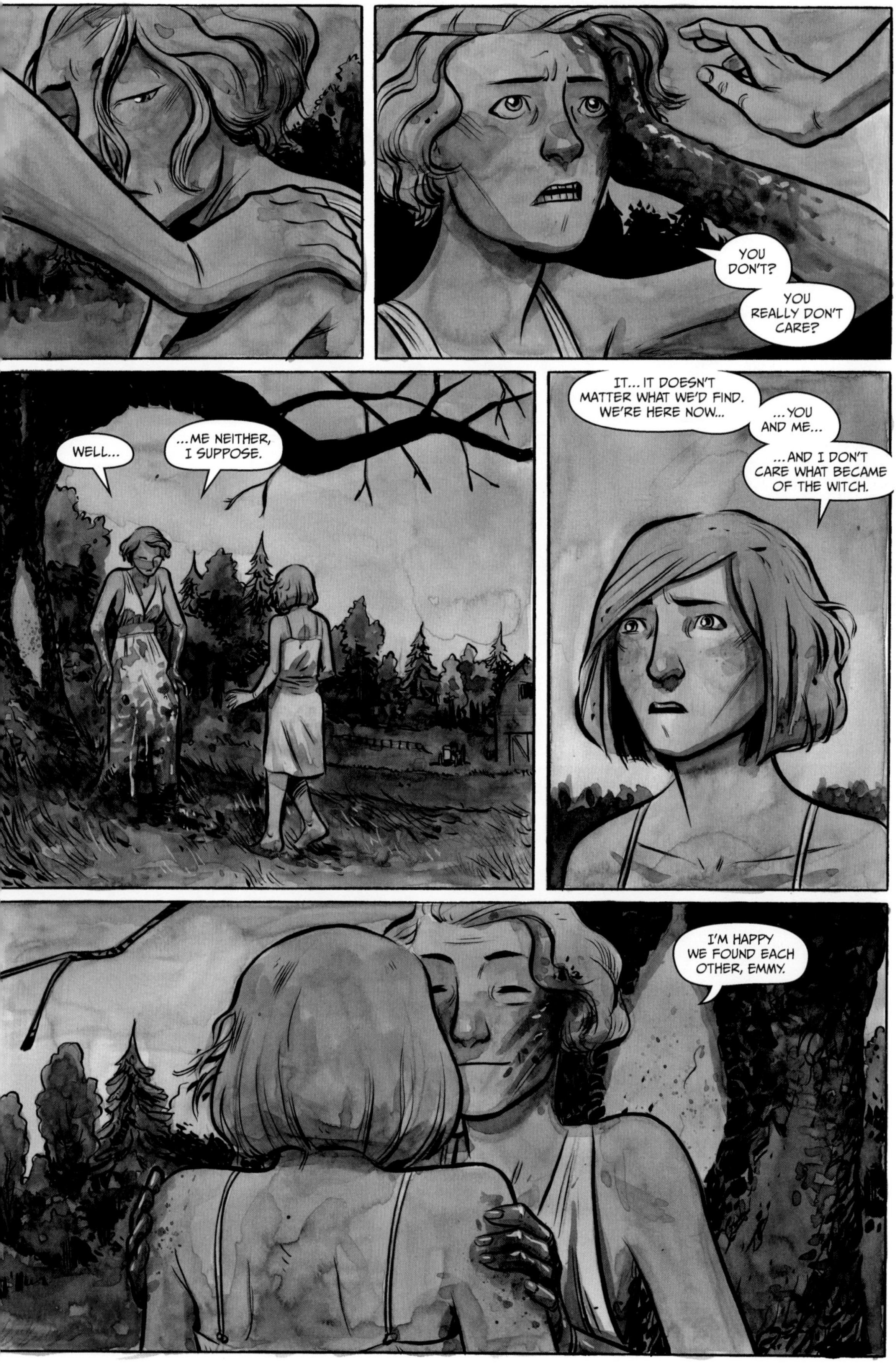
YOU DON'T?
YOU REALLY DON'T CARE?
WELL...
...ME NEITHER, I SUPPOSE.
IT... IT DOESN'T MATTER WHAT WE'D FIND. WE'RE HERE NOW...
...YOU AND ME...
...AND I DON'T CARE WHAT BECAME OF THE WITCH.
I'M HAPPY WE FOUND EACH OTHER, EMMY.

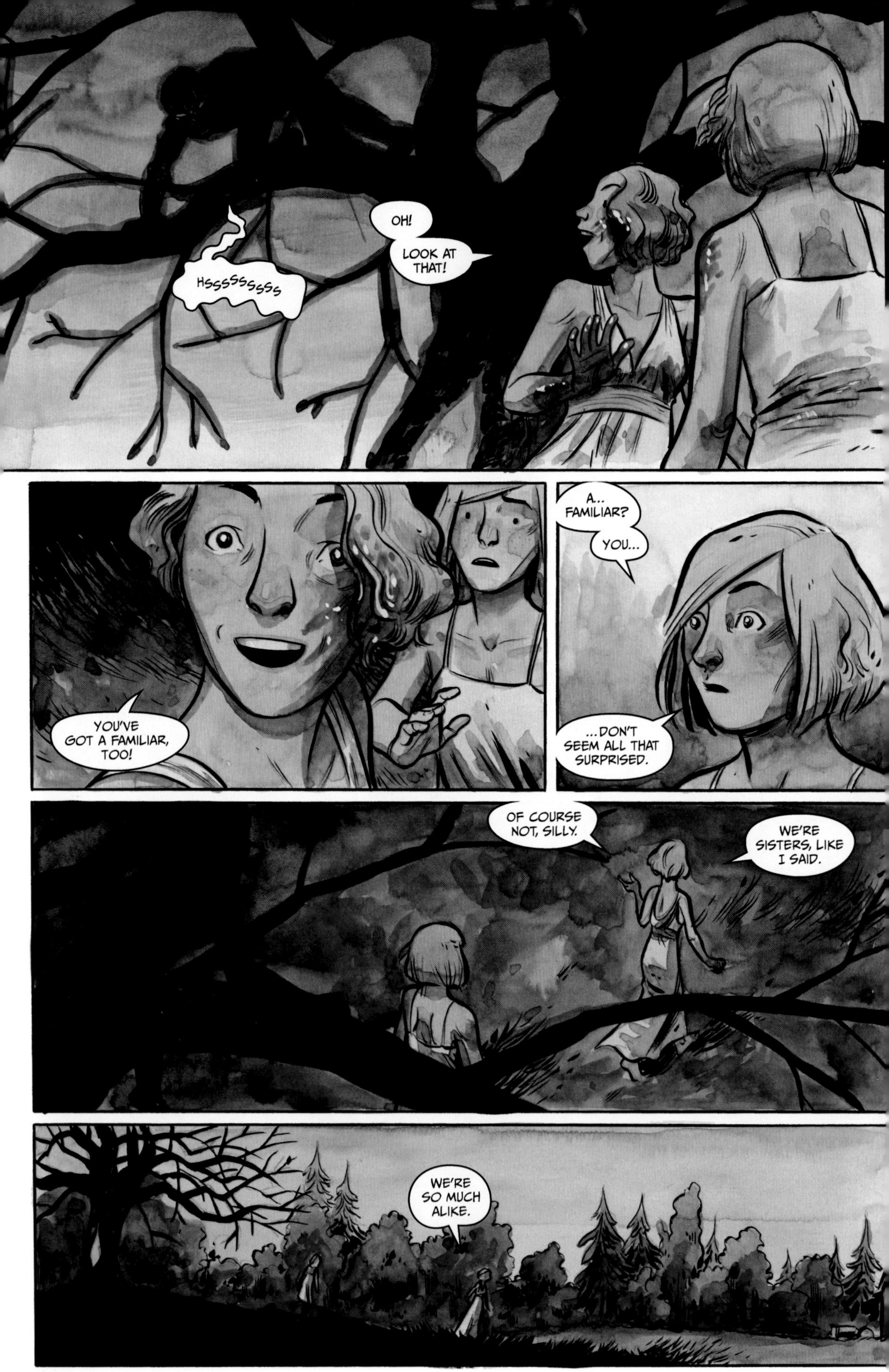
HSSSSSSSSS
OH!
LOOK AT THAT!
YOU'VE GOT A FAMILIAR, TOO!
A... FAMILIAR?
YOU...
...DON'T SEEM ALL THAT SURPRISED.
OF COURSE NOT, SILLY.
WE'RE SISTERS, LIKE I SAID.
WE'RE SO MUCH ALIKE.

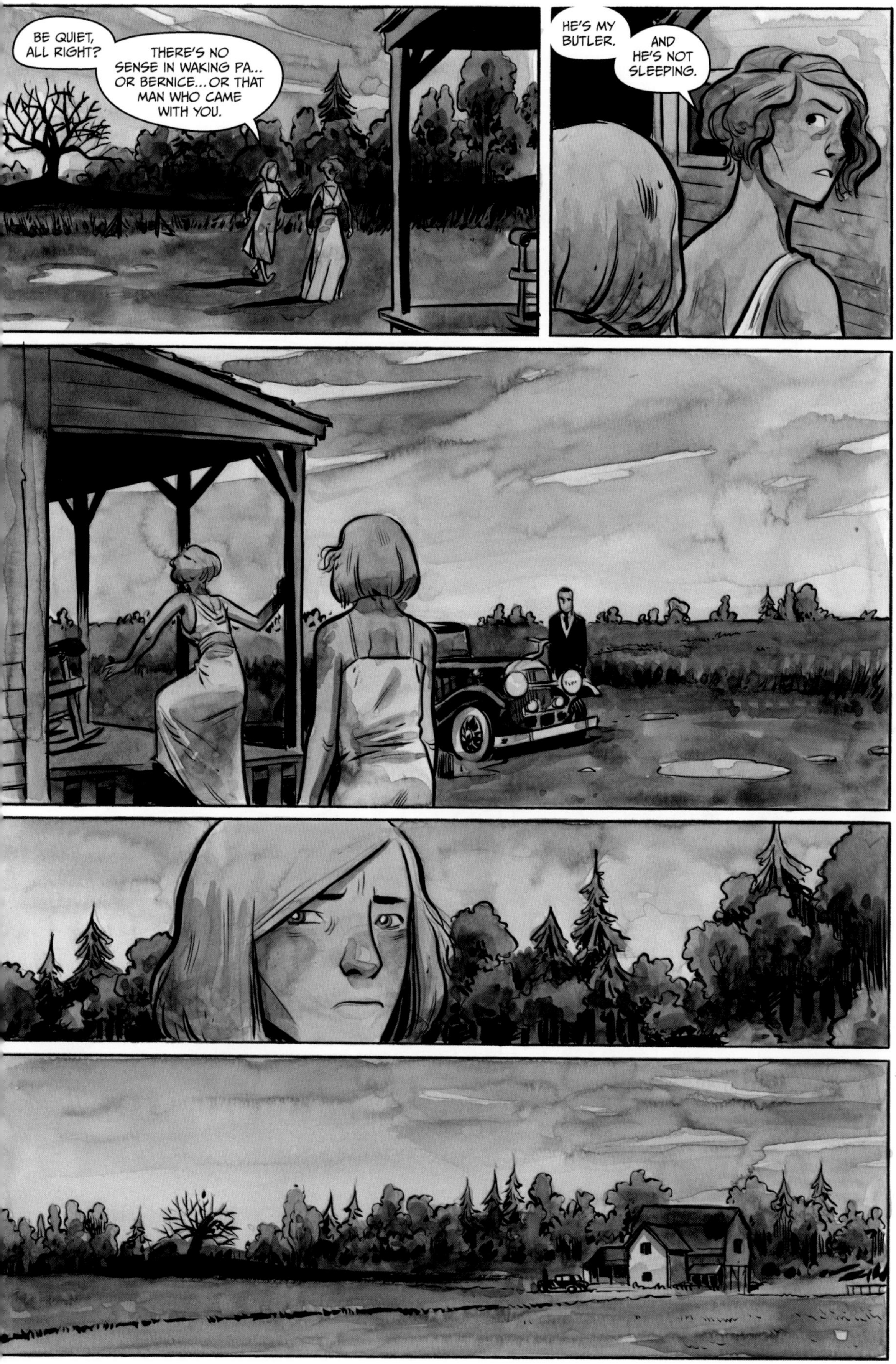
BE QUIET, ALL RIGHT?
THERE'S NO SENSE IN WAKING PA... OR BERNICE... OR THAT MAN WHO CAME WITH YOU.
HE'S MY BUTLER.
AND HE'S NOT SLEEPING.

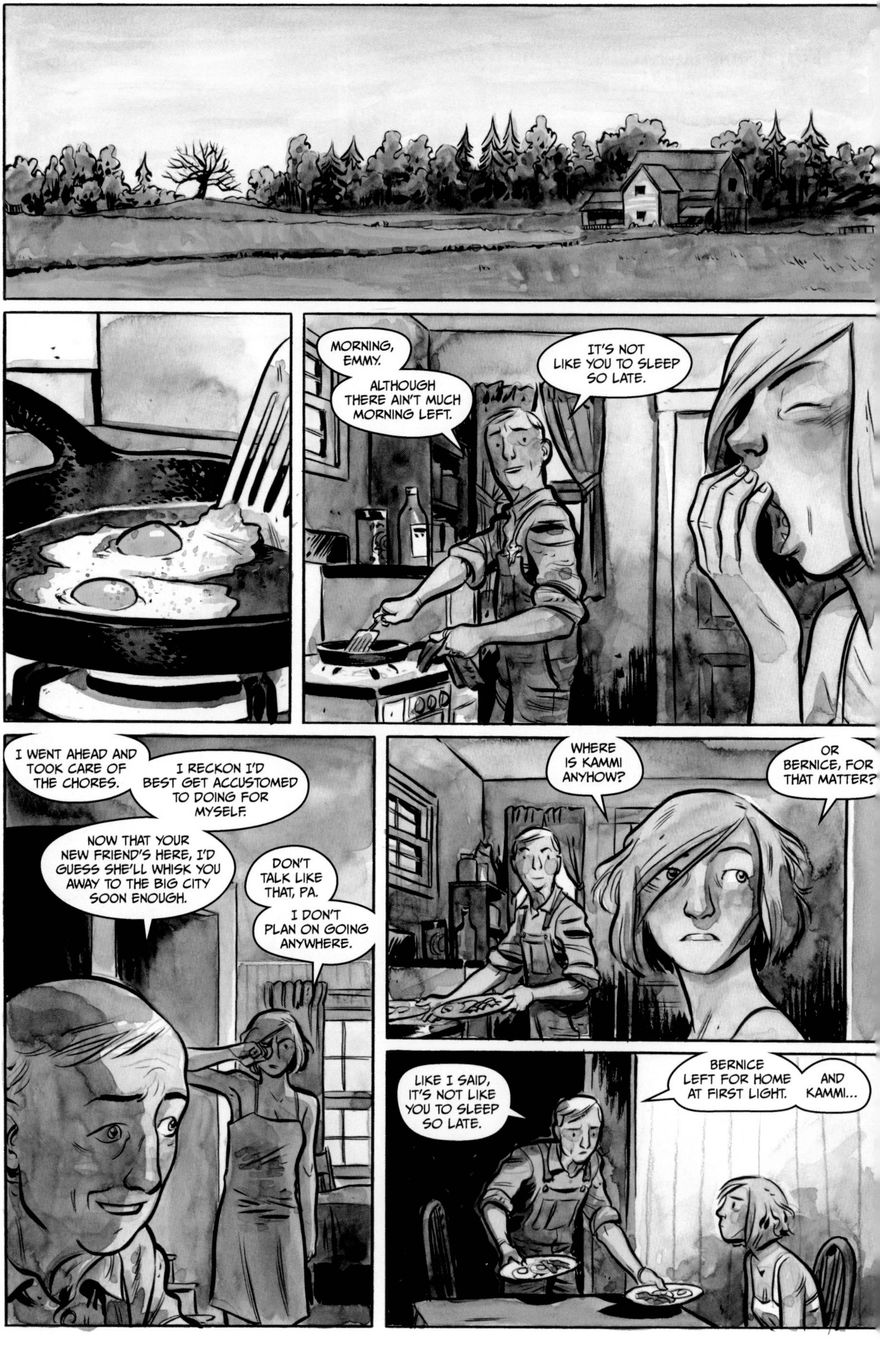
MORNING, EMMY.
ALTHOUGH THERE AIN'T MUCH MORNING LEFT.
IT'S NOT LIKE YOU TO SLEEP SO LATE.
I WENT AHEAD AND TOOK CARE OF THE CHORES.
I RECKON I'D BEST GET ACCUSTOMED TO DOING FOR MYSELF.
NOW THAT YOUR NEW FRIEND'S HERE, I'D GUESS SHE'LL WHISK YOU AWAY TO THE BIG CITY SOON ENOUGH.
DON'T TALK LIKE THAT, PA.
I DON'T PLAN ON GOING ANYWHERE.
WHERE IS KAMMI ANYHOW?
OR BERNICE, FOR THAT MATTER?
LIKE I SAID, IT'S NOT LIKE YOU TO SLEEP SO LATE.
BERNICE LEFT FOR HOME AT FIRST LIGHT.
AND KAMMI...

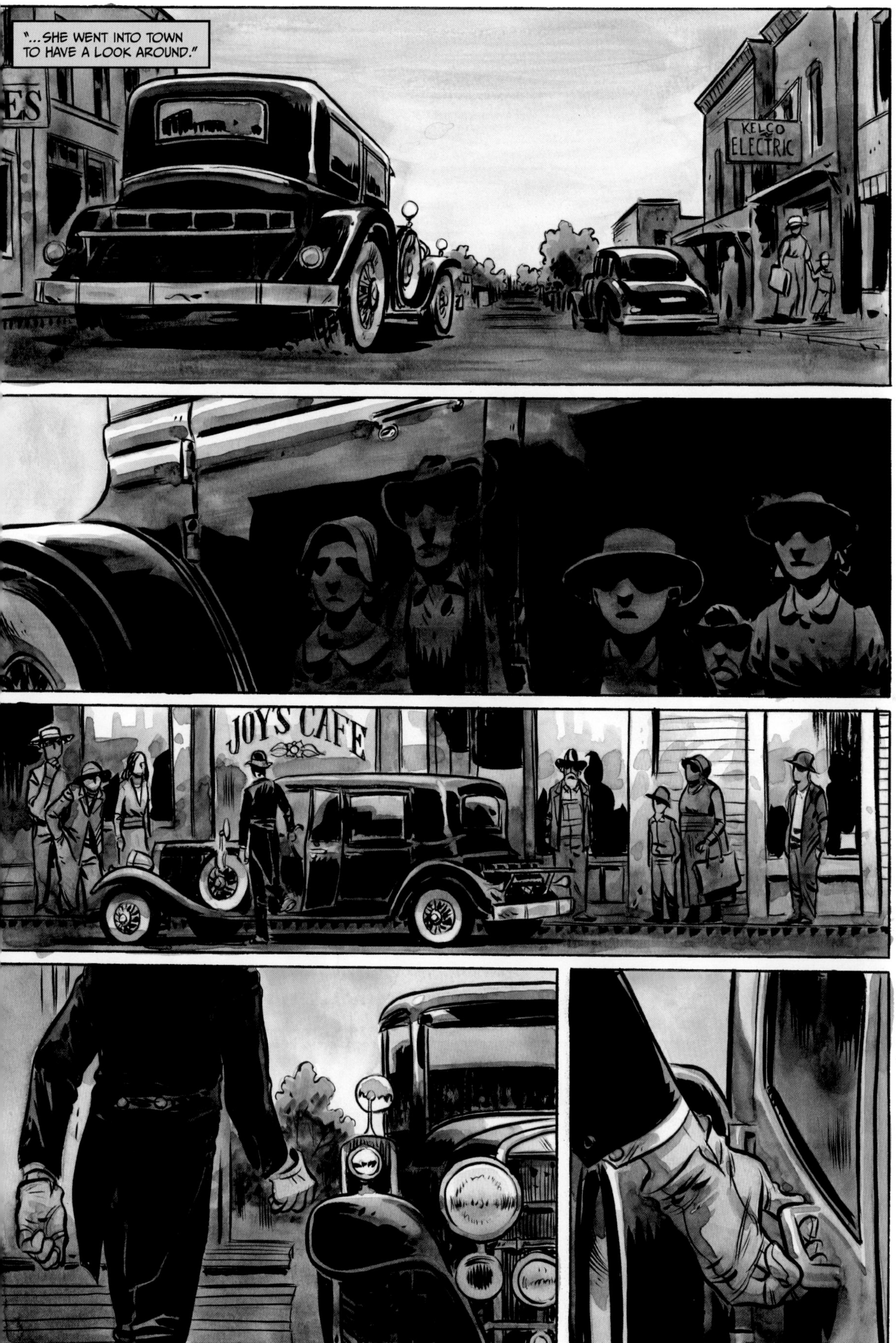
"...SHE WENT INTO TOWN TO HAVE A LOOK AROUND."
KELCO ELECTRIC
JOY'S CAFE

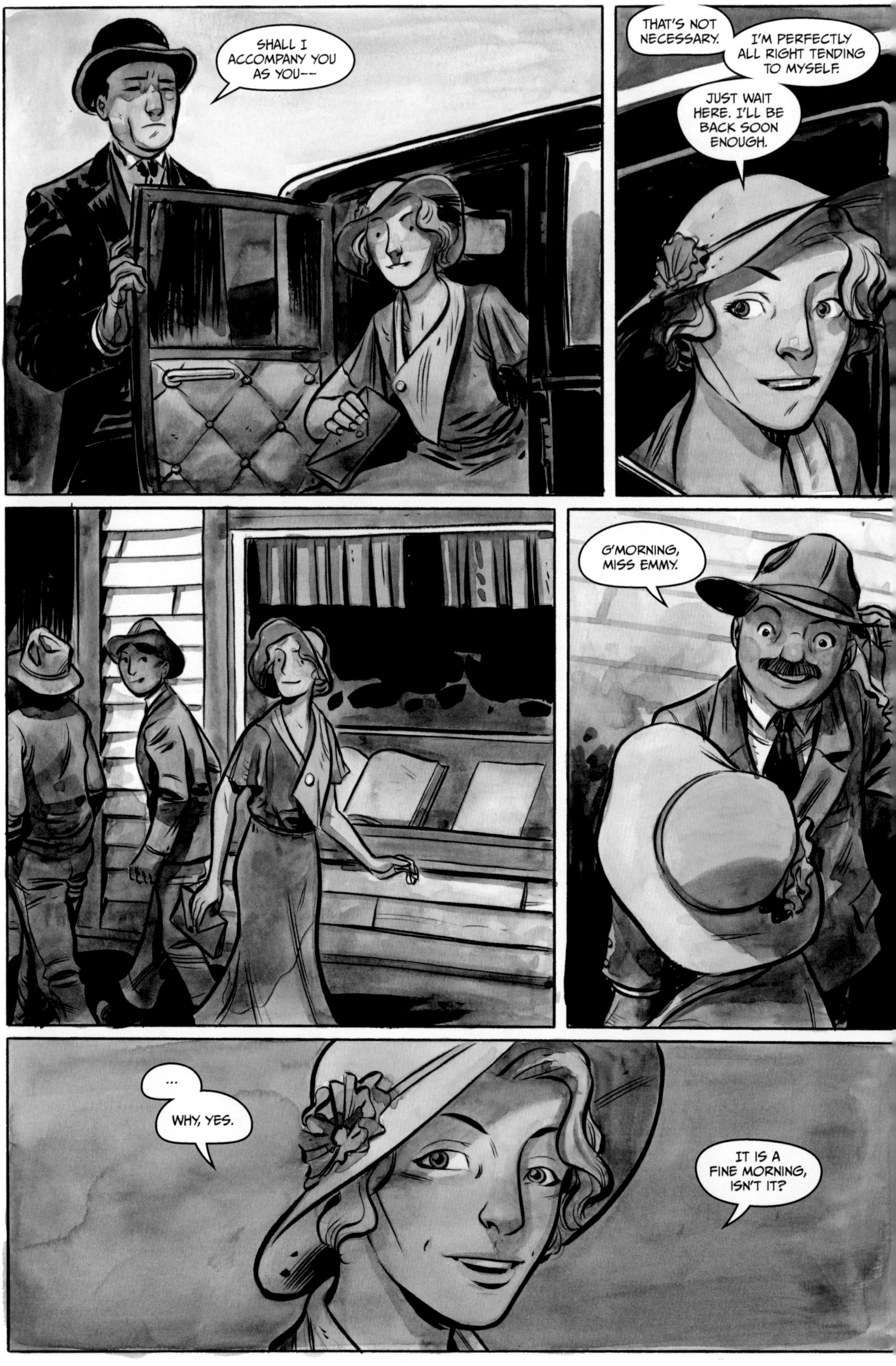
SHALL I ACCOMPANY YOU AS YOU--
THAT'S NOT NECESSARY.
I'M PERFECTLY ALL RIGHT TENDING TO MYSELF.
JUST WAIT HERE. I'LL BE BACK SOON ENOUGH.
G'MORNING, MISS EMMY.
...
WHY, YES.
IT IS A FINE MORNING, ISN'T IT?

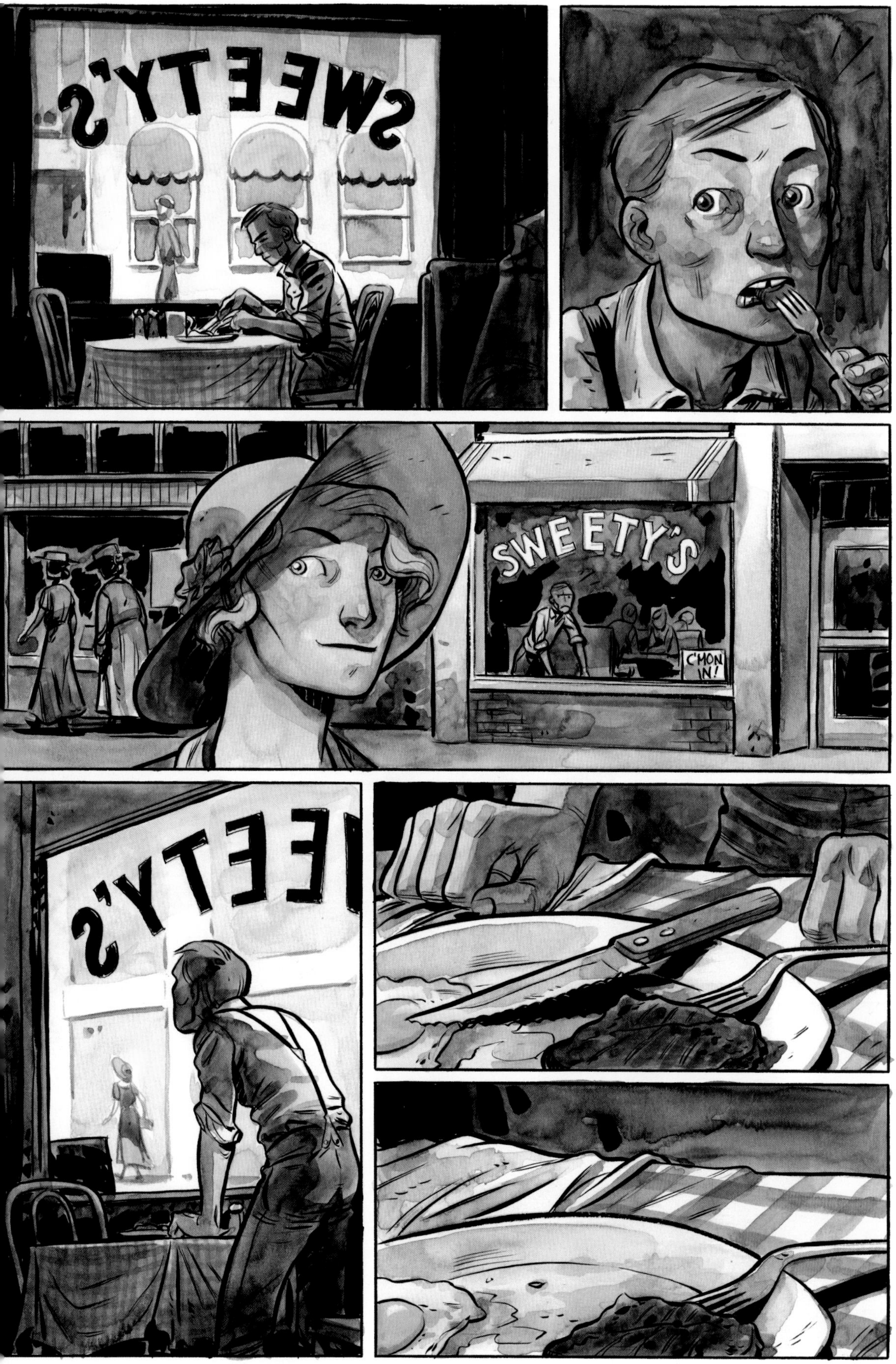
SWEETY'S
SWEETY'S
C'MON IN!

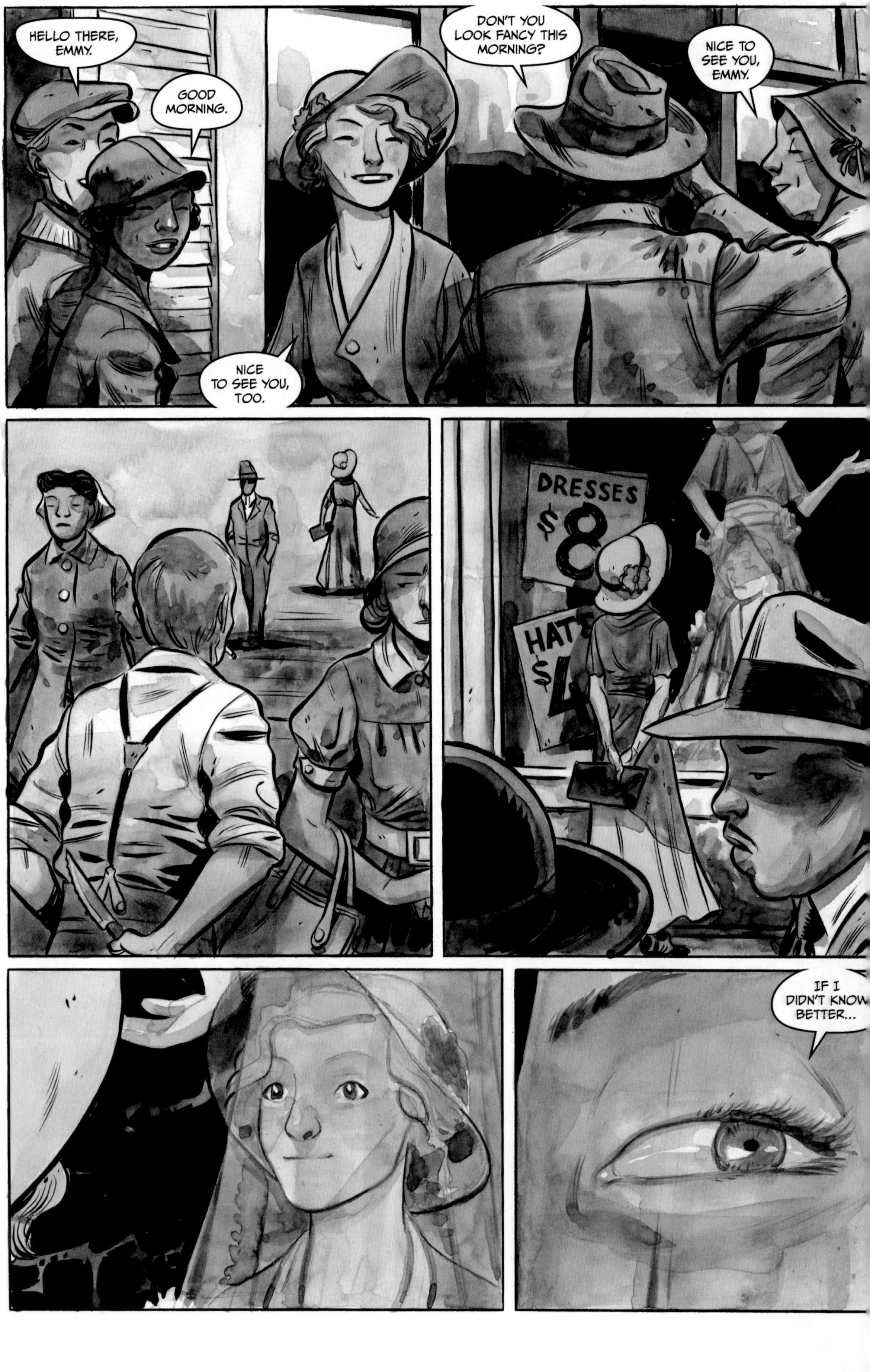
HELLO THERE, EMMY.
GOOD MORNING.
DON'T YOU LOOK FANCY THIS MORNING?
NICE TO SEE YOU, EMMY.
NICE TO SEE YOU, TOO.
DRESSES $8
HATS $4
IF I DIDN'T KNOW BETTER...

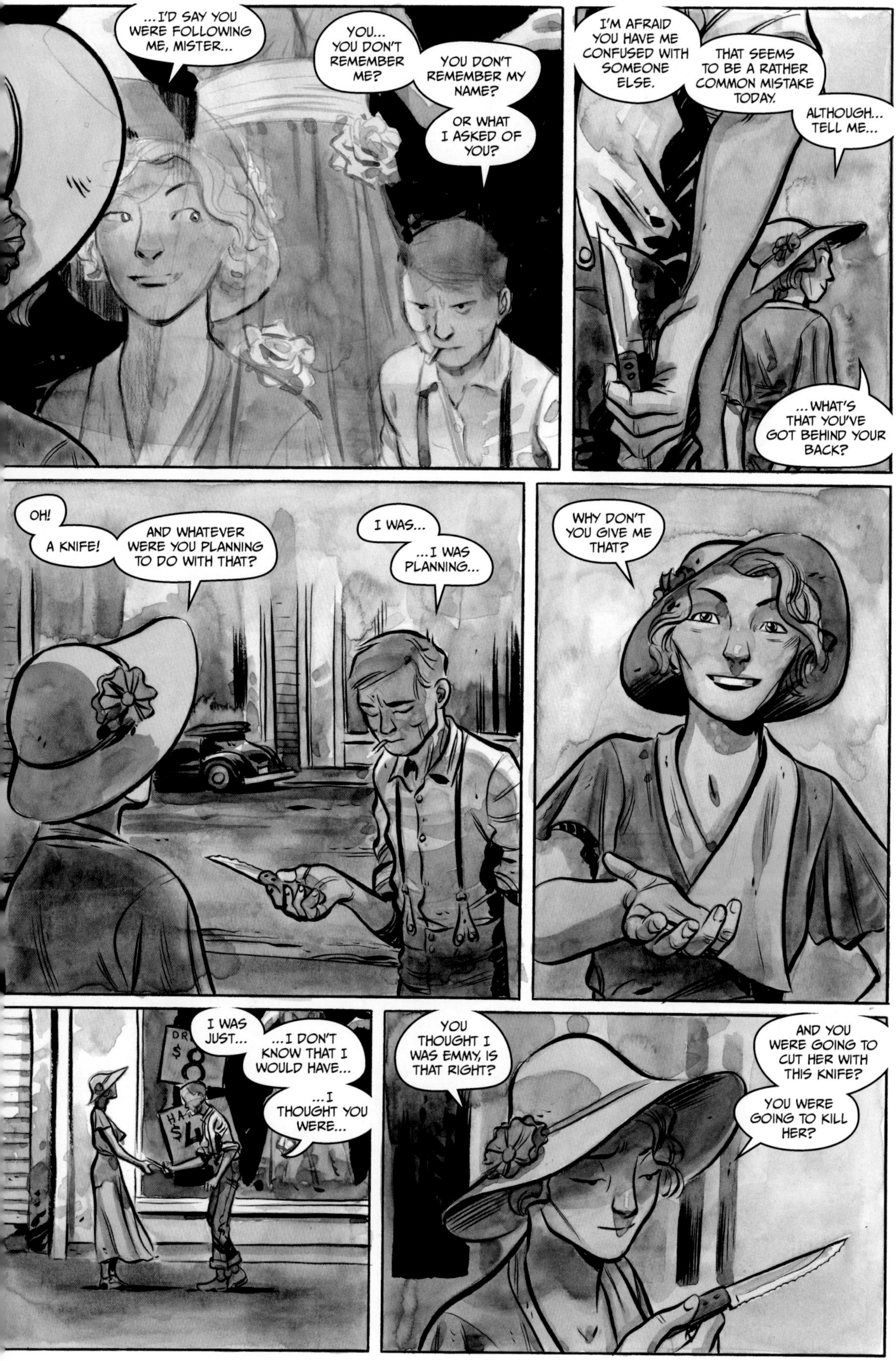
...I'D SAY YOU WERE FOLLOWING ME, MISTER...
YOU... YOU DON'T REMEMBER ME?
YOU DON'T REMEMBER MY NAME?
OR WHAT I ASKED OF YOU?
I'M AFRAID YOU HAVE ME CONFUSED WITH SOMEONE ELSE.
THAT SEEMS TO BE A RATHER COMMON MISTAKE TODAY.
ALTHOUGH... TELL ME...
...WHAT'S THAT YOU'VE GOT BEHIND YOUR BACK?
OH!
A KNIFE!
AND WHATEVER WERE YOU PLANNING TO DO WITH THAT?
I WAS...
...I WAS PLANNING...
WHY DON'T YOU GIVE ME THAT?
I WAS JUST...
...I DON'T KNOW THAT I WOULD HAVE...
...I THOUGHT YOU WERE...
YOU THOUGHT I WAS EMMY, IS THAT RIGHT?
AND YOU WERE GOING TO CUT HER WITH THIS KNIFE?
YOU WERE GOING TO KILL HER?

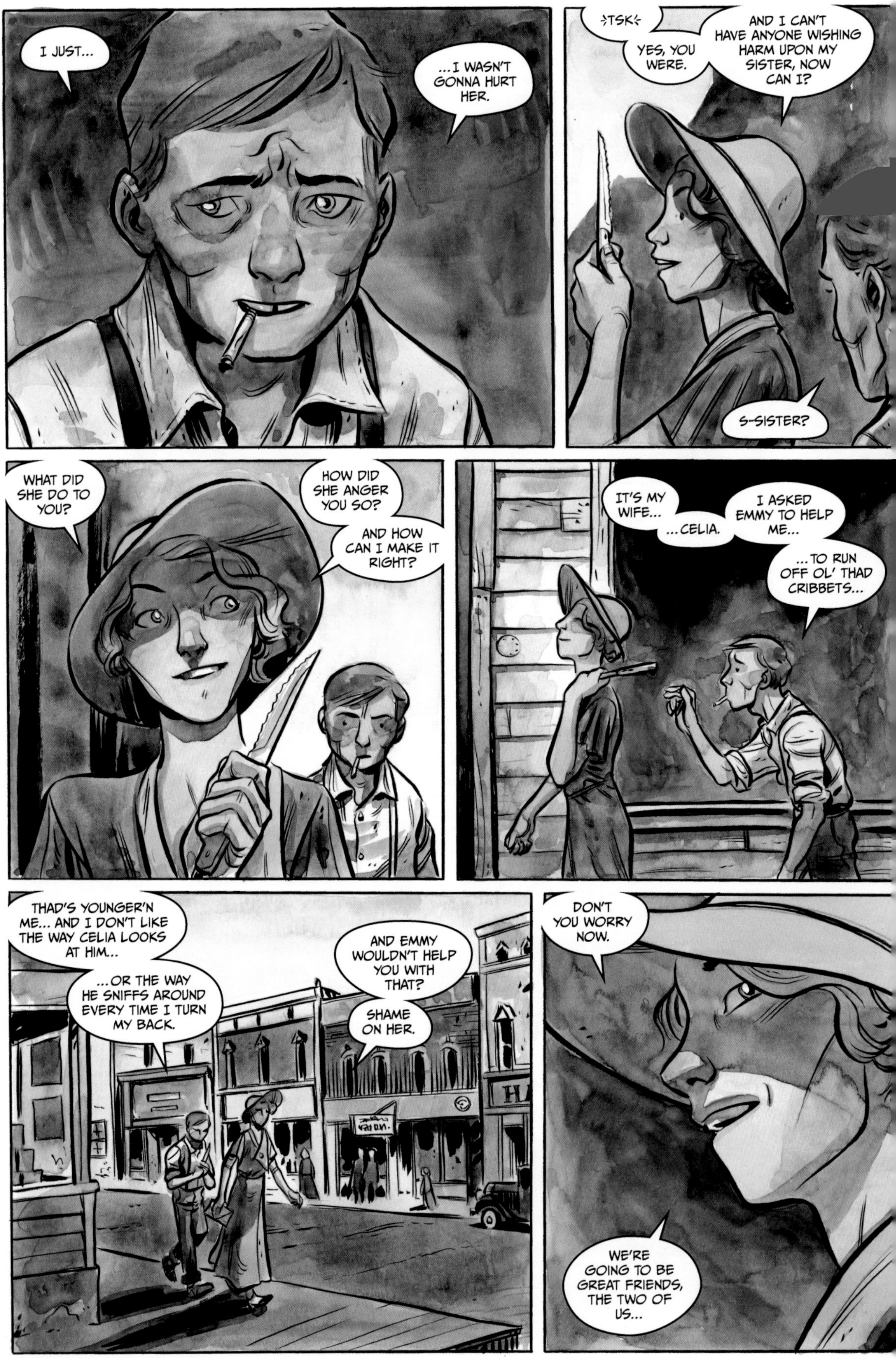
I JUST...
...I WASN'T GONNA HURT HER.
-TSK-
YES, YOU WERE.
AND I CAN'T HAVE ANYONE WISHING HARM UPON MY SISTER, NOW CAN I?
S-SISTER?
WHAT DID SHE DO TO YOU?
HOW DID SHE ANGER YOU SO?
AND HOW CAN I MAKE IT RIGHT?
IT'S MY WIFE...
...CELIA.
I ASKED EMMY TO HELP ME...
...TO RUN OFF OL' THAD CRIBBETS...
THAD'S YOUNGER'N ME... AND I DON'T LIKE THE WAY CELIA LOOKS AT HIM...
...OR THE WAY HE SNIFFS AROUND EVERY TIME I TURN MY BACK.
AND EMMY WOULDN'T HELP YOU WITH THAT?
SHAME ON HER.
DON'T YOU WORRY NOW.
WE'RE GOING TO BE GREAT FRIENDS, THE TWO OF US...

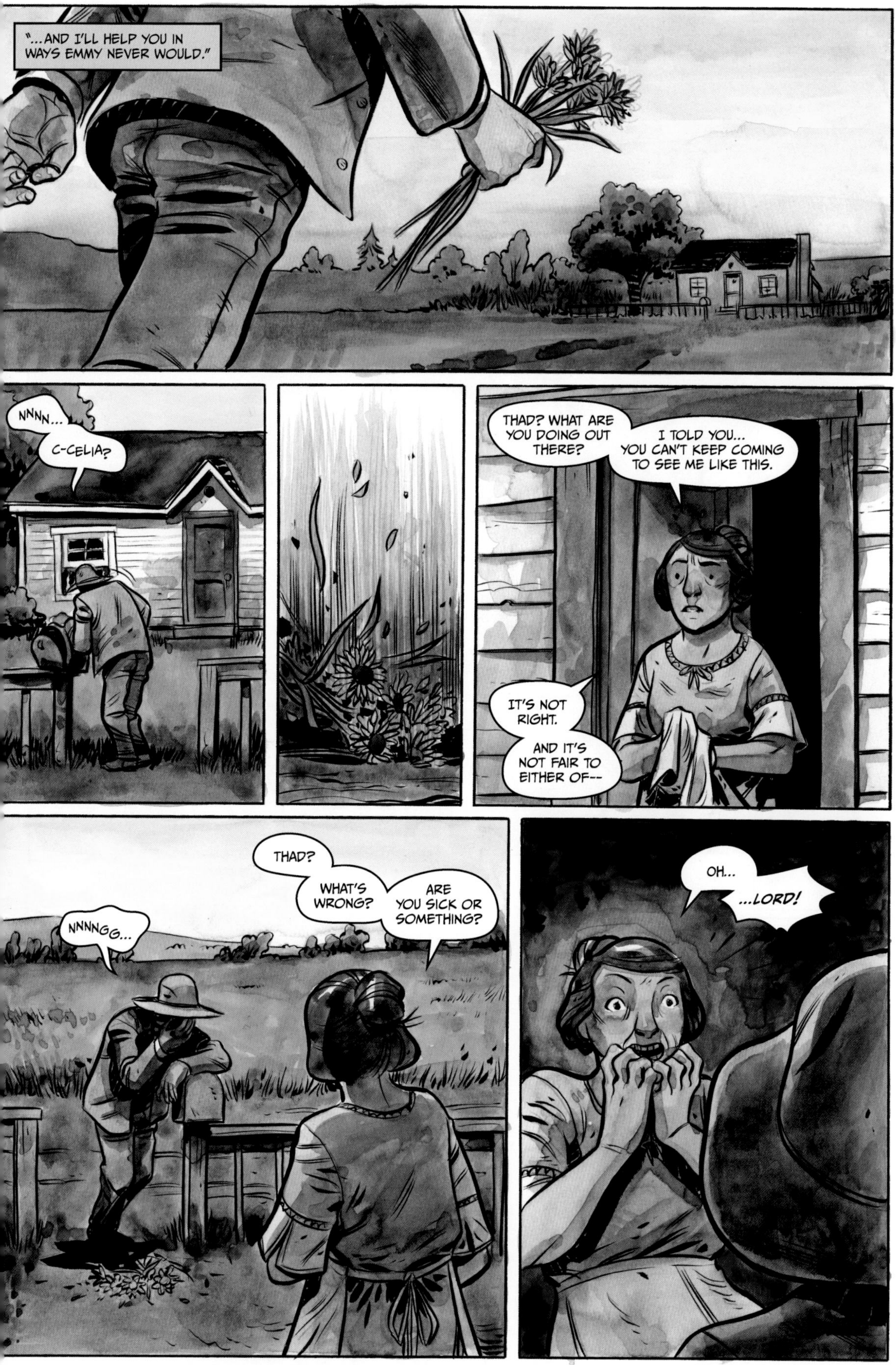
"...AND I'LL HELP YOU IN WAYS EMMY NEVER WOULD."
NNNN...
C-CELIA?
THAD? WHAT ARE YOU DOING OUT THERE?
I TOLD YOU... YOU CAN'T KEEP COMING TO SEE ME LIKE THIS.
IT'S NOT RIGHT.
AND IT'S NOT FAIR TO EITHER OF--
THAD?
WHAT'S WRONG?
ARE YOU SICK OR SOMETHING?
NNNNGG...
OH...
...LORD!

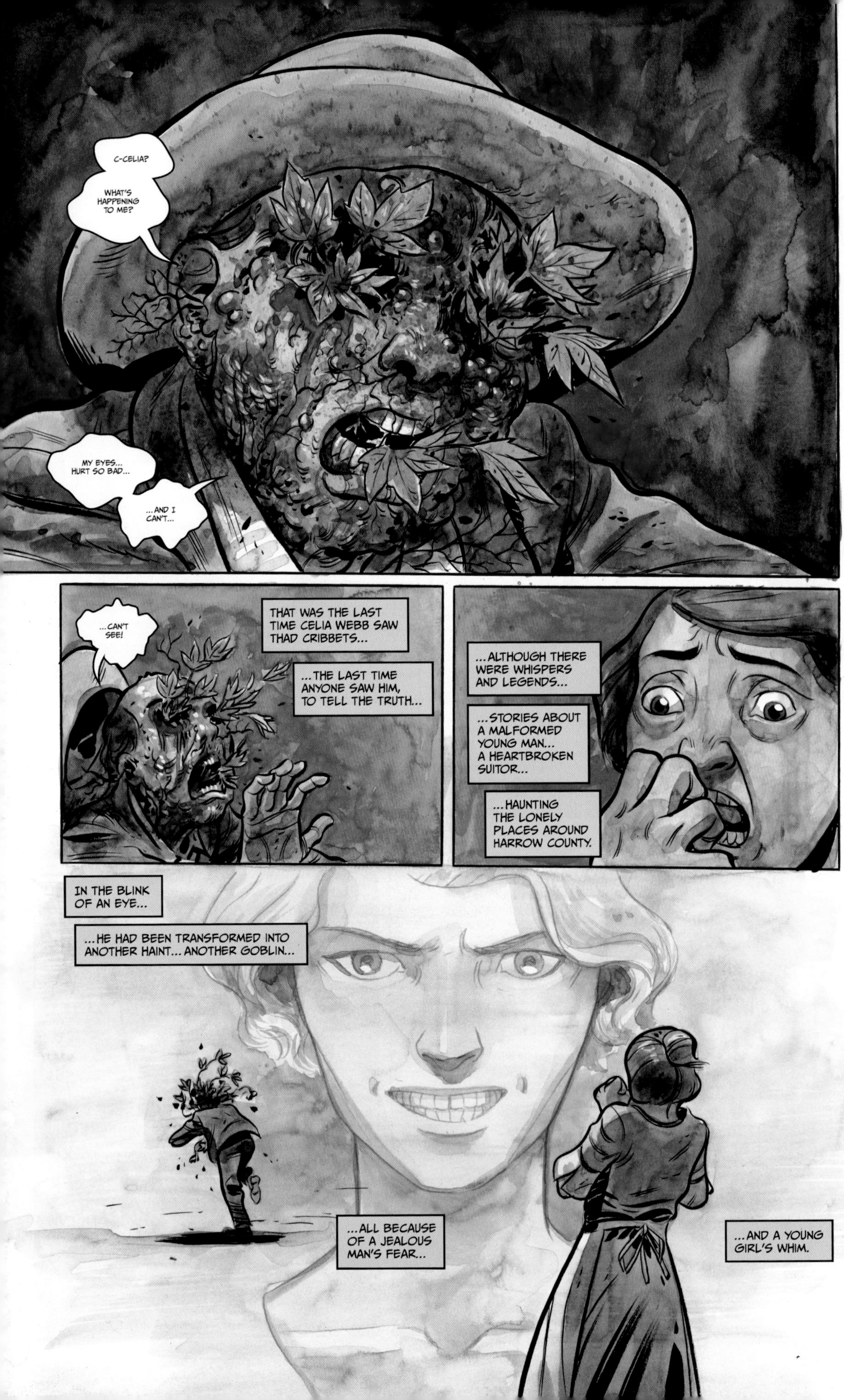
C-CELIA?
WHAT'S HAPPENING TO ME?
MY EYES... HURT SO BAD...
...AND I CAN'T...
...CAN'T SEE!
THAT WAS THE LAST TIME CELIA WEBB SAW THAD CRIBBETS...
...THE LAST TIME ANYONE SAW HIM, TO TELL THE TRUTH...
...ALTHOUGH THERE WERE WHISPERS AND LEGENDS...
...STORIES ABOUT A MALFORMED YOUNG MAN... A HEARTBROKEN SUITOR...
...HAUNTING THE LONELY PLACES AROUND HARROW COUNTY.
IN THE BLINK OF AN EYE...
...HE HAD BEEN TRANSFORMED INTO ANOTHER HAINT... ANOTHER GOBLIN...
...ALL BECAUSE OF A JEALOUS MAN'S FEAR...
...AND A YOUNG GIRL'S WHIM.

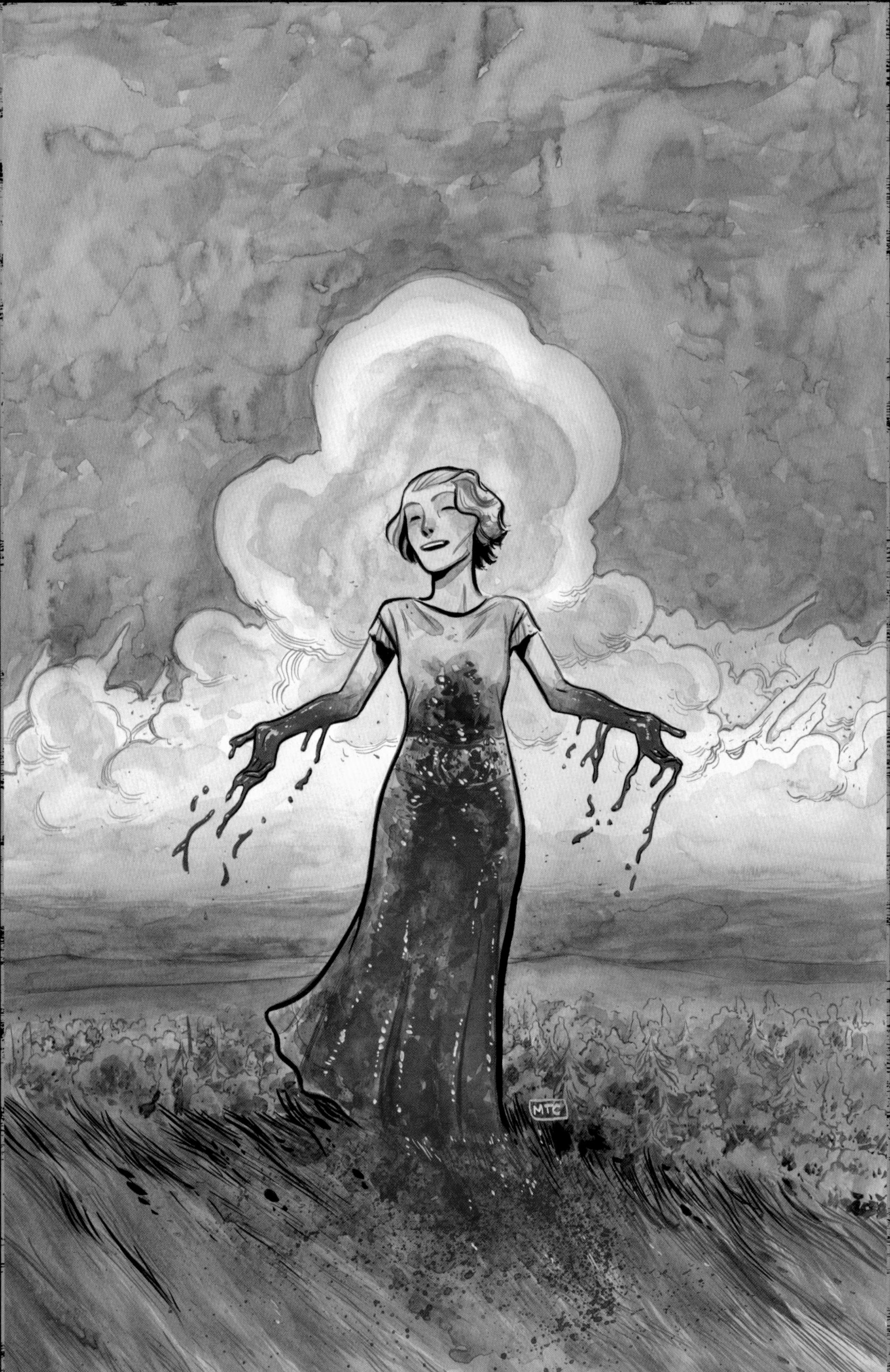
MTC

THREE

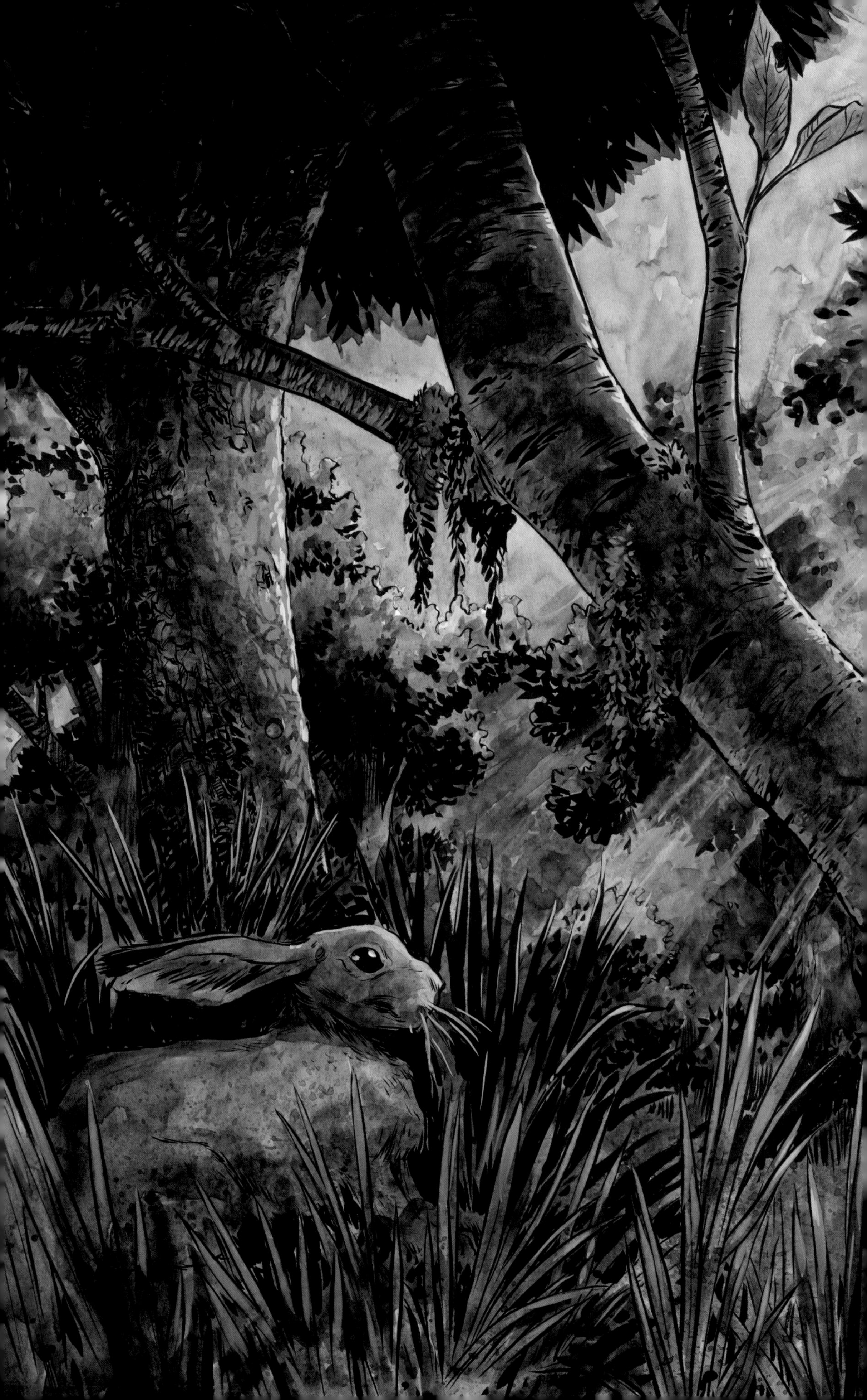

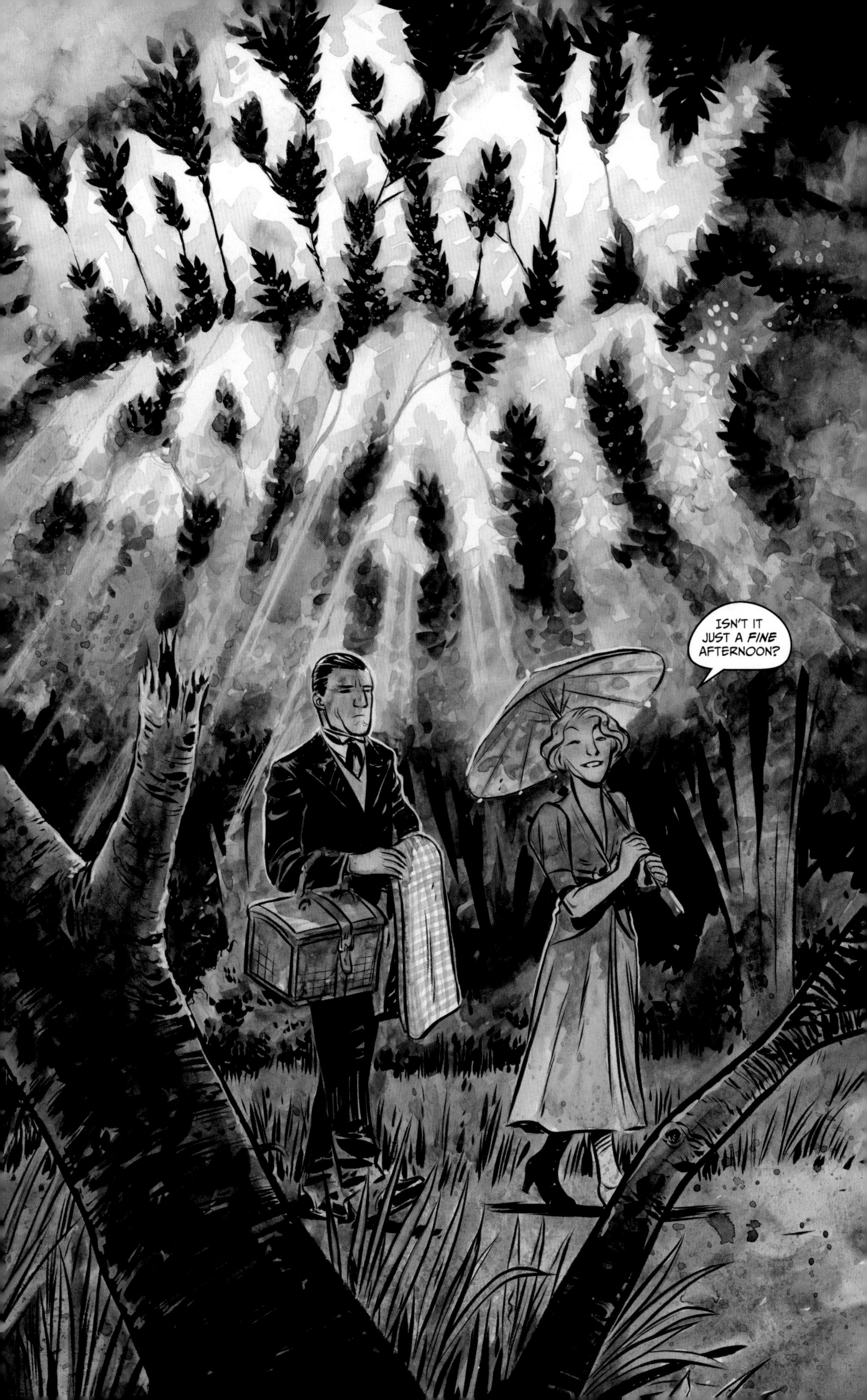
ISN'T IT JUST A *FINE* AFTERNOON?

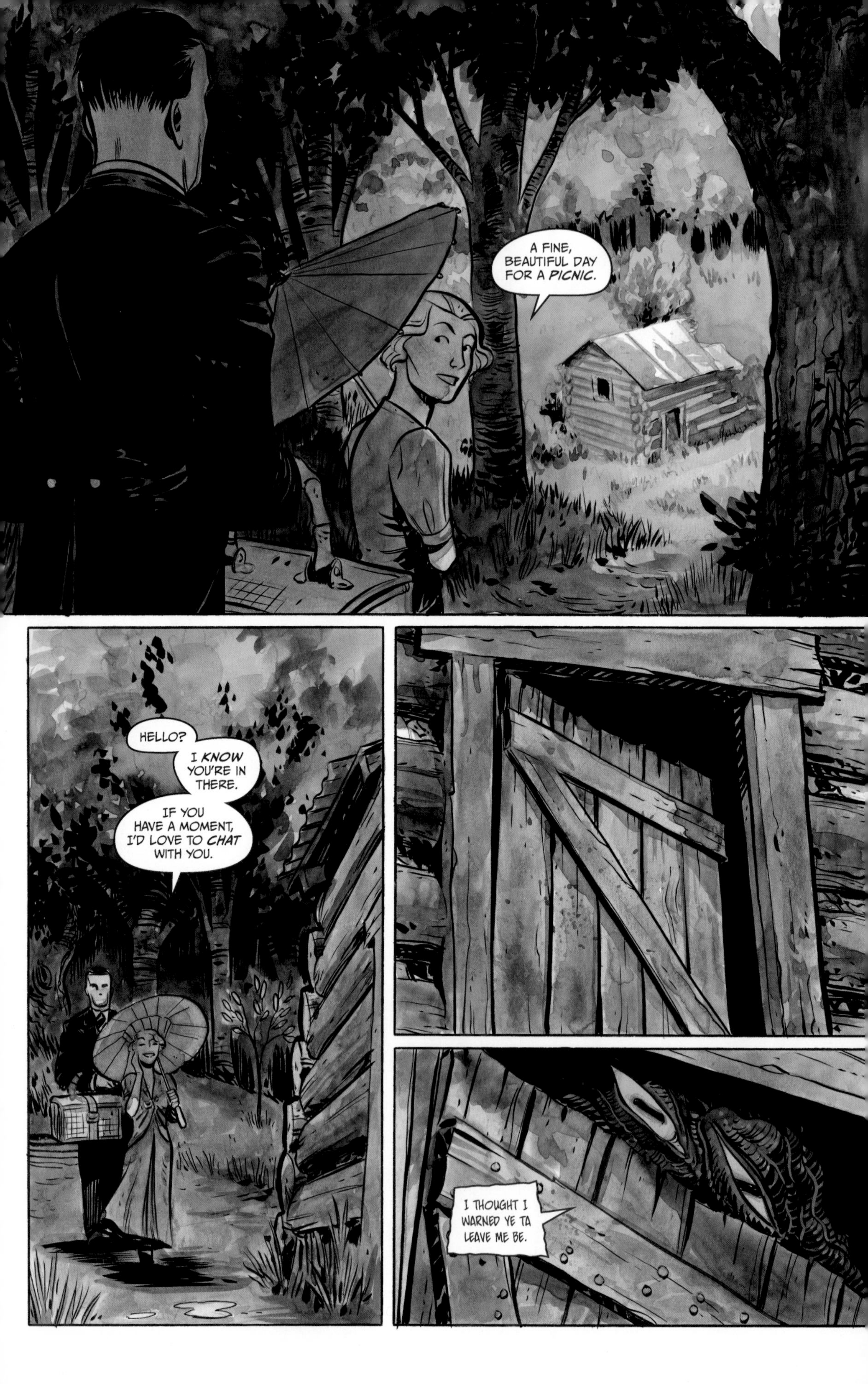
A FINE, BEAUTIFUL DAY FOR A *PICNIC*.
HELLO?
I *KNOW* YOU'RE IN THERE.
IF YOU HAVE A MOMENT, I'D LOVE TO *CHAT* WITH YOU.
I THOUGHT I WARNED YE TA LEAVE ME BE.

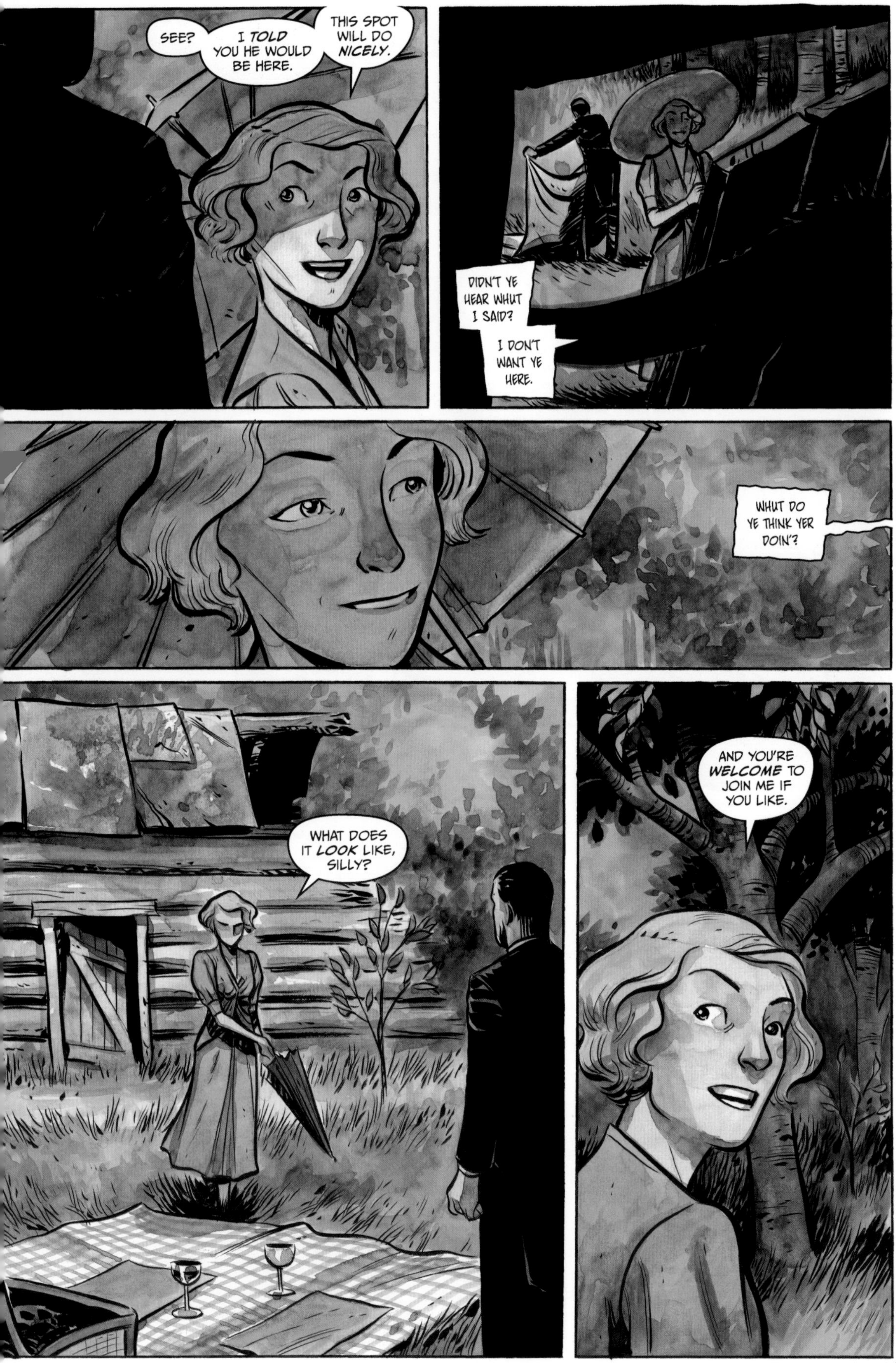
SEE?
I *TOLD* YOU HE WOULD BE HERE.
THIS SPOT WILL DO *NICELY*.
DIDN'T YE HEAR WHUT I SAID?
I DON'T WANT YE HERE.
WHUT DO YE THINK YER DOIN'?
WHAT DOES IT *LOOK* LIKE, SILLY?
AND YOU'RE *WELCOME* TO JOIN ME IF YOU LIKE.

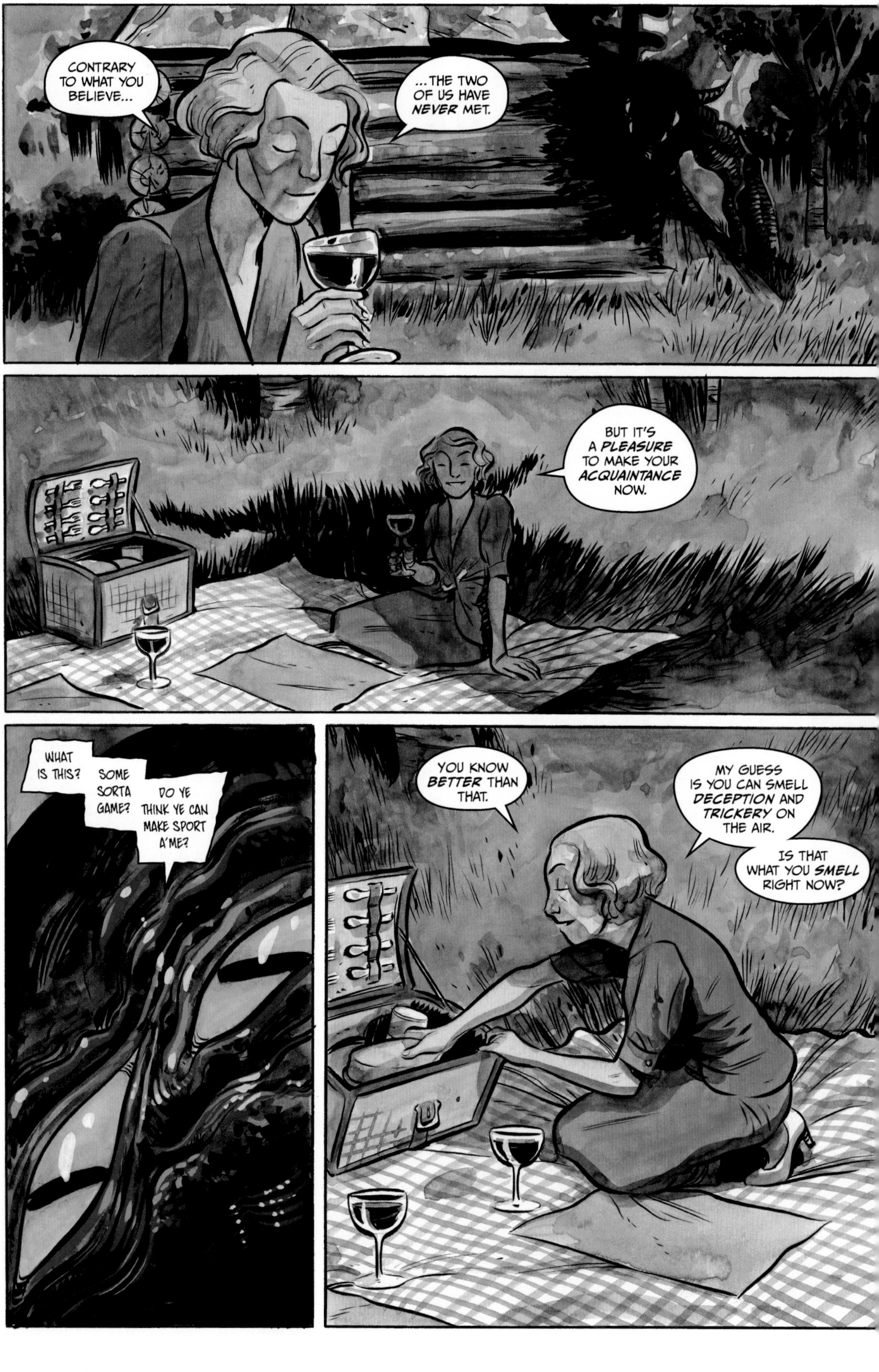
CONTRARY TO WHAT YOU BELIEVE...
...THE TWO OF US HAVE *NEVER* MET.
BUT IT'S A *PLEASURE* TO MAKE YOUR *ACQUAINTANCE* NOW.
WHAT IS THIS?
SOME SORTA GAME?
DO YE THINK YE CAN MAKE SPORT A'ME?
YOU KNOW *BETTER* THAN THAT.
MY GUESS IS YOU CAN SMELL *DECEPTION* AND *TRICKERY* ON THE AIR.
IS THAT WHAT YOU *SMELL* RIGHT NOW?

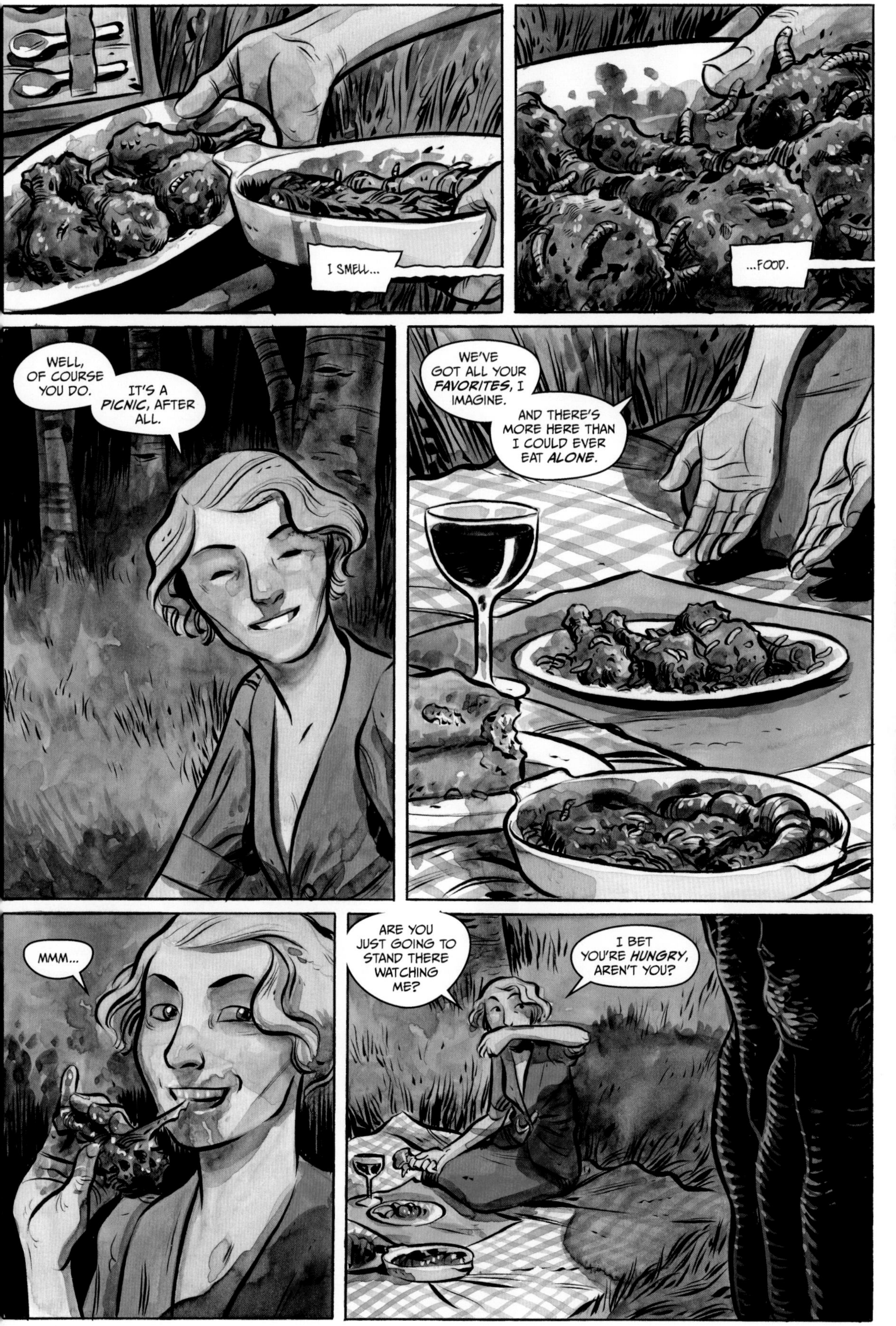
I SMELL...
...FOOD.
WELL, OF COURSE YOU DO.
IT'S A *PICNIC*, AFTER ALL.
WE'VE GOT ALL YOUR *FAVORITES*, I IMAGINE.
AND THERE'S MORE HERE THAN I COULD EVER EAT *ALONE*.
MMM...
ARE YOU JUST GOING TO STAND THERE WATCHING ME?
I BET YOU'RE *HUNGRY*, AREN'T YOU?

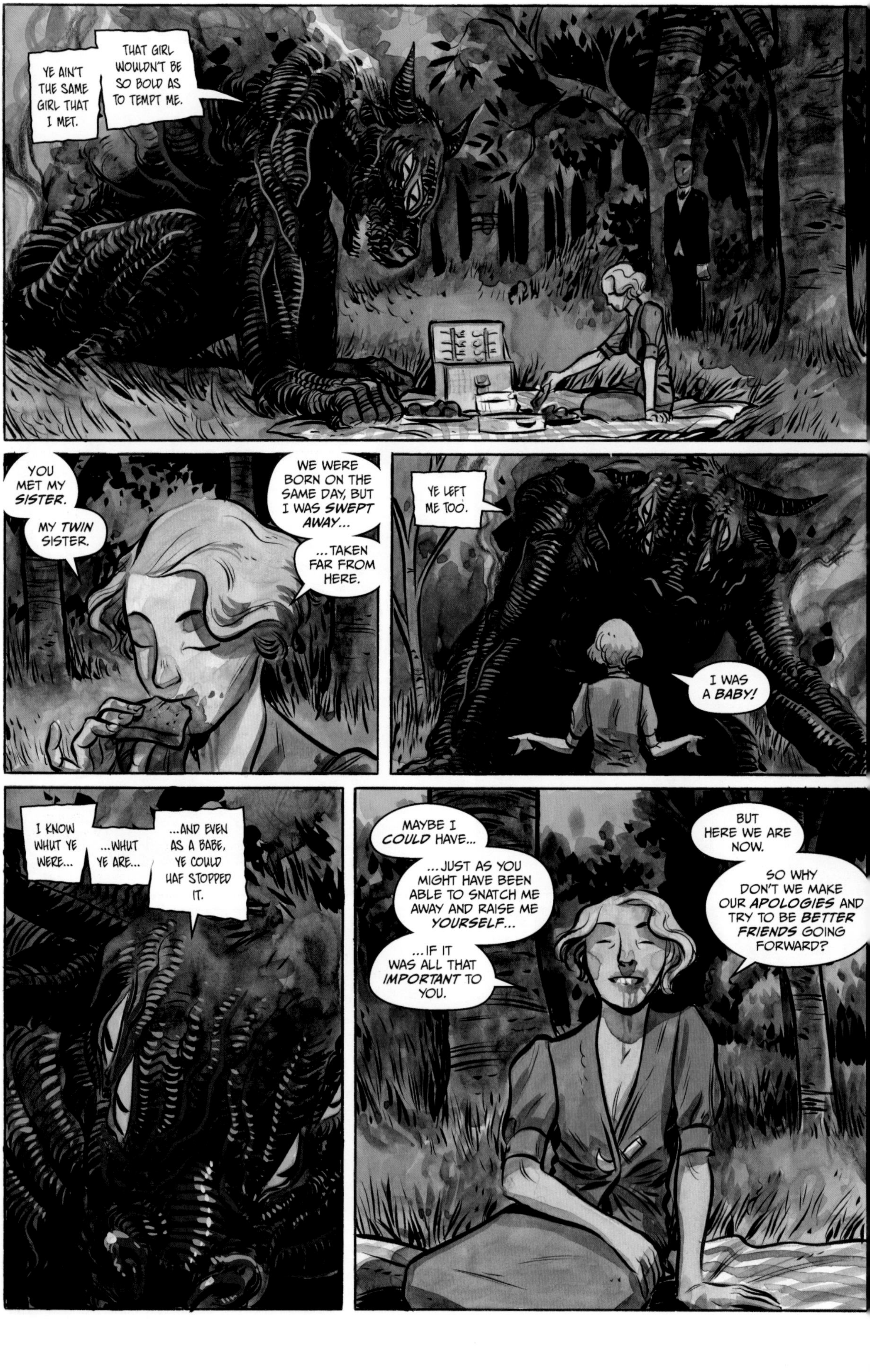
YE AIN'T THE SAME GIRL THAT I MET.
THAT GIRL WOULDN'T BE SO BOLD AS TO TEMPT ME.
YOU MET MY SISTER.
MY TWIN SISTER.
WE WERE BORN ON THE SAME DAY, BUT I WAS SWEPT AWAY...
...TAKEN FAR FROM HERE.
YE LEFT ME TOO.
I WAS A BABY!
I KNOW WHUT YE WERE...
...WHUT YE ARE...
...AND EVEN AS A BABE, YE COULD HAF STOPPED IT.
MAYBE I COULD HAVE...
...JUST AS YOU MIGHT HAVE BEEN ABLE TO SNATCH ME AWAY AND RAISE ME YOURSELF...
...IF IT WAS ALL THAT IMPORTANT TO YOU.
BUT HERE WE ARE NOW.
SO WHY DON'T WE MAKE OUR APOLOGIES AND TRY TO BE BETTER FRIENDS GOING FORWARD?

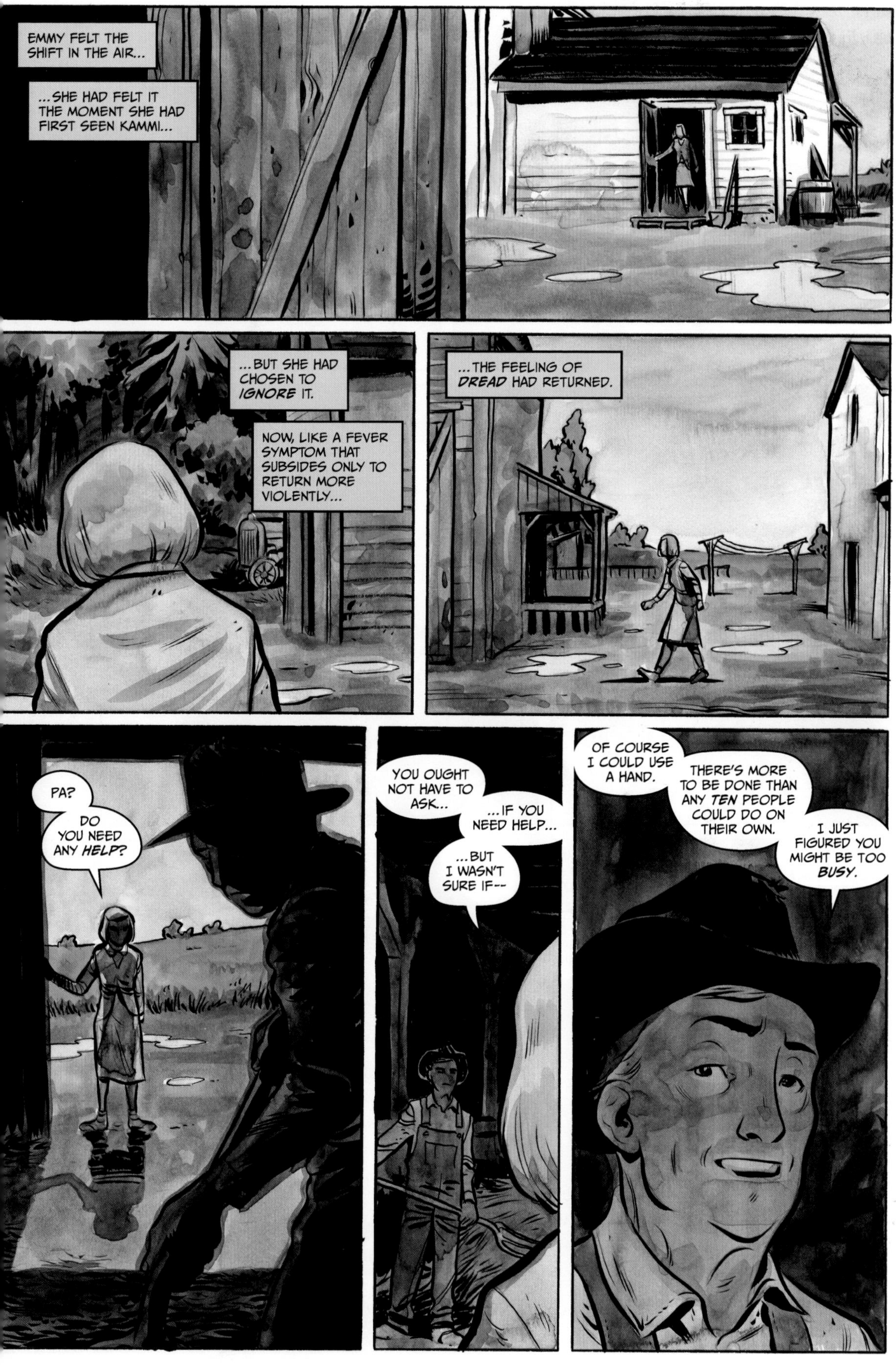
EMMY FELT THE SHIFT IN THE AIR...
...SHE HAD FELT IT THE MOMENT SHE HAD FIRST SEEN KAMMI...
...BUT SHE HAD CHOSEN TO *IGNORE* IT.
NOW, LIKE A FEVER SYMPTOM THAT SUBSIDES ONLY TO RETURN MORE VIOLENTLY...
...THE FEELING OF *DREAD* HAD RETURNED.
PA?
DO YOU NEED ANY *HELP?*
YOU OUGHT NOT HAVE TO ASK...
...IF YOU NEED HELP...
...BUT I WASN'T SURE IF--
OF COURSE I COULD USE A HAND.
THERE'S MORE TO BE DONE THAN ANY *TEN* PEOPLE COULD DO ON THEIR OWN.
I JUST FIGURED YOU MIGHT BE TOO *BUSY*.

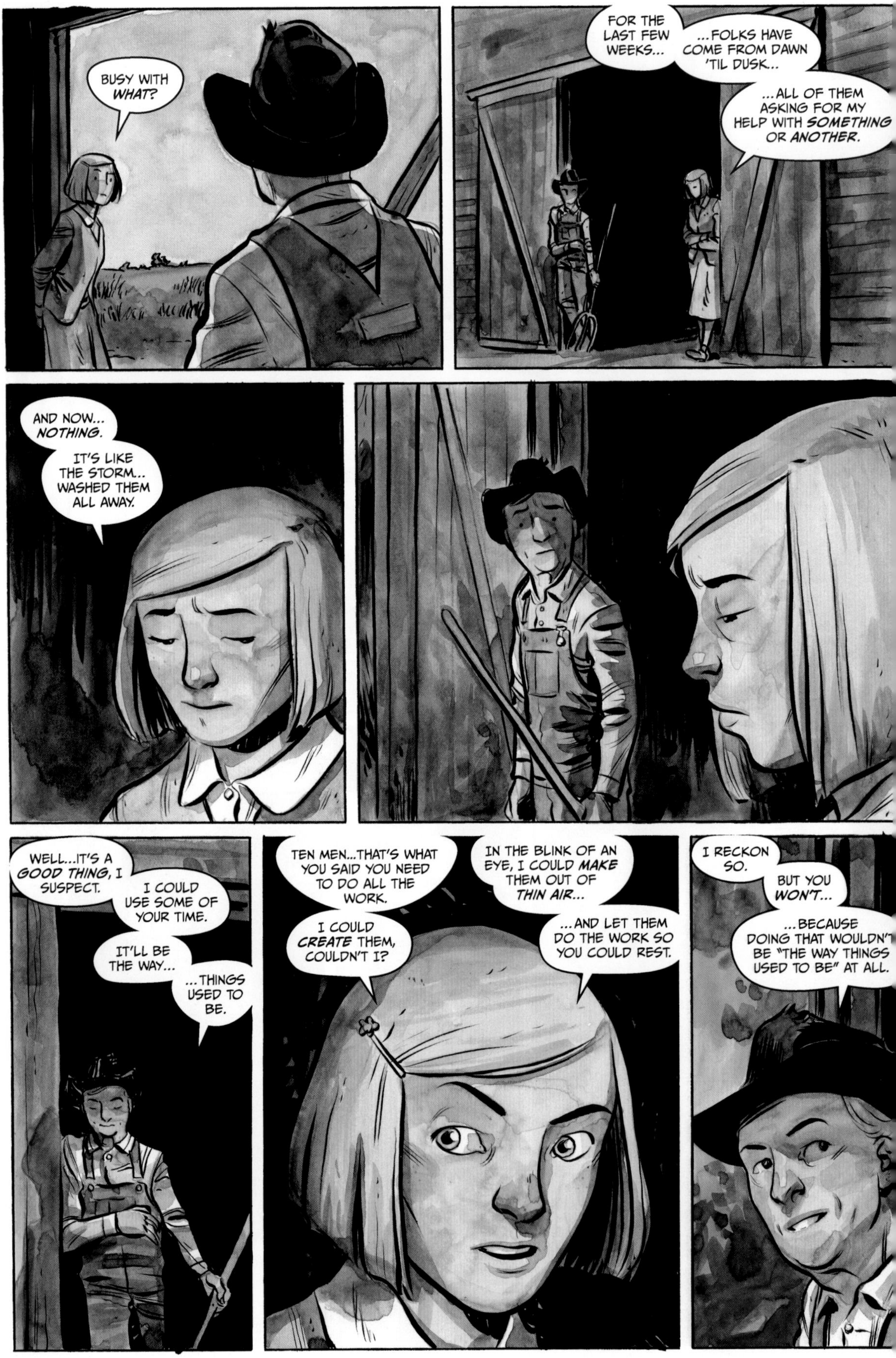
BUSY WITH *WHAT?*
FOR THE LAST FEW WEEKS...
...FOLKS HAVE COME FROM DAWN 'TIL DUSK...
...ALL OF THEM ASKING FOR MY HELP WITH *SOMETHING* OR *ANOTHER.*
AND NOW... *NOTHING.*
IT'S LIKE THE STORM... WASHED THEM ALL AWAY.
WELL...IT'S A *GOOD THING,* I SUSPECT.
I COULD USE SOME OF YOUR TIME.
IT'LL BE THE WAY...
...THINGS USED TO BE.
TEN MEN...THAT'S WHAT YOU SAID YOU NEED TO DO ALL THE WORK.
I COULD *CREATE* THEM, COULDN'T I?
IN THE BLINK OF AN EYE, I COULD *MAKE* THEM OUT OF *THIN AIR...*
...AND LET THEM DO THE WORK SO YOU COULD REST.
I RECKON SO.
BUT YOU *WON'T...*
...BECAUSE DOING THAT WOULDN'T BE "THE WAY THINGS USED TO BE" AT ALL.

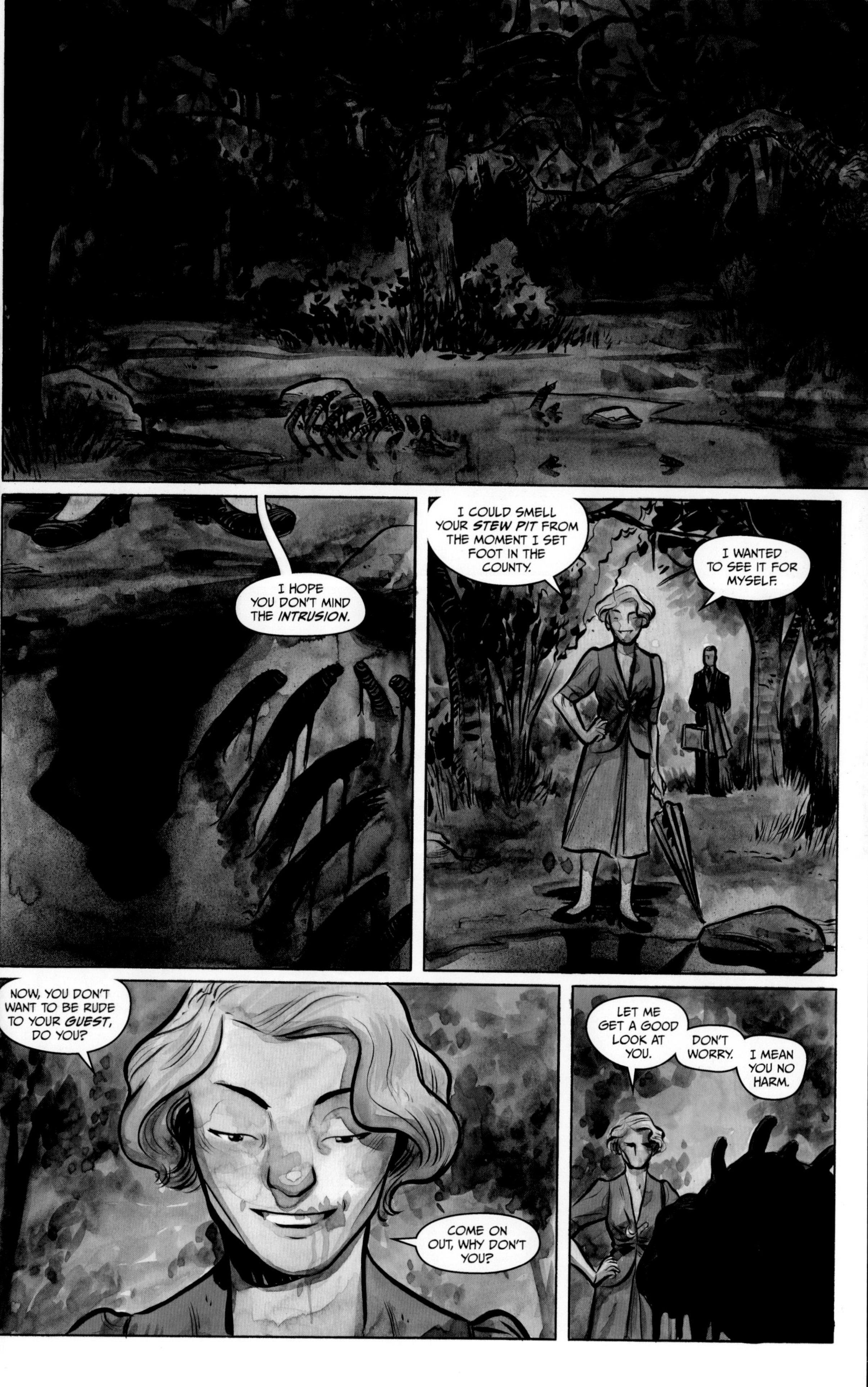
I HOPE YOU DON'T MIND THE *INTRUSION*.
I COULD SMELL YOUR ***STEW PIT*** FROM THE MOMENT I SET FOOT IN THE COUNTY.
I WANTED TO SEE IT FOR MYSELF.
NOW, YOU DON'T WANT TO BE RUDE TO YOUR ***GUEST***, DO YOU?
COME ON OUT, WHY DON'T YOU?
LET ME GET A GOOD LOOK AT YOU.
DON'T WORRY.
I MEAN YOU NO HARM.

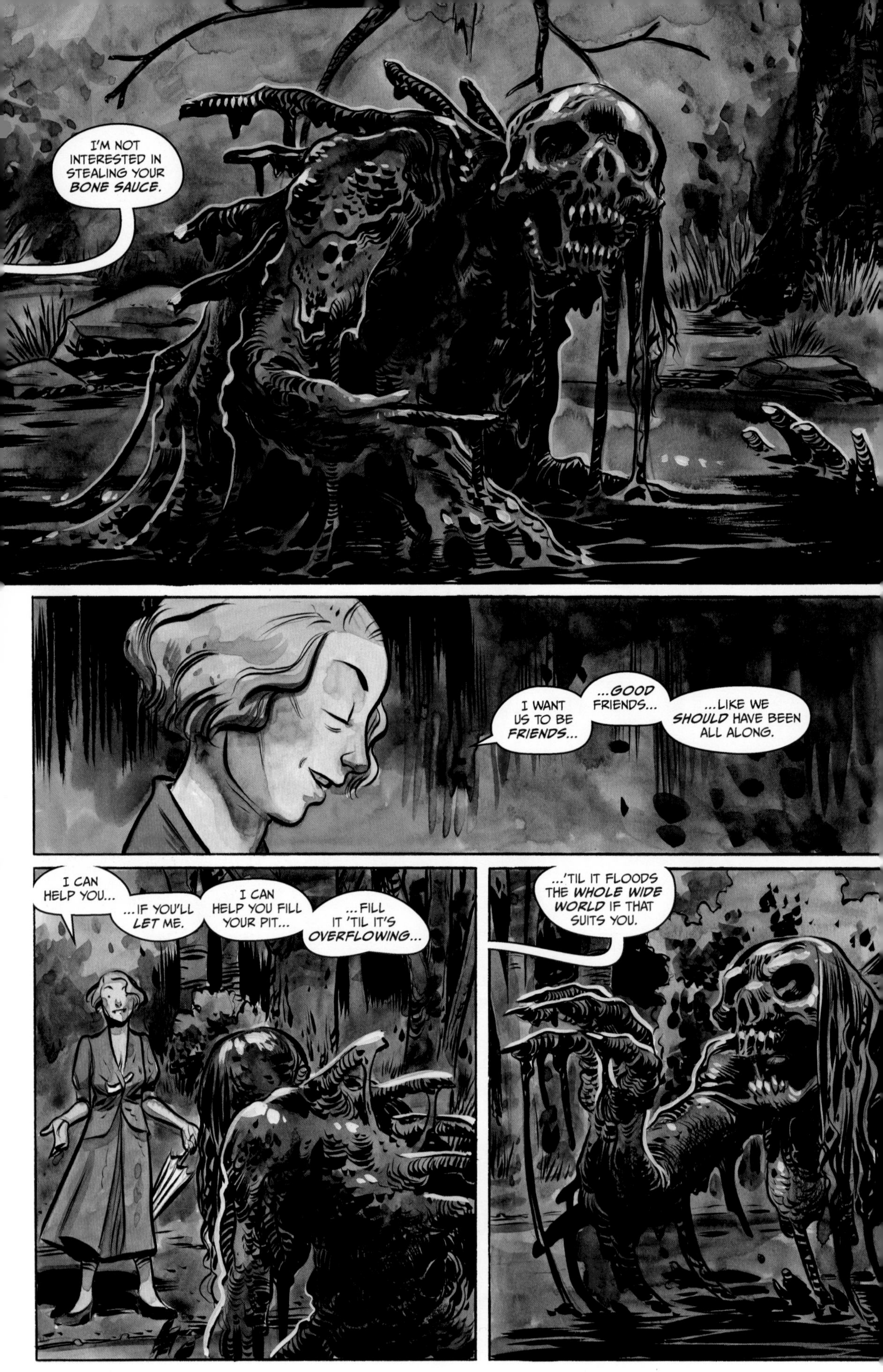
I'M NOT INTERESTED IN STEALING YOUR *BONE SAUCE*.
I WANT US TO BE *FRIENDS*...
...*GOOD* FRIENDS...
...LIKE WE *SHOULD* HAVE BEEN ALL ALONG.
I CAN HELP YOU...
...IF YOU'LL *LET* ME.
I CAN HELP YOU FILL YOUR PIT...
...FILL IT 'TIL IT'S *OVERFLOWING*...
...'TIL IT FLOODS THE *WHOLE WIDE WORLD* IF THAT SUITS YOU.

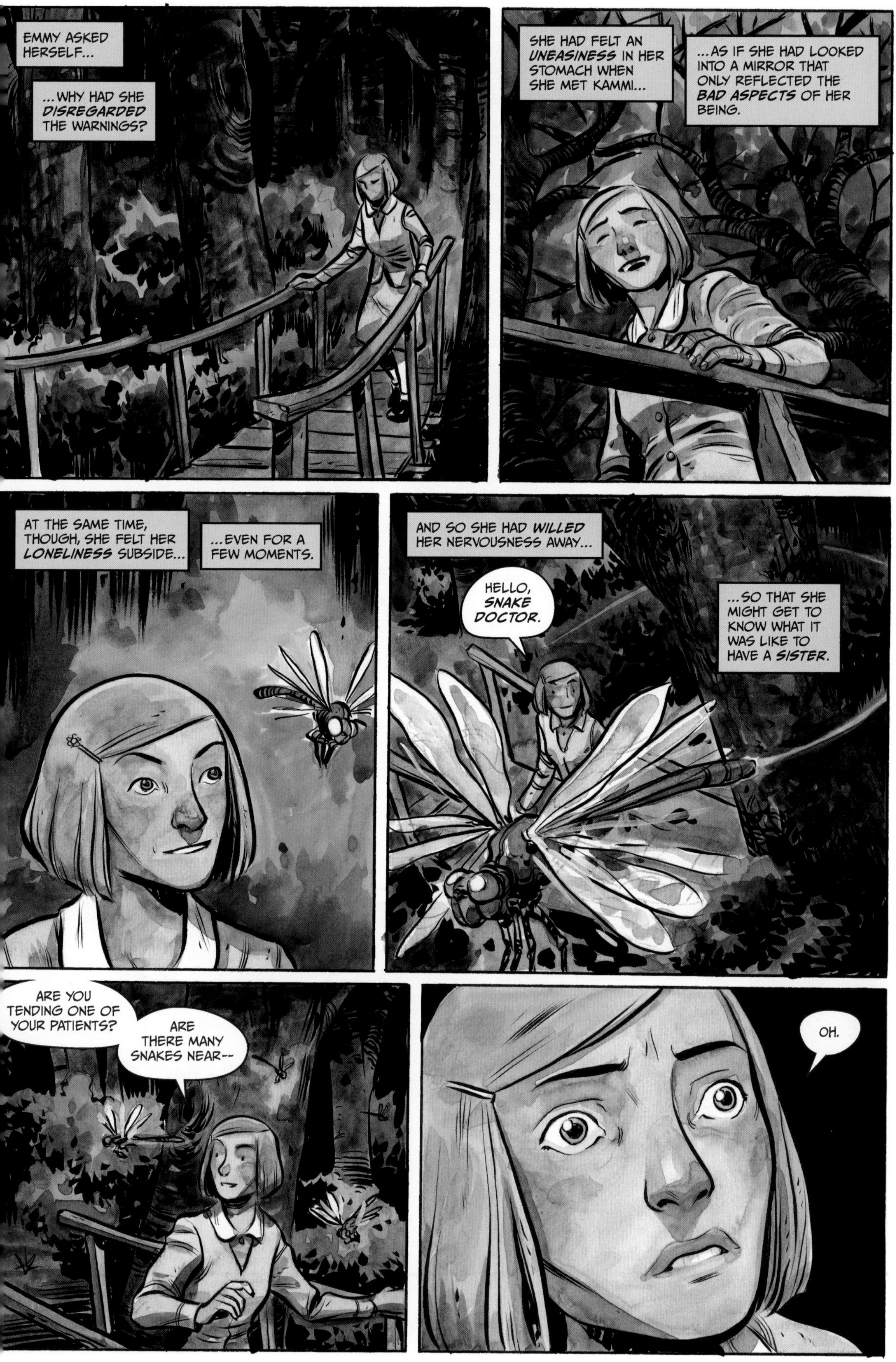
EMMY ASKED HERSELF...
...WHY HAD SHE DISREGARDED THE WARNINGS?
SHE HAD FELT AN UNEASINESS IN HER STOMACH WHEN SHE MET KAMMI...
...AS IF SHE HAD LOOKED INTO A MIRROR THAT ONLY REFLECTED THE BAD ASPECTS OF HER BEING.
AT THE SAME TIME, THOUGH, SHE FELT HER LONELINESS SUBSIDE...
...EVEN FOR A FEW MOMENTS.
AND SO SHE HAD WILLED HER NERVOUSNESS AWAY...
HELLO, SNAKE DOCTOR.
...SO THAT SHE MIGHT GET TO KNOW WHAT IT WAS LIKE TO HAVE A SISTER.
ARE YOU TENDING ONE OF YOUR PATIENTS?
ARE THERE MANY SNAKES NEAR--
OH.

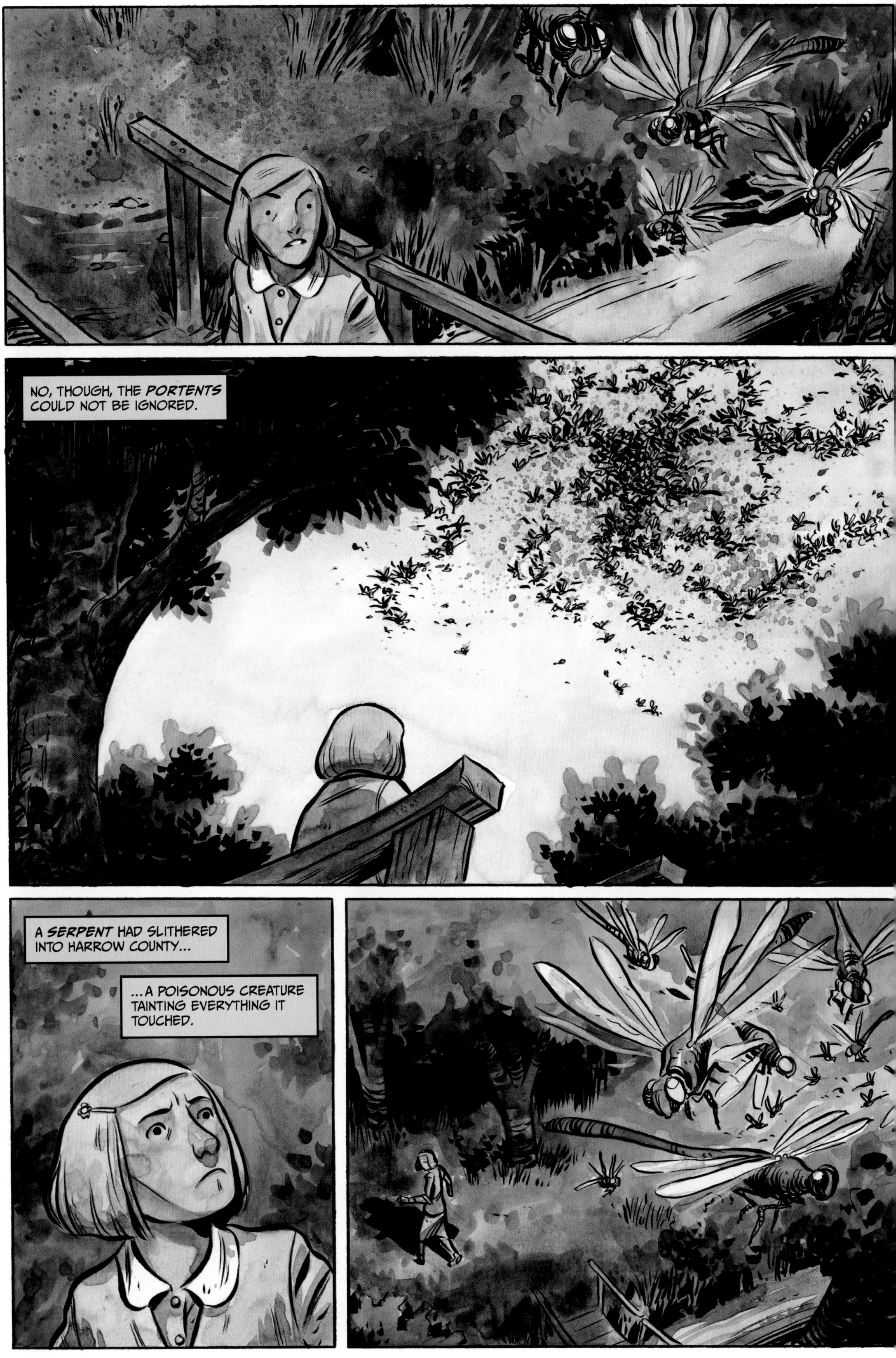
NO, THOUGH, THE *PORTENTS* COULD NOT BE IGNORED.
A *SERPENT* HAD SLITHERED INTO HARROW COUNTY...
...A POISONOUS CREATURE TAINTING EVERYTHING IT TOUCHED.

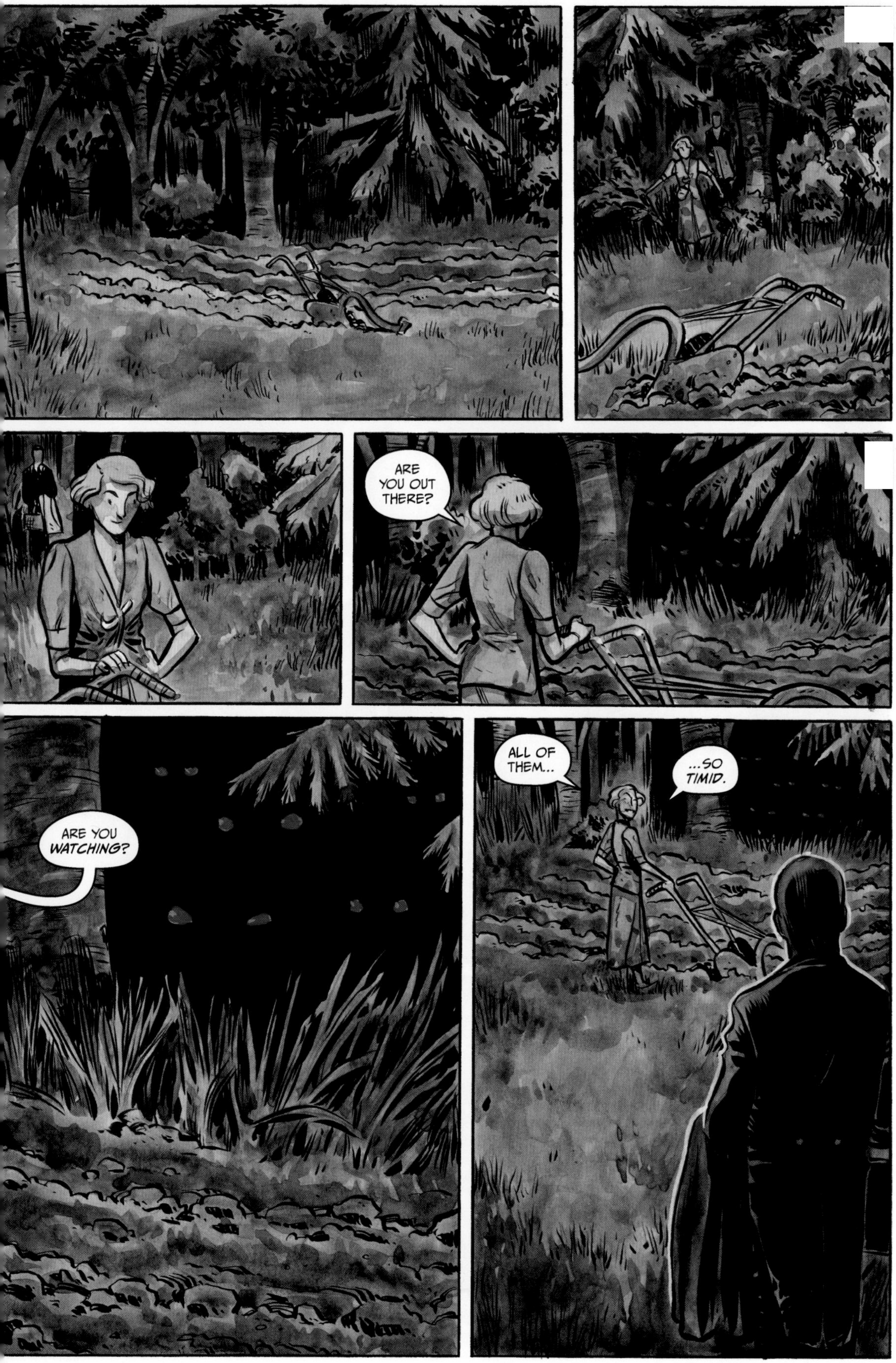
ARE YOU OUT THERE?
ARE YOU WATCHING?
ALL OF THEM...
...SO TIMID.

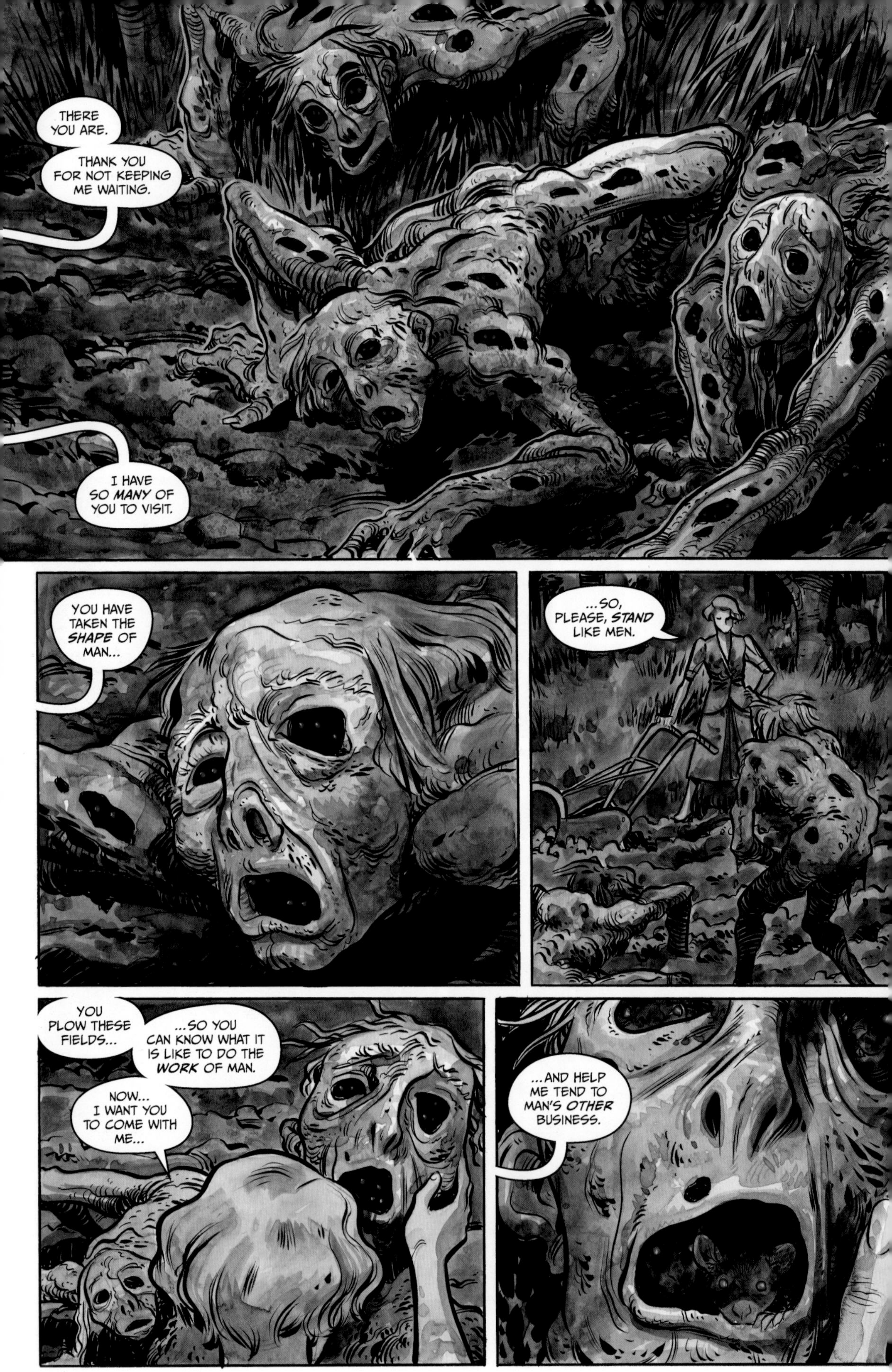

THERE YOU ARE.
THANK YOU FOR NOT KEEPING ME WAITING.
I HAVE SO *MANY* OF YOU TO VISIT.
YOU HAVE TAKEN THE *SHAPE* OF MAN...
...SO, PLEASE, *STAND* LIKE MEN.
YOU PLOW THESE FIELDS...
...SO YOU CAN KNOW WHAT IT IS LIKE TO DO THE *WORK* OF MAN.
NOW... I WANT YOU TO COME WITH ME...
...AND HELP ME TEND TO MAN'S *OTHER* BUSINESS.

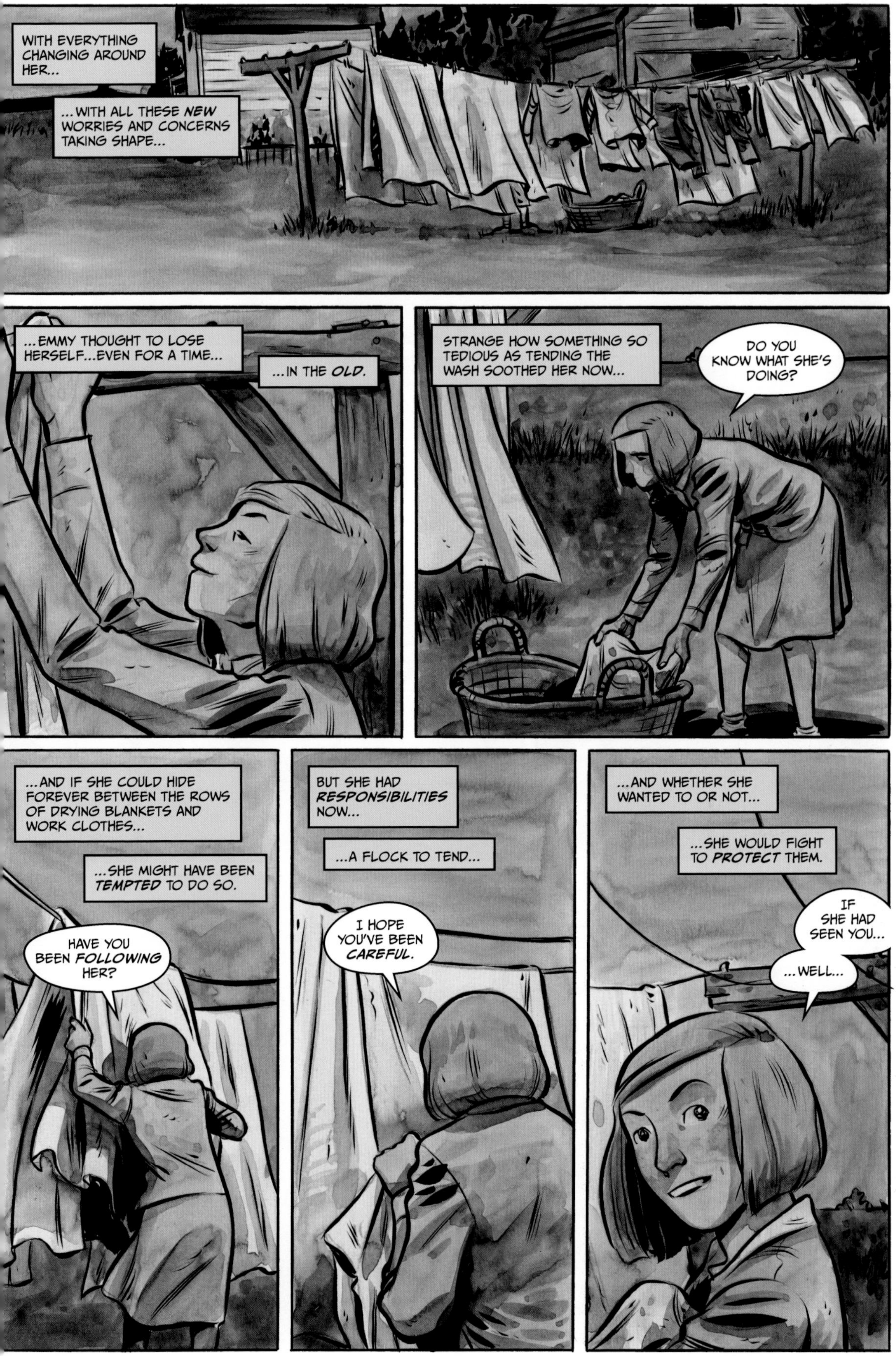
WITH EVERYTHING CHANGING AROUND HER...
...WITH ALL THESE NEW WORRIES AND CONCERNS TAKING SHAPE...
...EMMY THOUGHT TO LOSE HERSELF...EVEN FOR A TIME...
...IN THE OLD.
STRANGE HOW SOMETHING SO TEDIOUS AS TENDING THE WASH SOOTHED HER NOW...
DO YOU KNOW WHAT SHE'S DOING?
...AND IF SHE COULD HIDE FOREVER BETWEEN THE ROWS OF DRYING BLANKETS AND WORK CLOTHES...
...SHE MIGHT HAVE BEEN TEMPTED TO DO SO.
HAVE YOU BEEN FOLLOWING HER?
BUT SHE HAD RESPONSIBILITIES NOW...
...A FLOCK TO TEND...
I HOPE YOU'VE BEEN CAREFUL.
...AND WHETHER SHE WANTED TO OR NOT...
...SHE WOULD FIGHT TO PROTECT THEM.
IF SHE HAD SEEN YOU...
...WELL...

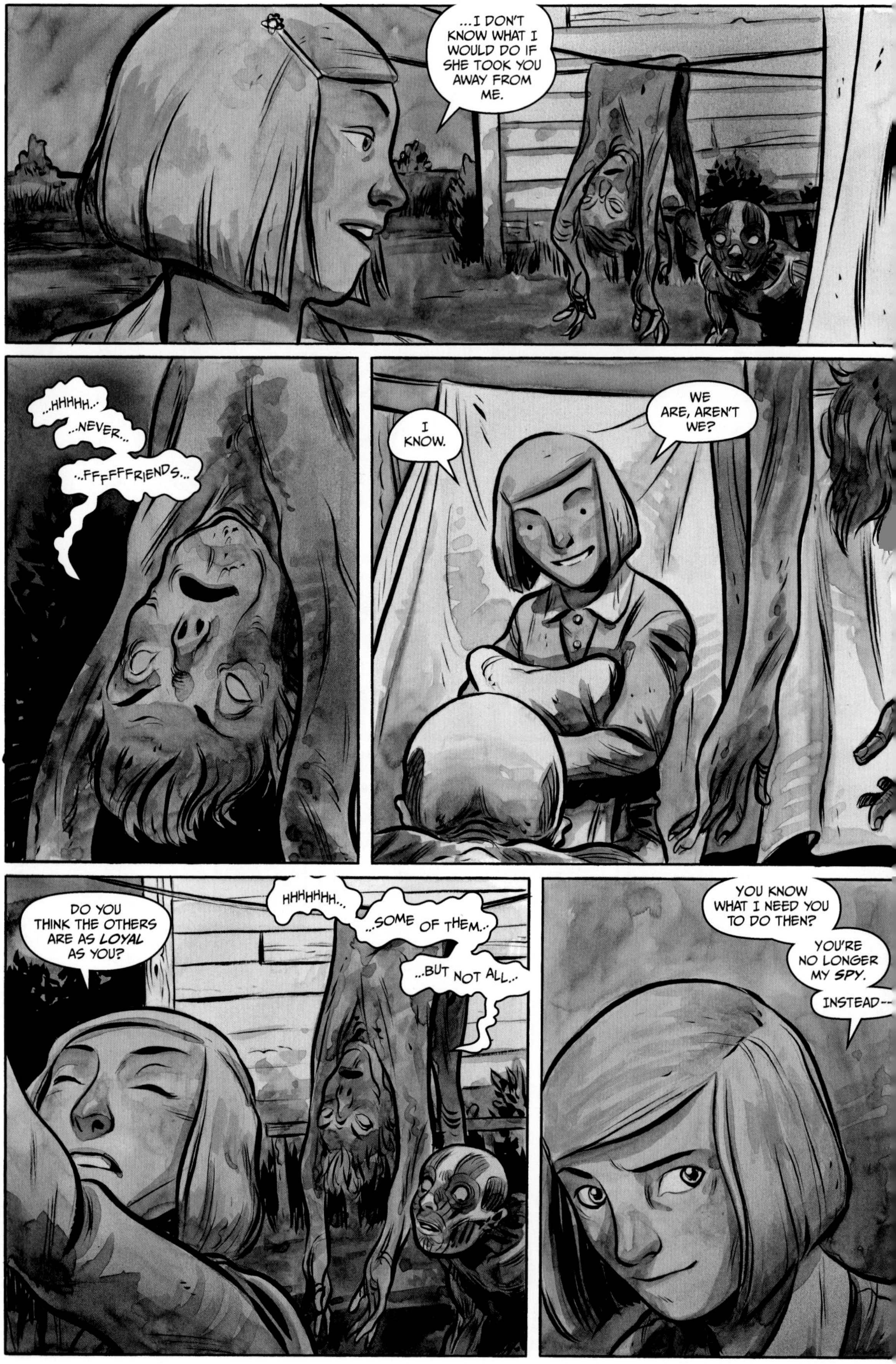
...I DON'T KNOW WHAT I WOULD DO IF SHE TOOK YOU AWAY FROM ME.
...HHHHH...
...NEVER...
...FFFFFFRIENDS...
I KNOW.
WE ARE, AREN'T WE?
DO YOU THINK THE OTHERS ARE AS LOYAL AS YOU?
HHHHHHH...
...SOME OF THEM...
...BUT NOT ALL...
YOU KNOW WHAT I NEED YOU TO DO THEN?
YOU'RE NO LONGER MY SPY.
INSTEAD--

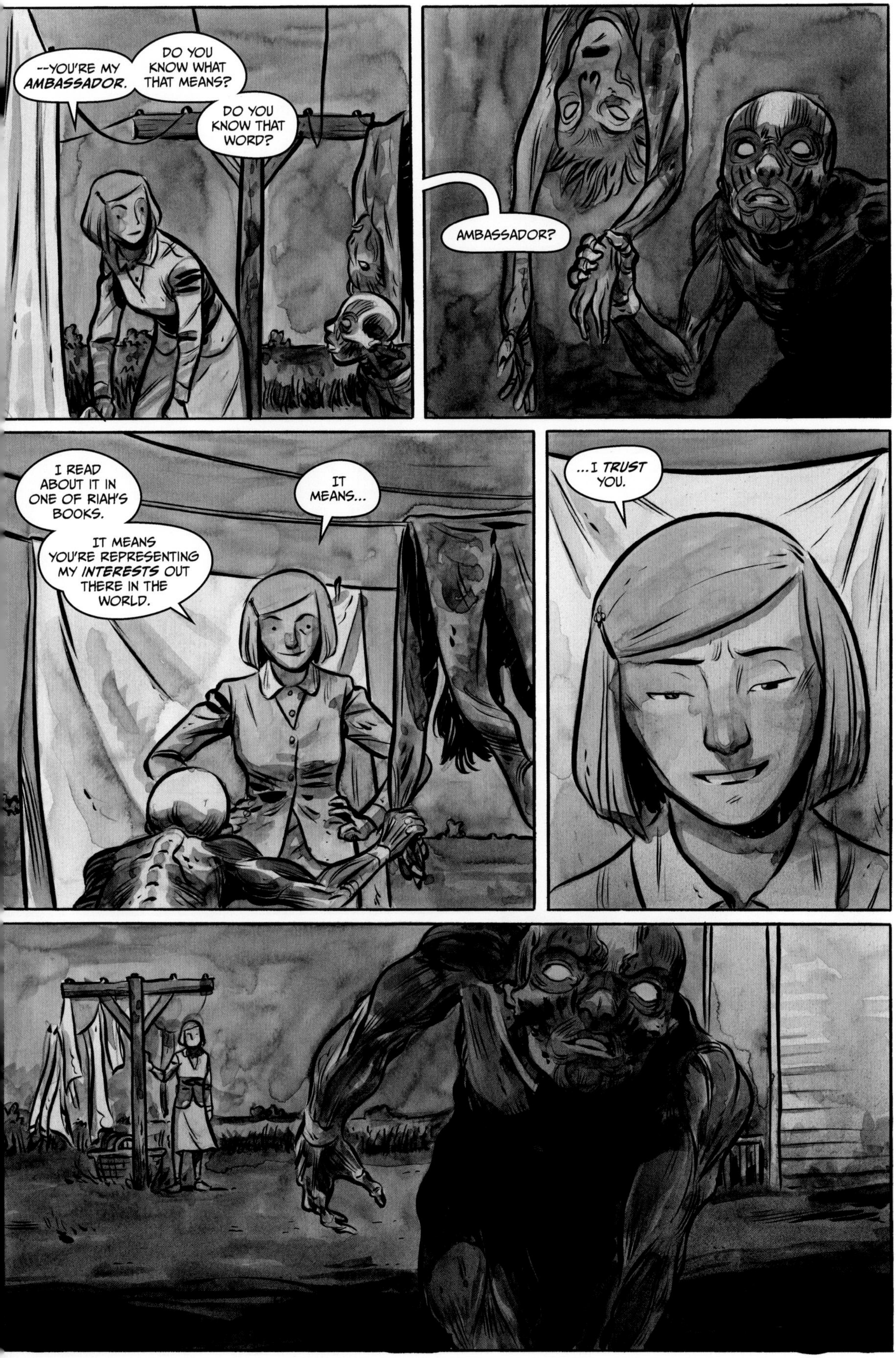
--YOU'RE MY AMBASSADOR.
DO YOU KNOW WHAT THAT MEANS?
DO YOU KNOW THAT WORD?
AMBASSADOR?
I READ ABOUT IT IN ONE OF RIAH'S BOOKS.
IT MEANS YOU'RE REPRESENTING MY INTERESTS OUT THERE IN THE WORLD.
IT MEANS...
...I TRUST YOU.

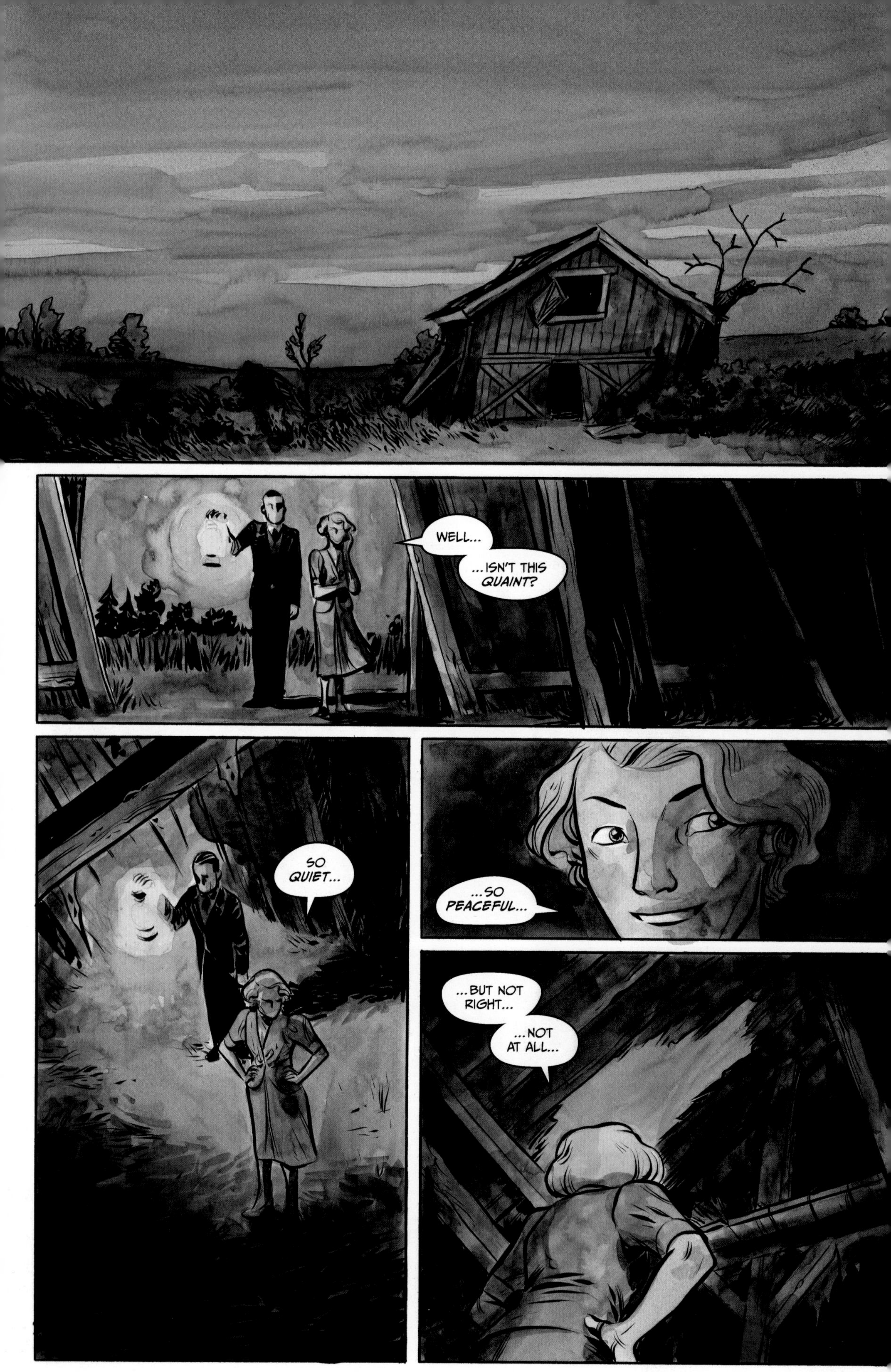
WELL...
...ISN'T THIS QUAINT?
SO QUIET...
...SO PEACEFUL...
...BUT NOT RIGHT...
...NOT AT ALL...

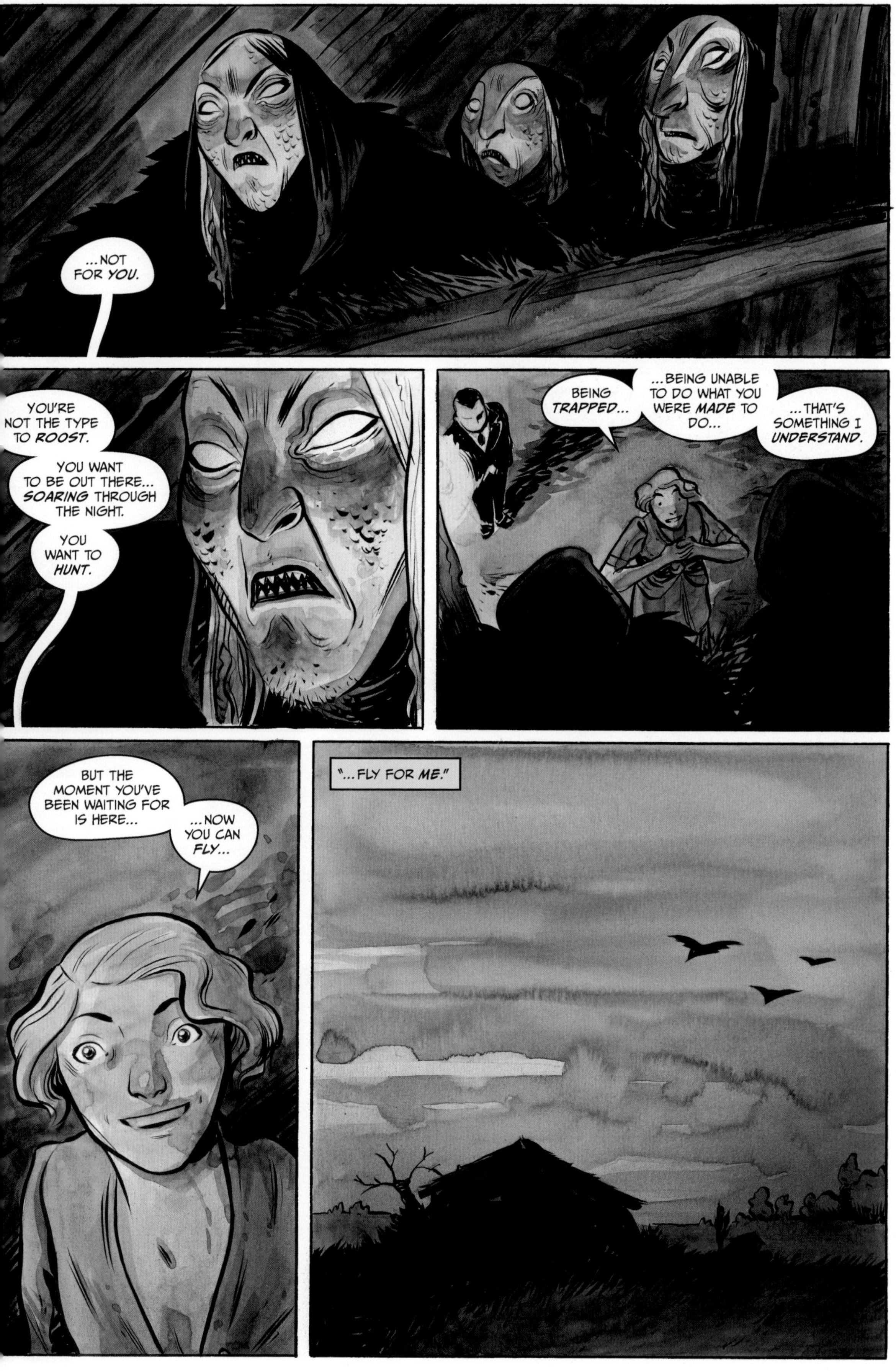
...NOT FOR YOU.
YOU'RE NOT THE TYPE TO ROOST.
YOU WANT TO BE OUT THERE... SOARING THROUGH THE NIGHT.
YOU WANT TO HUNT.
BEING TRAPPED...
...BEING UNABLE TO DO WHAT YOU WERE MADE TO DO...
...THAT'S SOMETHING I UNDERSTAND.
BUT THE MOMENT YOU'VE BEEN WAITING FOR IS HERE...
...NOW YOU CAN FLY...
"...FLY FOR ME."

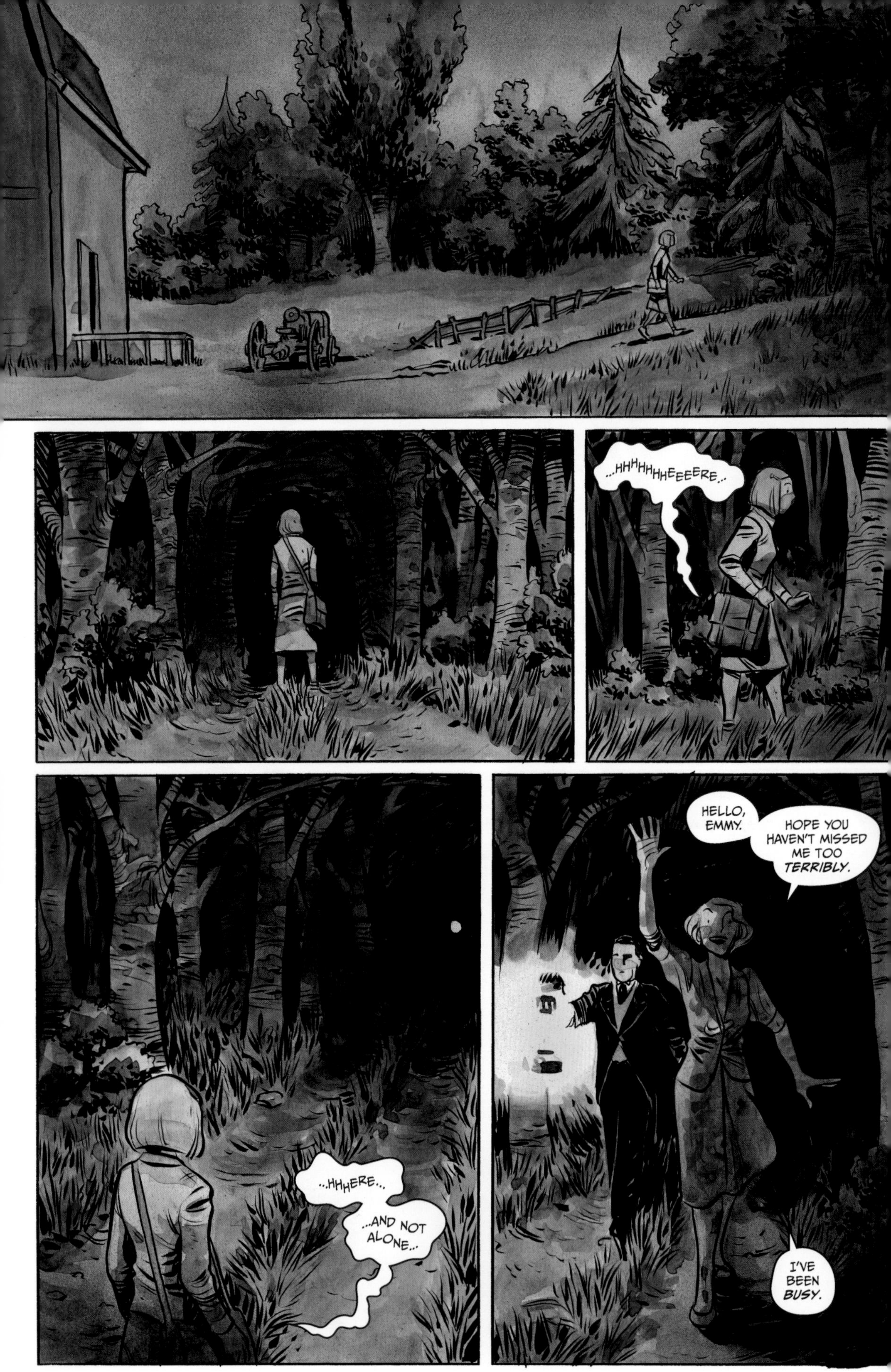
...HHHHHHHEEEERE...
...HHHERE...
...AND NOT ALONE...
HELLO, EMMY.
HOPE YOU HAVEN'T MISSED ME TOO TERRIBLY.
I'VE BEEN BUSY.

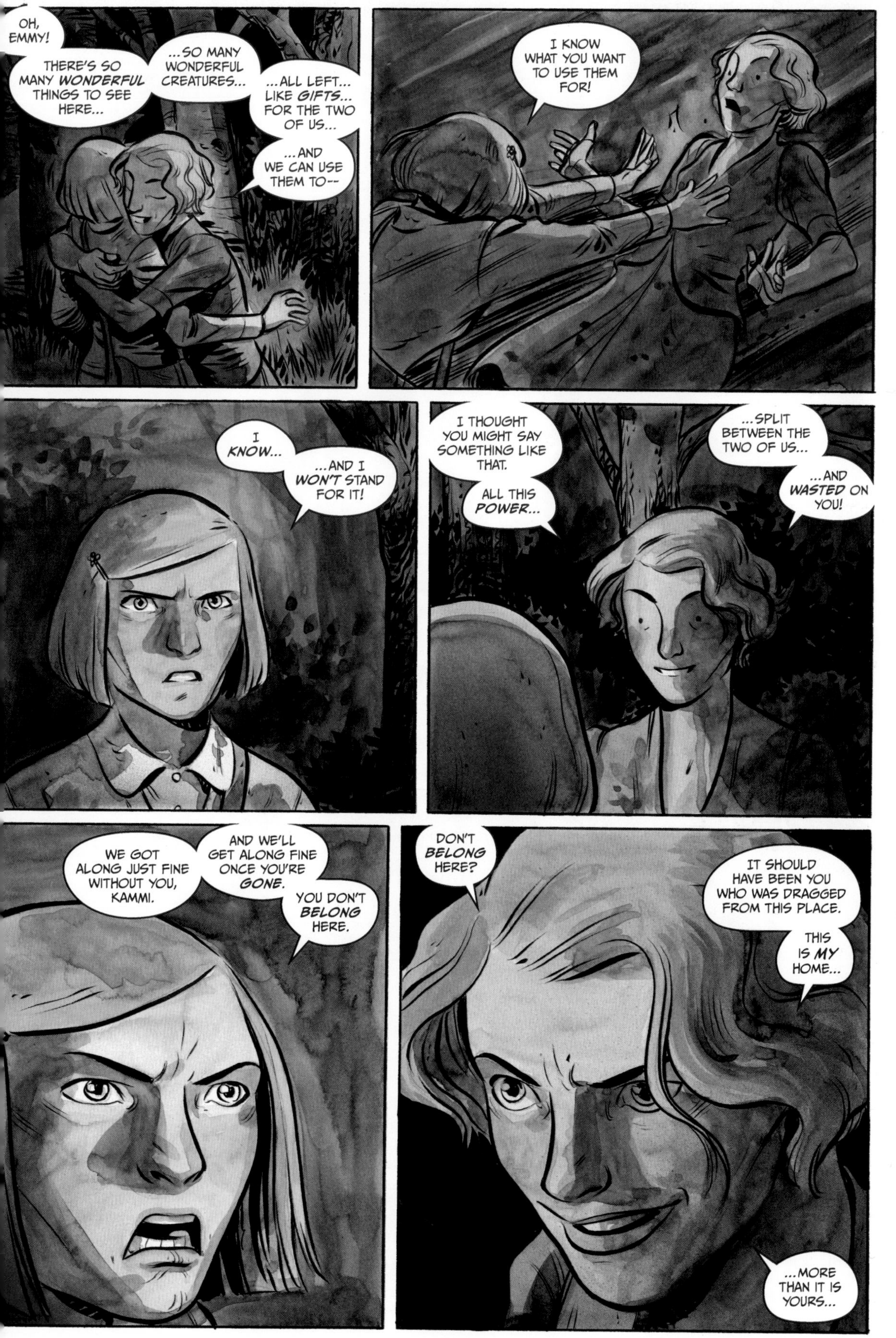
OH, EMMY!
THERE'S SO MANY WONDERFUL THINGS TO SEE HERE...
...SO MANY WONDERFUL CREATURES...
...ALL LEFT... LIKE GIFTS... FOR THE TWO OF US...
...AND WE CAN USE THEM TO--
I KNOW WHAT YOU WANT TO USE THEM FOR!
I KNOW...
...AND I WON'T STAND FOR IT!
I THOUGHT YOU MIGHT SAY SOMETHING LIKE THAT.
ALL THIS POWER...
...SPLIT BETWEEN THE TWO OF US...
...AND WASTED ON YOU!
WE GOT ALONG JUST FINE WITHOUT YOU, KAMMI.
AND WE'LL GET ALONG FINE ONCE YOU'RE GONE.
YOU DON'T BELONG HERE.
DON'T BELONG HERE?
IT SHOULD HAVE BEEN YOU WHO WAS DRAGGED FROM THIS PLACE.
THIS IS MY HOME...
...MORE THAN IT IS YOURS...

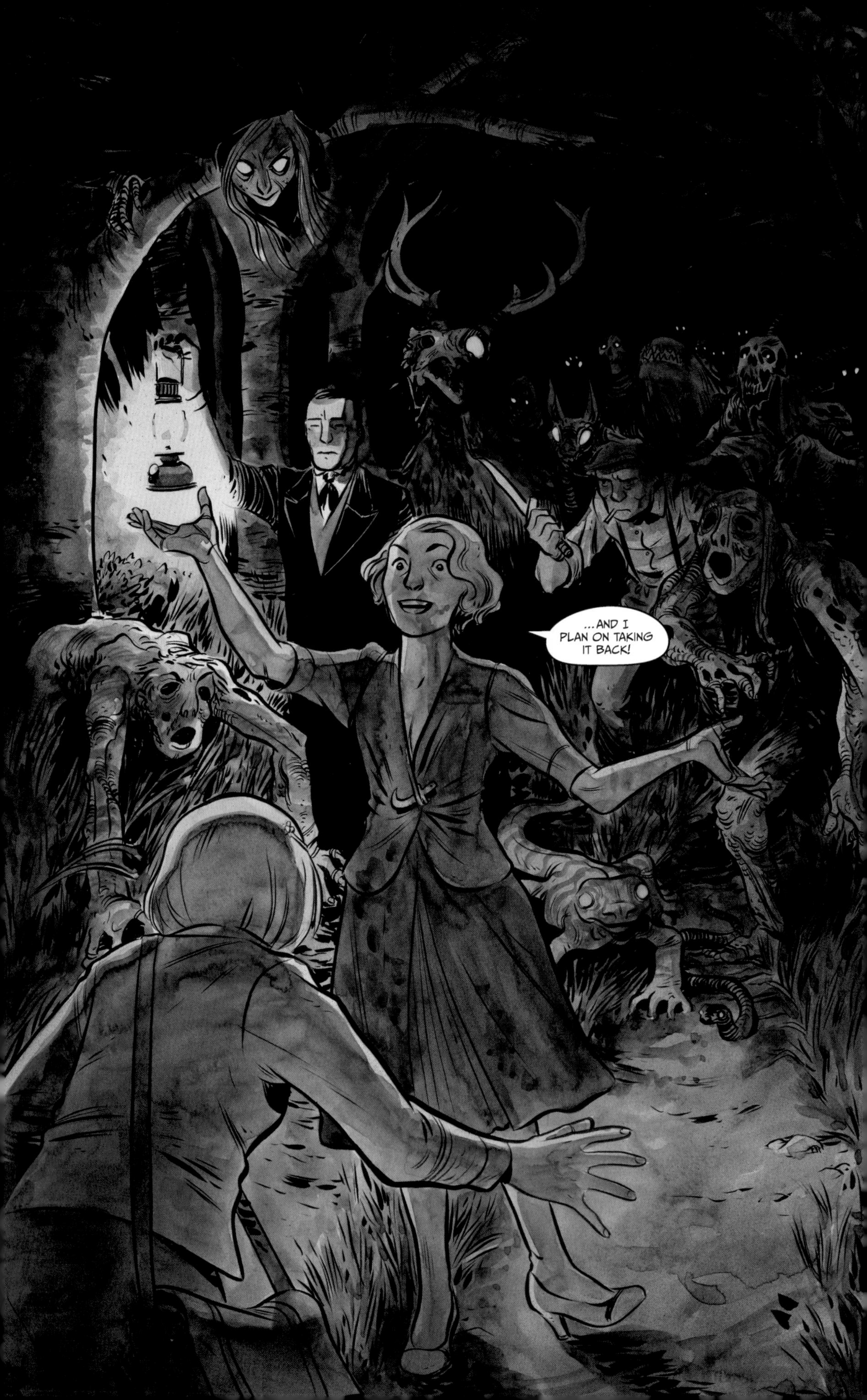
...AND I PLAN ON TAKING IT BACK!

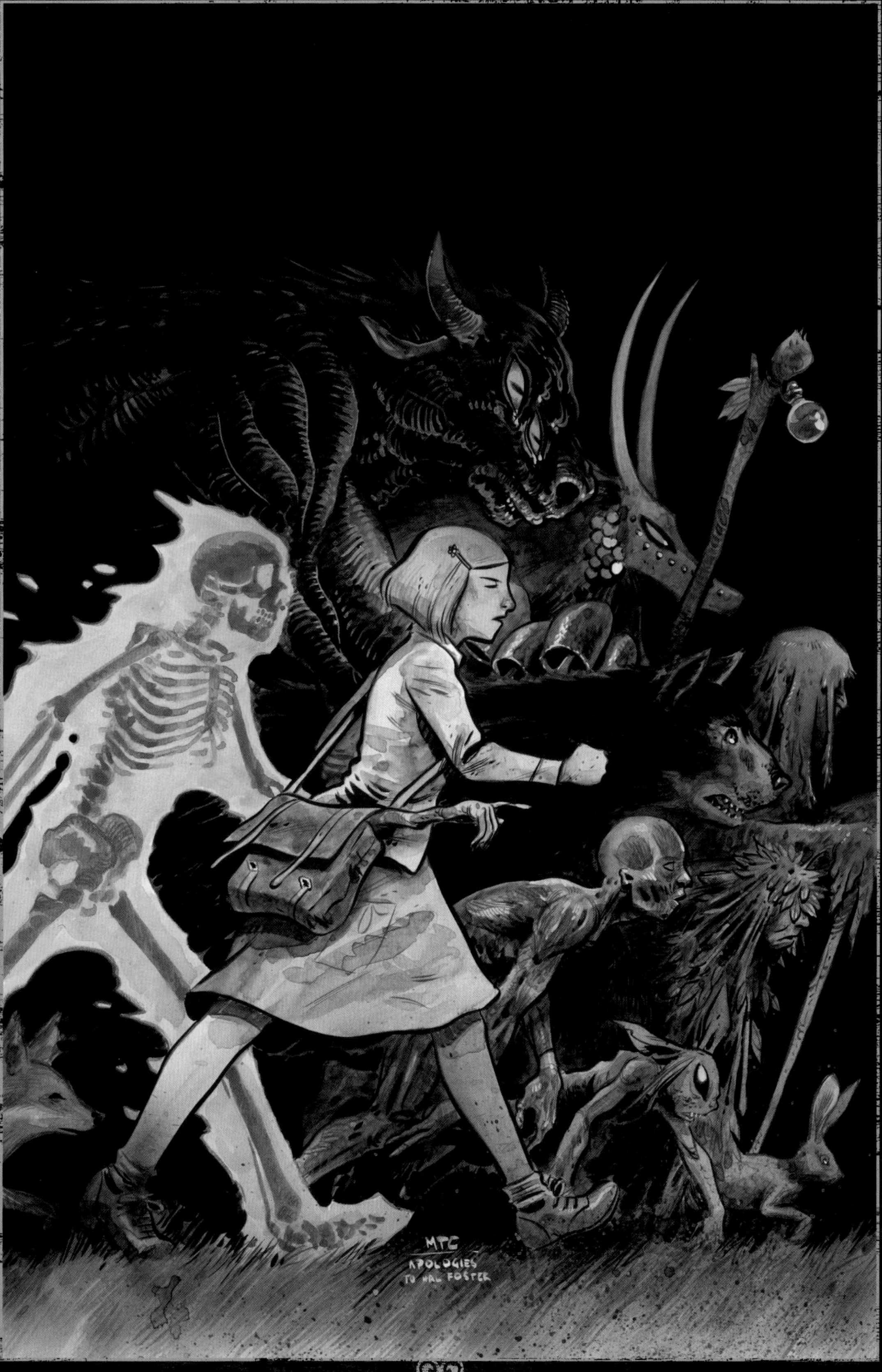
MPC
APOLOGIES TO HAL FOSTER

FOUR

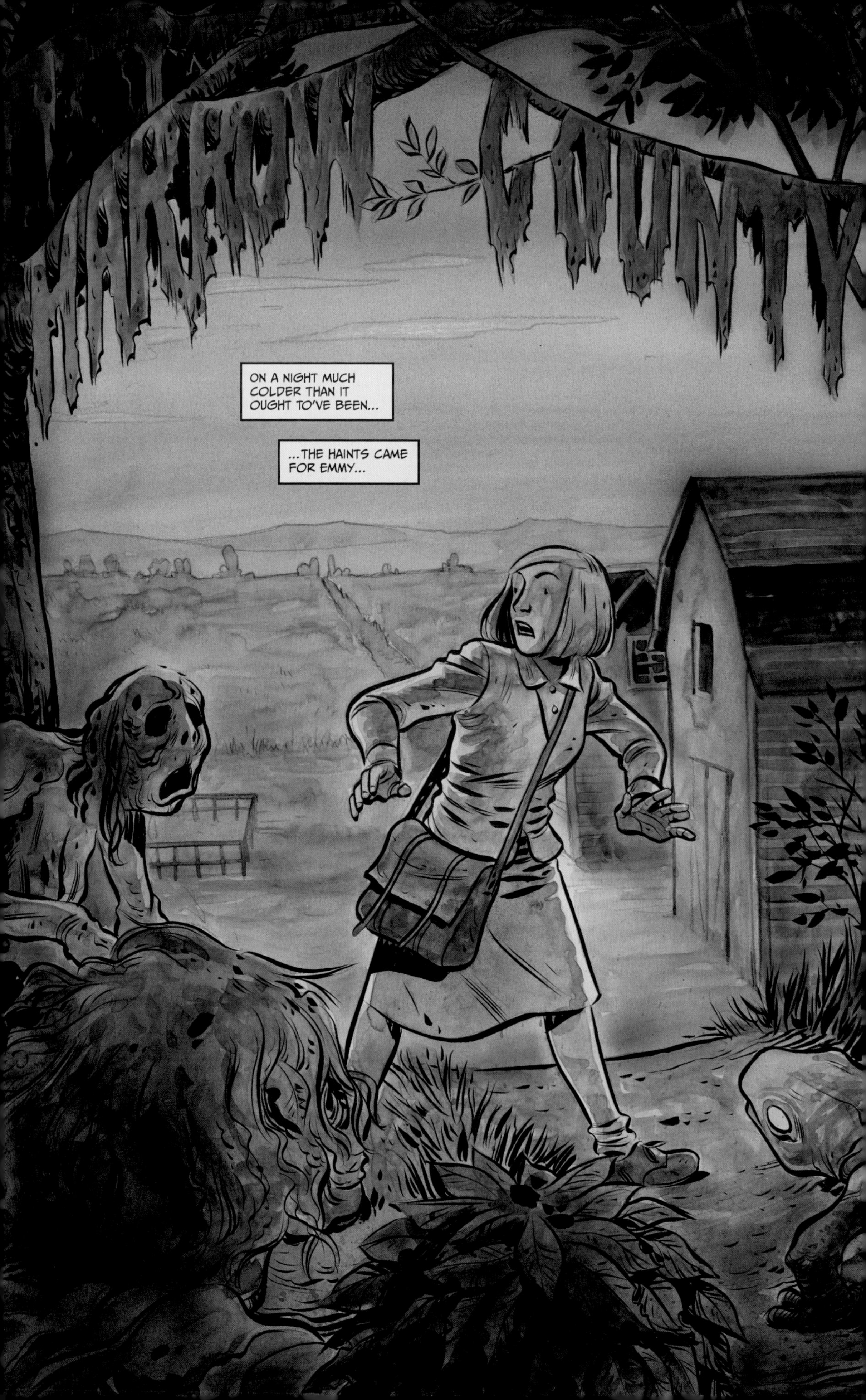
HARROW COUNTY
ON A NIGHT MUCH COLDER THAN IT OUGHT TO'VE BEEN...
...THE HAINTS CAME FOR EMMY...

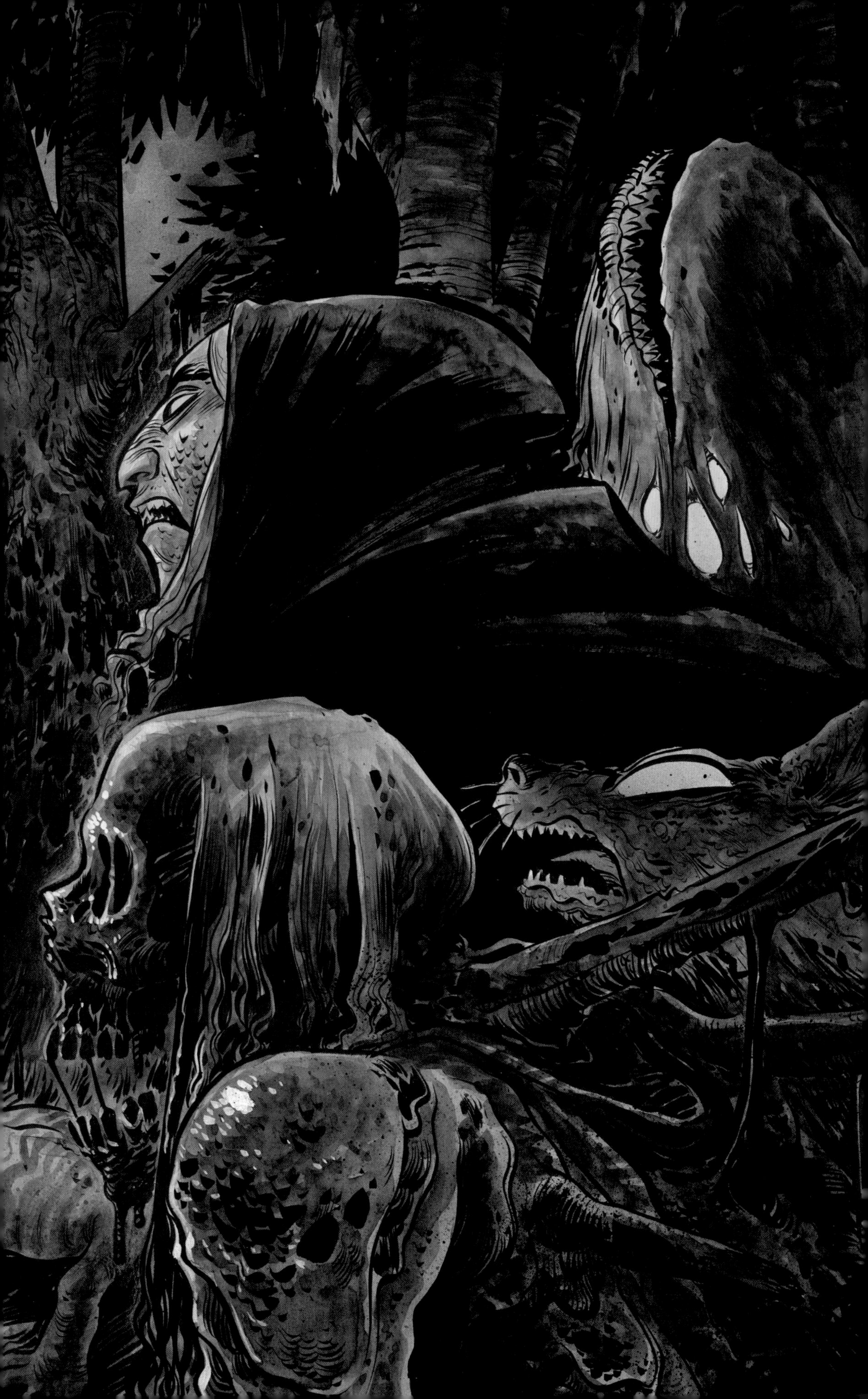

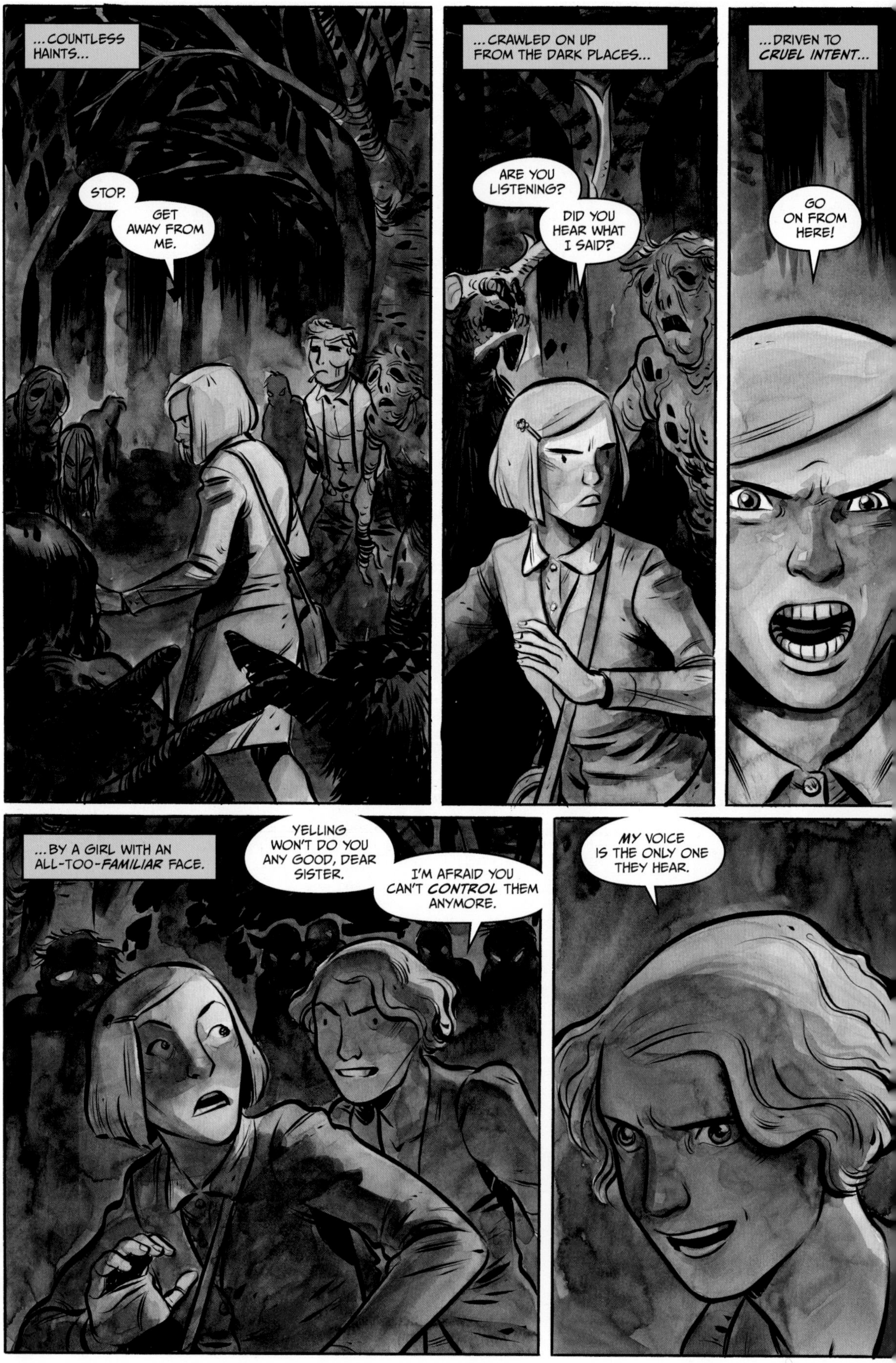
...COUNTLESS HAINTS...
STOP.
GET AWAY FROM ME.
...CRAWLED ON UP FROM THE DARK PLACES...
ARE YOU LISTENING?
DID YOU HEAR WHAT I SAID?
...DRIVEN TO CRUEL INTENT...
GO ON FROM HERE!
...BY A GIRL WITH AN ALL-TOO-FAMILIAR FACE.
YELLING WON'T DO YOU ANY GOOD, DEAR SISTER.
I'M AFRAID YOU CAN'T CONTROL THEM ANYMORE.
MY VOICE IS THE ONLY ONE THEY HEAR.

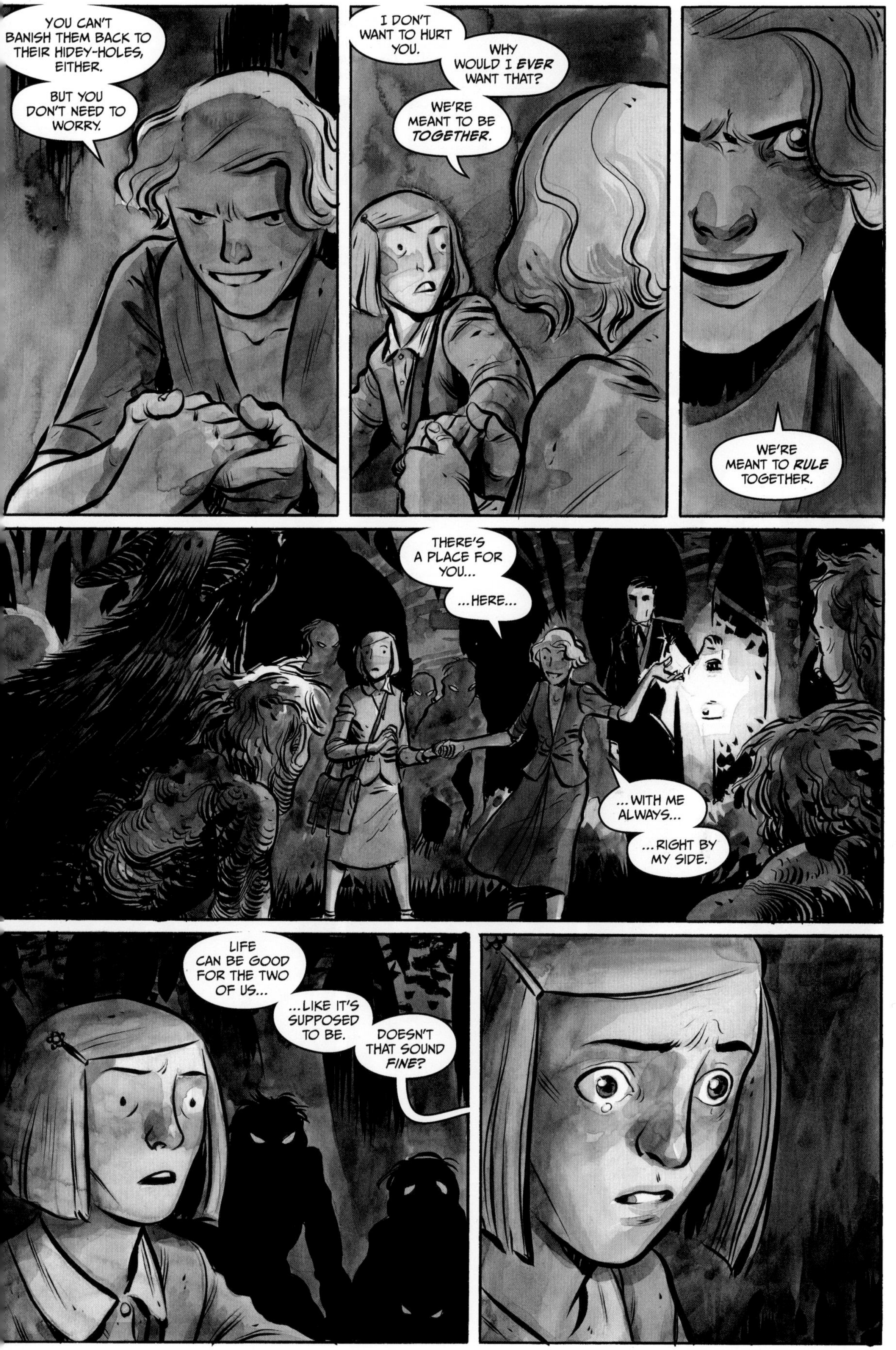
YOU CAN'T BANISH THEM BACK TO THEIR HIDEY-HOLES, EITHER.
BUT YOU DON'T NEED TO WORRY.
I DON'T WANT TO HURT YOU.
WHY WOULD I EVER WANT THAT?
WE'RE MEANT TO BE TOGETHER.
WE'RE MEANT TO RULE TOGETHER.
THERE'S A PLACE FOR YOU...
...HERE...
...WITH ME ALWAYS...
...RIGHT BY MY SIDE.
LIFE CAN BE GOOD FOR THE TWO OF US...
...LIKE IT'S SUPPOSED TO BE.
DOESN'T THAT SOUND FINE?

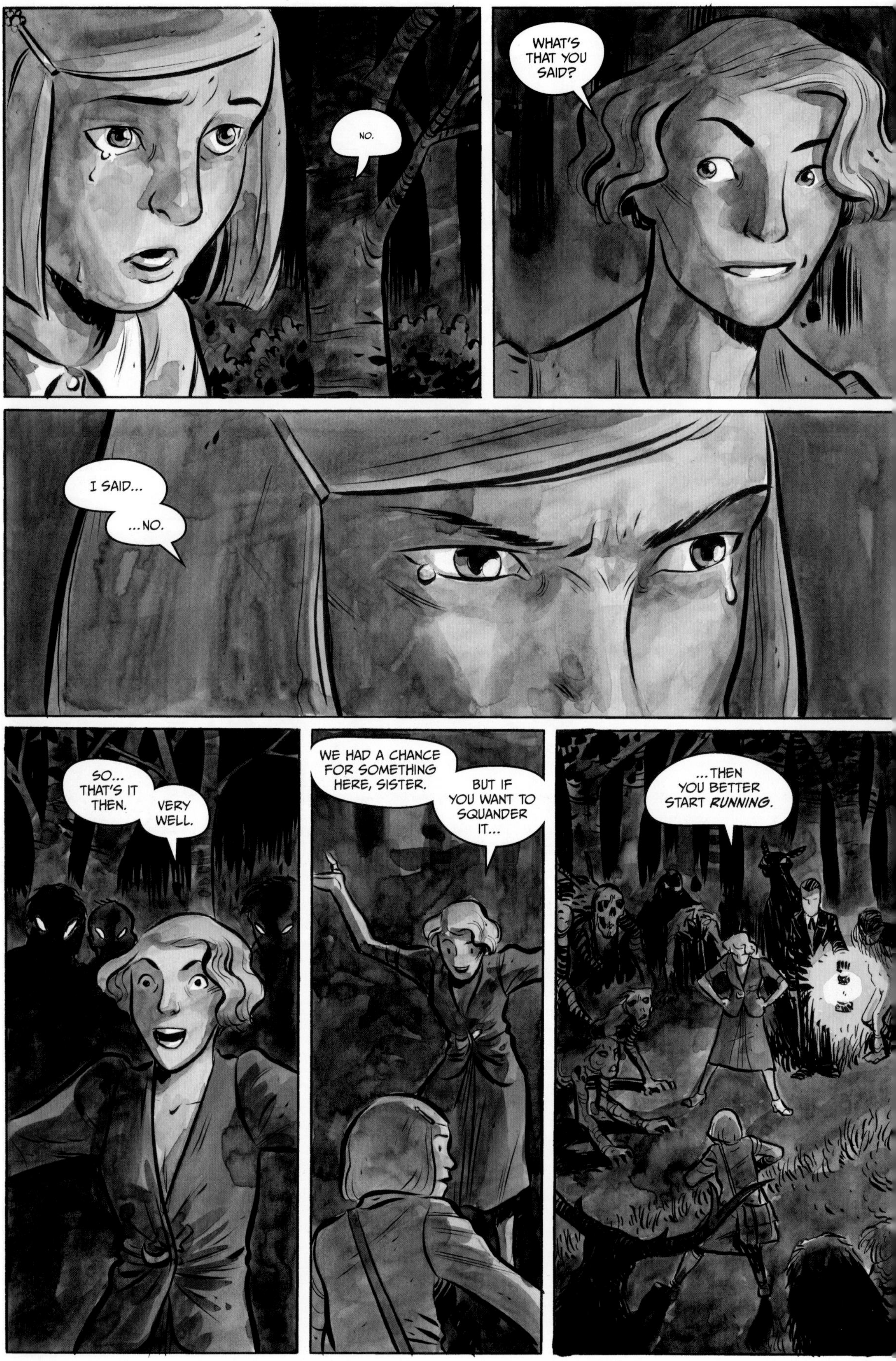
NO.
WHAT'S THAT YOU SAID?
I SAID...
...NO.
SO... THAT'S IT THEN.
VERY WELL.
WE HAD A CHANCE FOR SOMETHING HERE, SISTER.
BUT IF YOU WANT TO SQUANDER IT...
...THEN YOU BETTER START *RUNNING*.

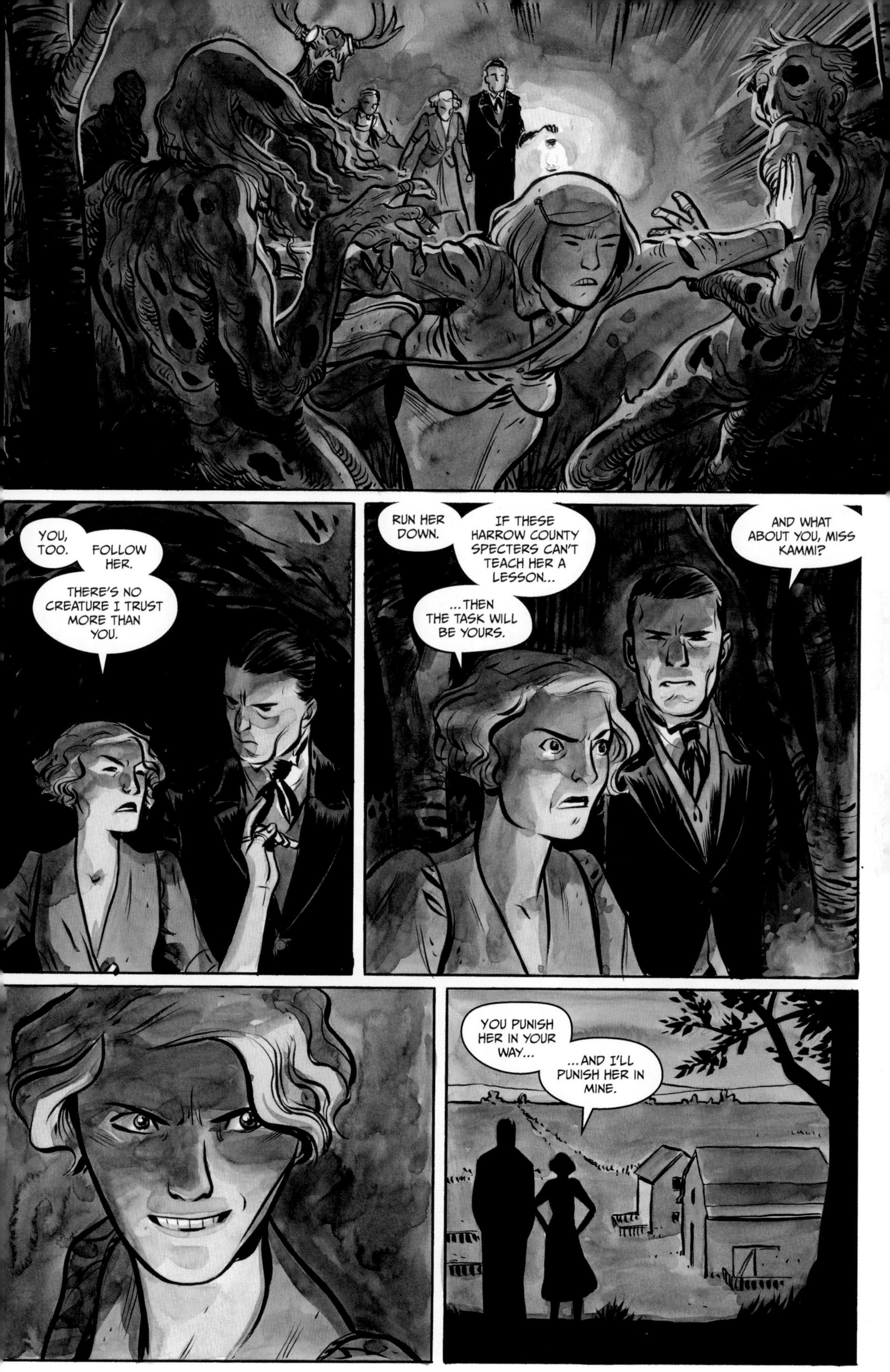
YOU, TOO.
FOLLOW HER.
THERE'S NO CREATURE I TRUST MORE THAN YOU.
RUN HER DOWN.
IF THESE HARROW COUNTY SPECTERS CAN'T TEACH HER A LESSON...
...THEN THE TASK WILL BE YOURS.
AND WHAT ABOUT YOU, MISS KAMMI?
YOU PUNISH HER IN YOUR WAY...
...AND I'LL PUNISH HER IN MINE.

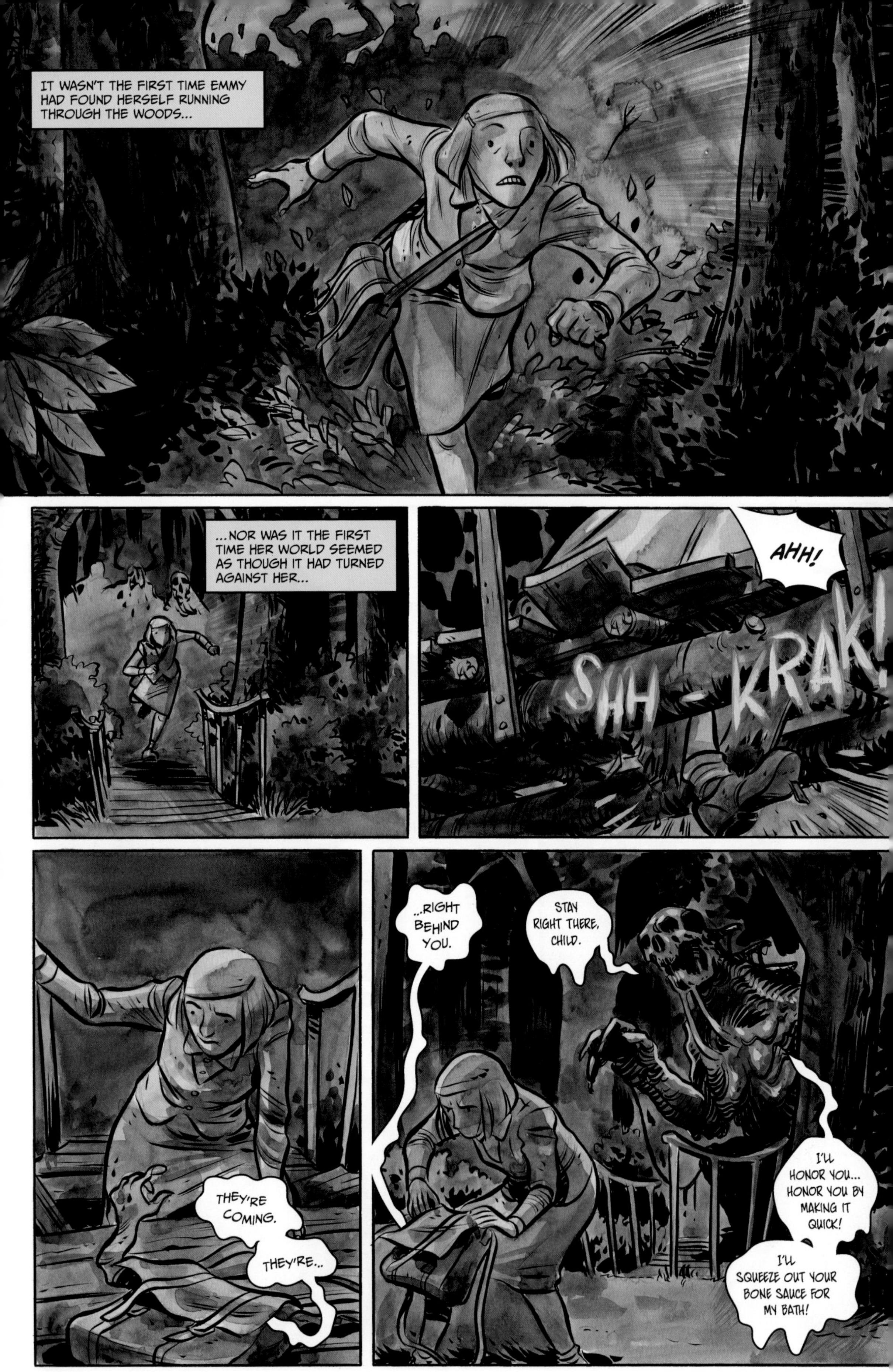
IT WASN'T THE FIRST TIME EMMY HAD FOUND HERSELF RUNNING THROUGH THE WOODS...
...NOR WAS IT THE FIRST TIME HER WORLD SEEMED AS THOUGH IT HAD TURNED AGAINST HER...
AHH!
SHH - KRAK!
THEY'RE COMING.
THEY'RE...
...RIGHT BEHIND YOU.
STAY RIGHT THERE, CHILD.
I'LL HONOR YOU... HONOR YOU BY MAKING IT QUICK!
I'LL SQUEEZE OUT YOUR BONE SAUCE FOR MY BATH!

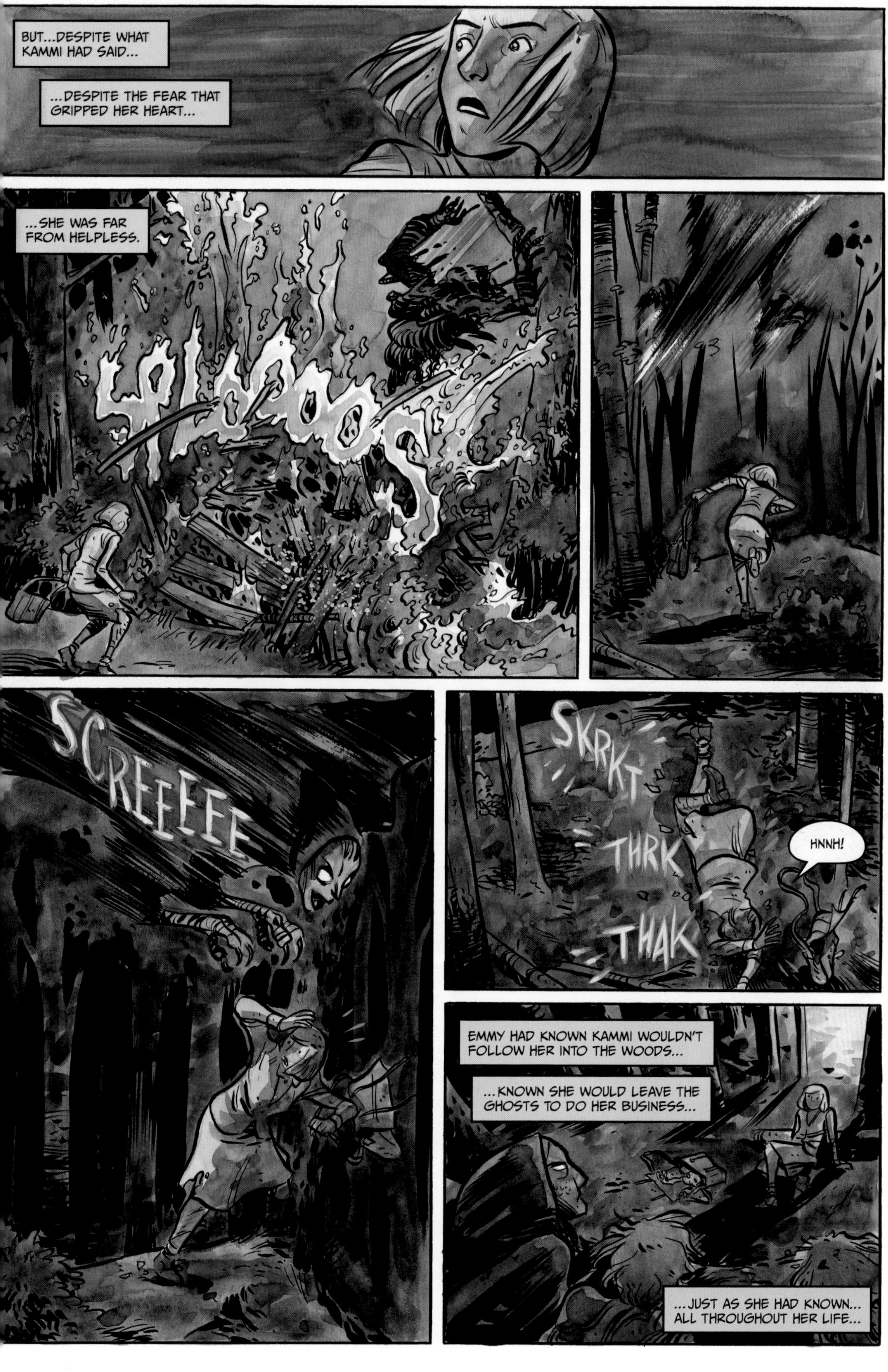
BUT...DESPITE WHAT KAMMI HAD SAID...
...DESPITE THE FEAR THAT GRIPPED HER HEART...
...SHE WAS FAR FROM HELPLESS.
SPLOOOSH
SCREEEEE
SKRKT
THRK
THAK
HNNH!
EMMY HAD KNOWN KAMMI WOULDN'T FOLLOW HER INTO THE WOODS...
...KNOWN SHE WOULD LEAVE THE GHOSTS TO DO HER BUSINESS...
...JUST AS SHE HAD KNOWN... ALL THROUGHOUT HER LIFE...

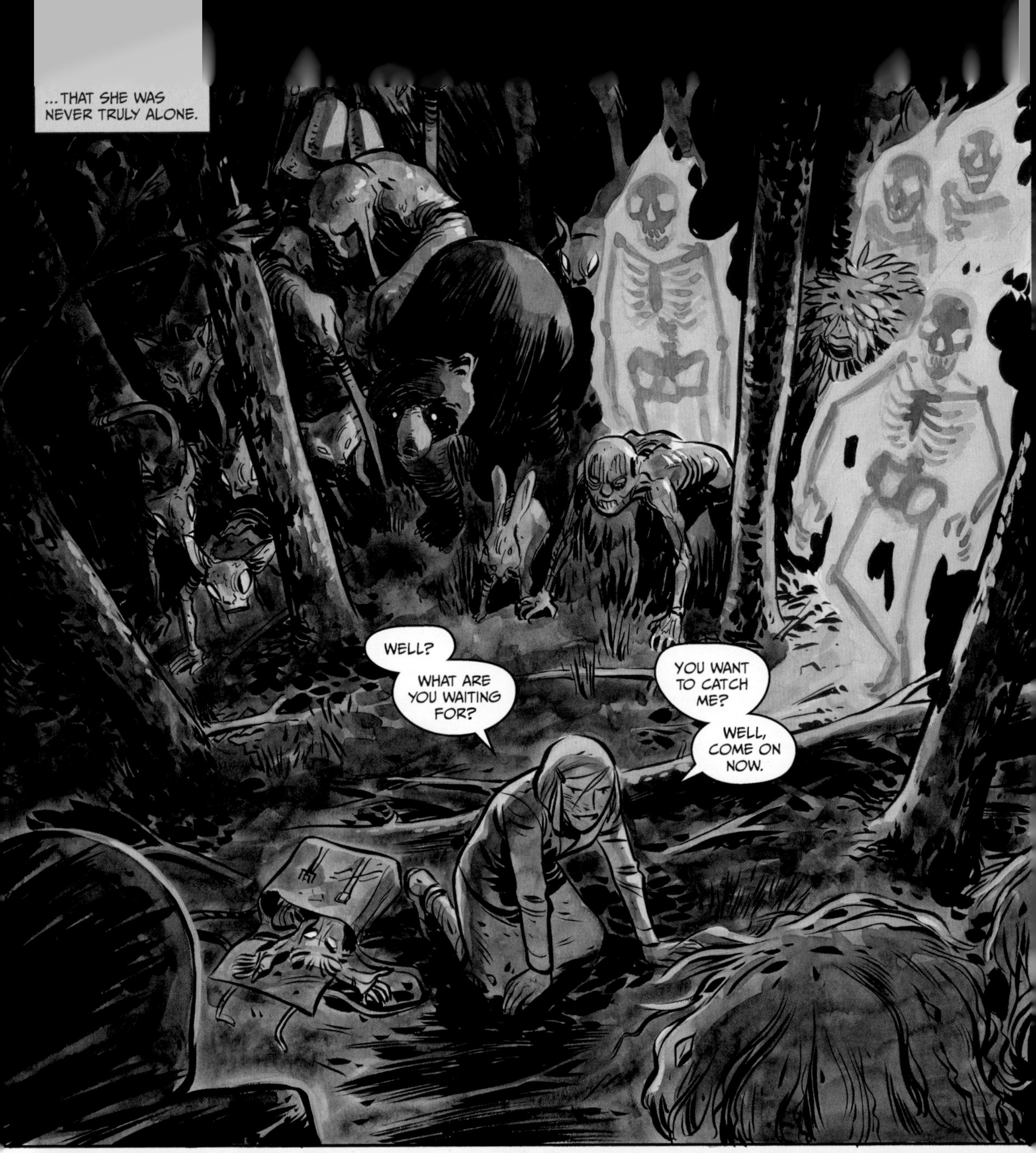
...THAT SHE WAS
NEVER TRULY ALONE.
WELL?
WHAT ARE YOU WAITING FOR?
YOU WANT TO CATCH ME?
WELL, COME ON NOW.

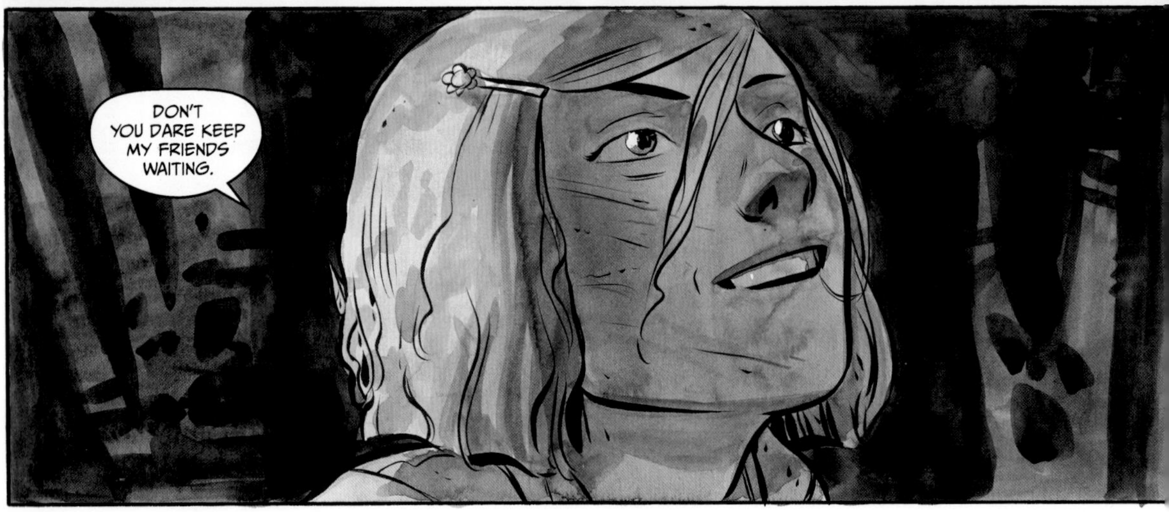
DON'T YOU DARE KEEP MY FRIENDS WAITING.

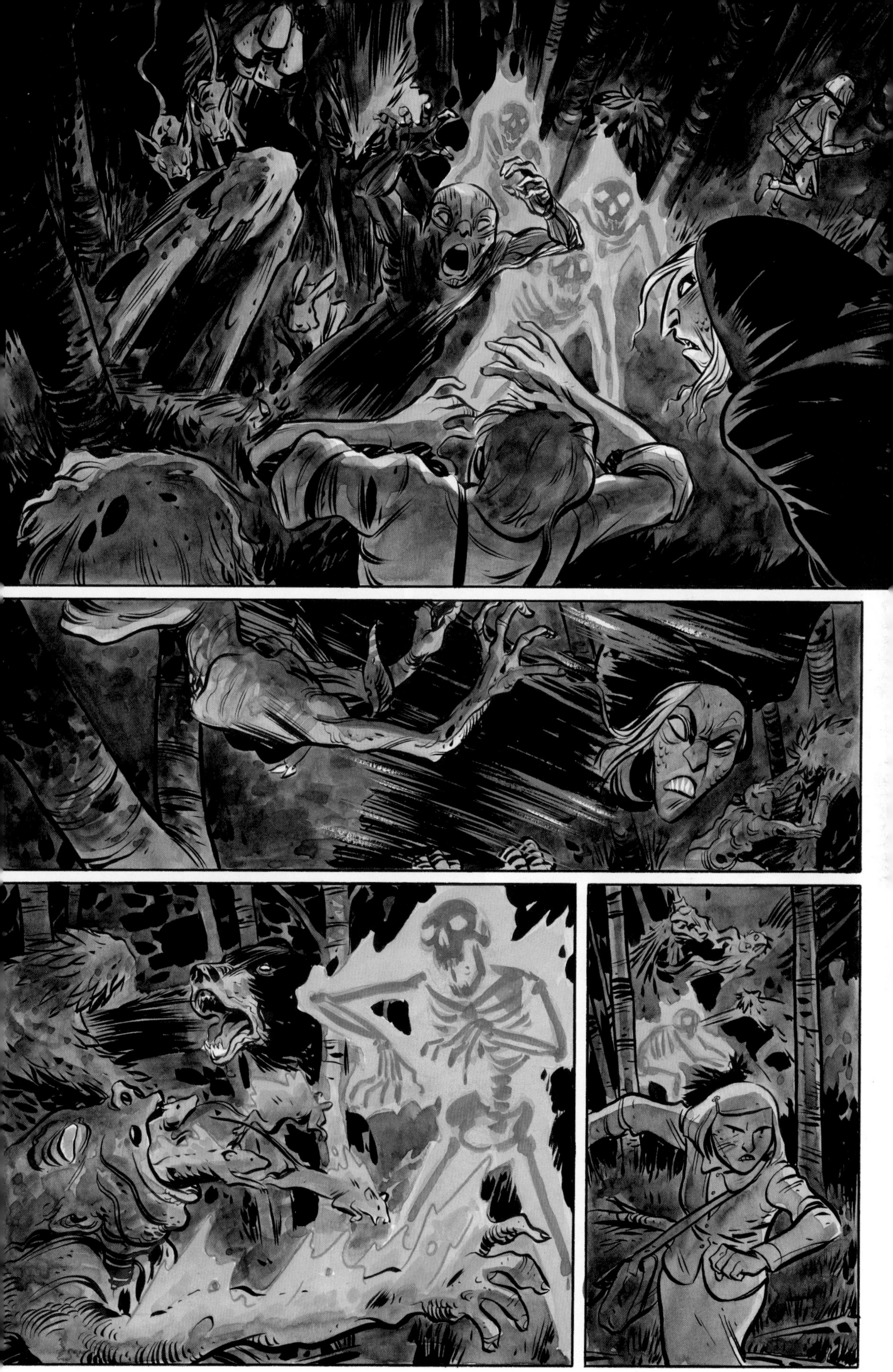

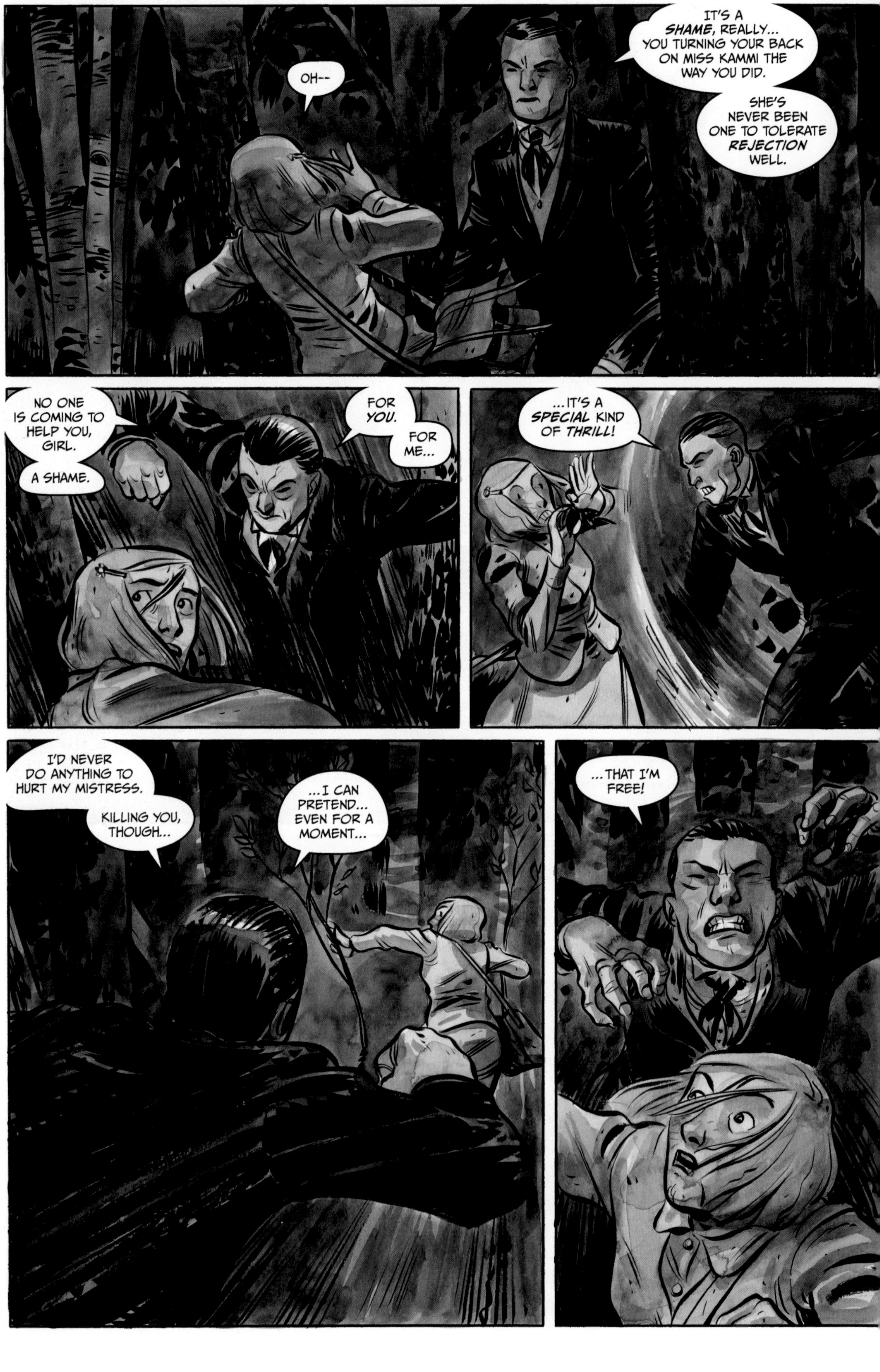
OH--
IT'S A SHAME, REALLY... YOU TURNING YOUR BACK ON MISS KAMMI THE WAY YOU DID.
SHE'S NEVER BEEN ONE TO TOLERATE REJECTION WELL.
NO ONE IS COMING TO HELP YOU, GIRL.
A SHAME.
FOR YOU.
FOR ME...
...IT'S A SPECIAL KIND OF THRILL!
I'D NEVER DO ANYTHING TO HURT MY MISTRESS.
KILLING YOU, THOUGH...
...I CAN PRETEND... EVEN FOR A MOMENT...
...THAT I'M FREE!

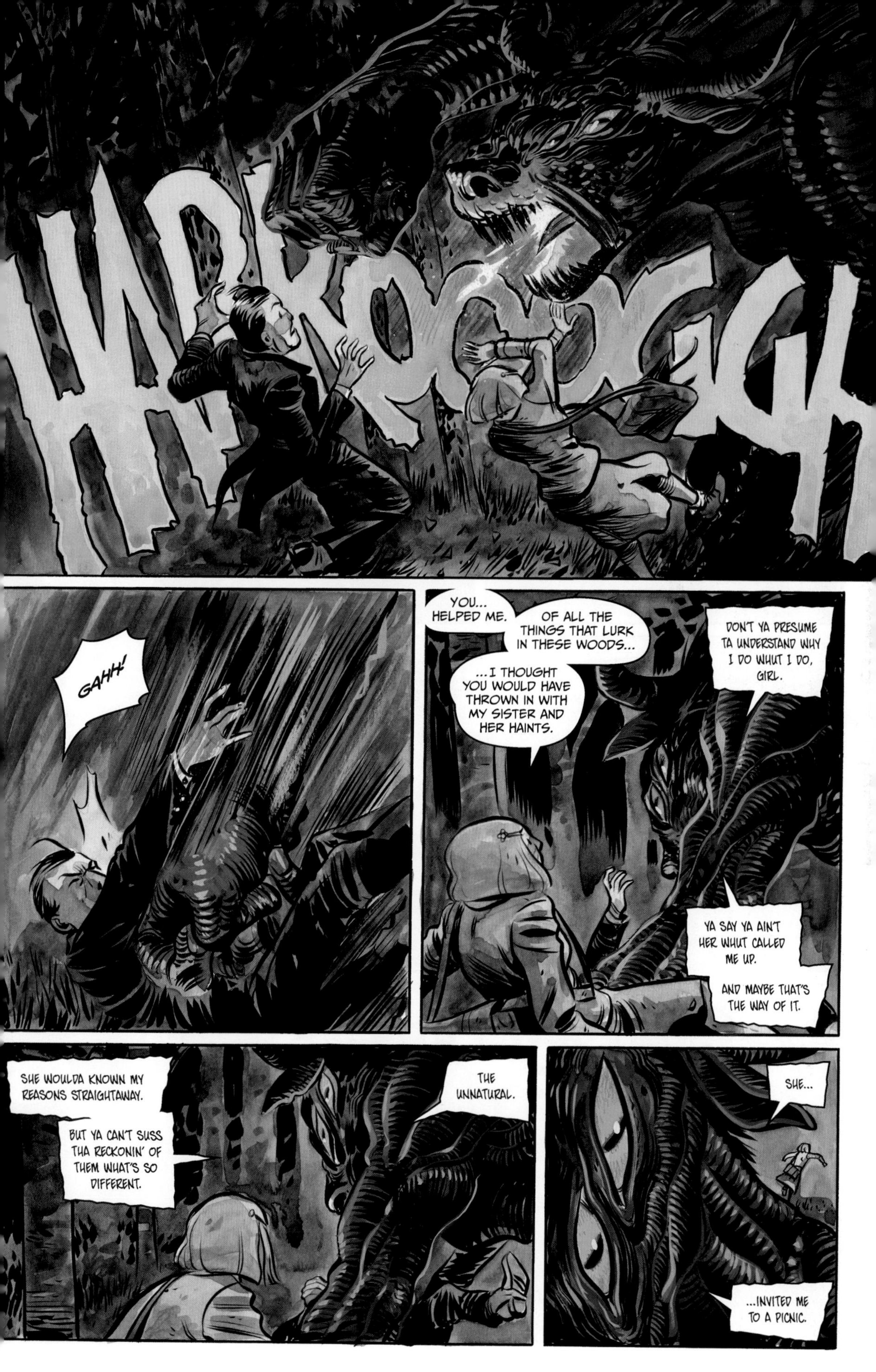
GAHH!
YOU... HELPED ME.
OF ALL THE THINGS THAT LURK IN THESE WOODS...
...I THOUGHT YOU WOULD HAVE THROWN IN WITH MY SISTER AND HER HAINTS.
DON'T YA PRESUME TA UNDERSTAND WHY I DO WHUT I DO, GIRL.
YA SAY YA AIN'T HER WHUT CALLED ME UP.
AND MAYBE THAT'S THE WAY OF IT.
SHE WOULDA KNOWN MY REASONS STRAIGHTAWAY.
BUT YA CAN'T SUSS THA RECKONIN' OF THEM WHAT'S SO DIFFERENT.
THE UNNATURAL.
SHE...
...INVITED ME TO A PICNIC.

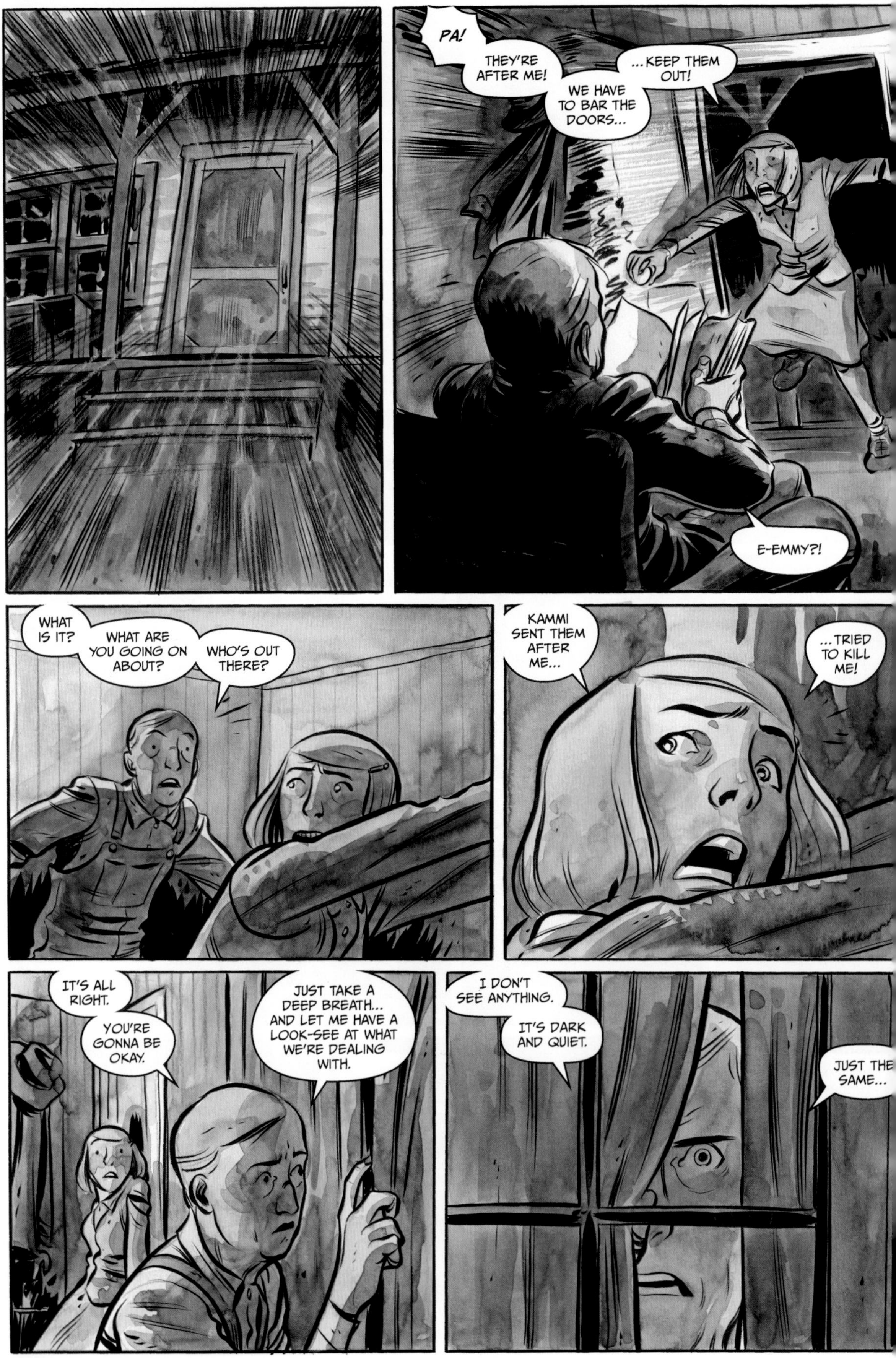
PA!
THEY'RE AFTER ME!
WE HAVE TO BAR THE DOORS...
...KEEP THEM OUT!
E-EMMY?!
WHAT IS IT?
WHAT ARE YOU GOING ON ABOUT?
WHO'S OUT THERE?
KAMMI SENT THEM AFTER ME...
...TRIED TO KILL ME!
IT'S ALL RIGHT.
YOU'RE GONNA BE OKAY.
JUST TAKE A DEEP BREATH... AND LET ME HAVE A LOOK-SEE AT WHAT WE'RE DEALING WITH.
I DON'T SEE ANYTHING.
IT'S DARK AND QUIET.
JUST THE SAME...

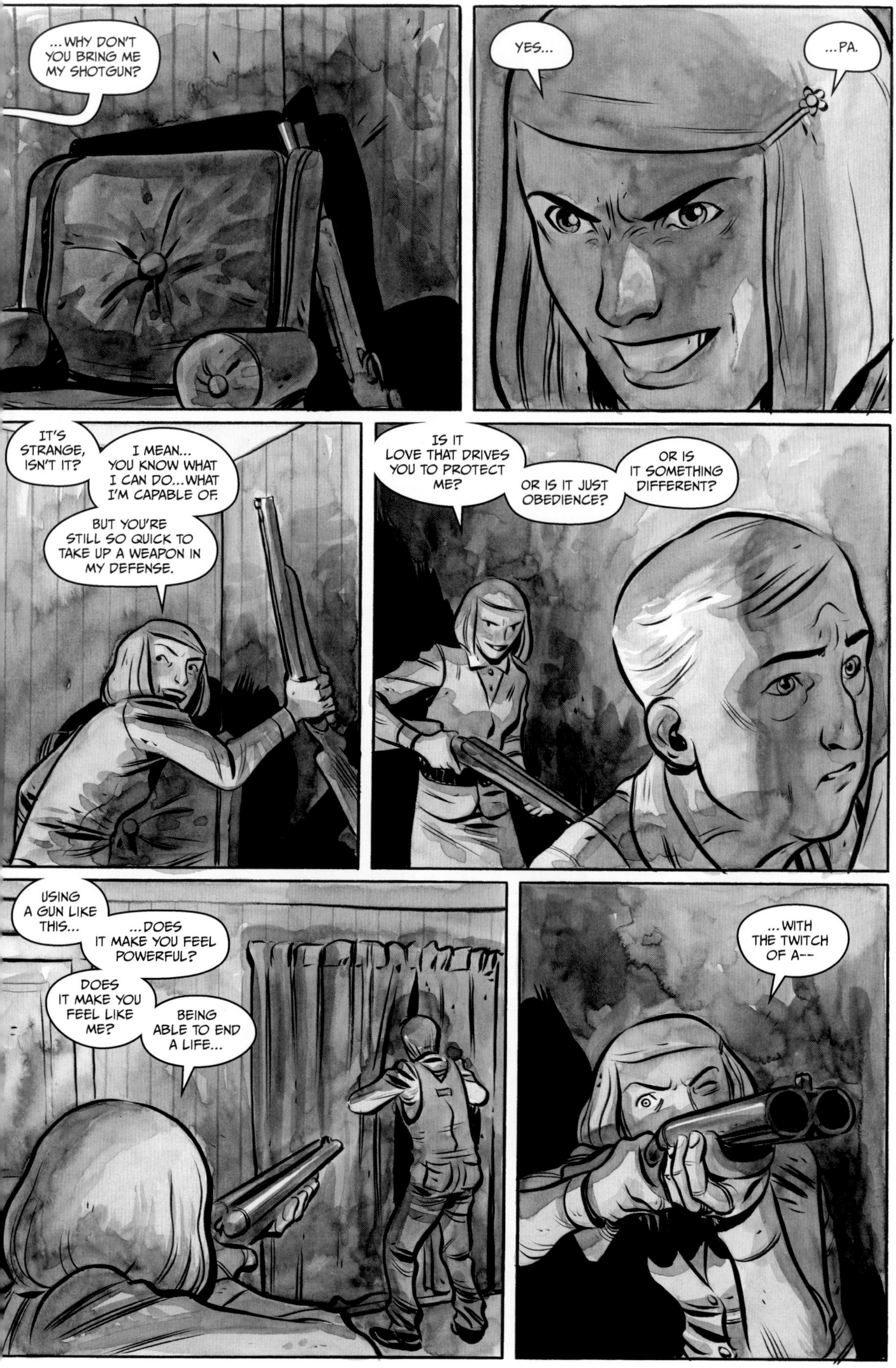
...WHY DON'T YOU BRING ME MY SHOTGUN?
YES...
...PA.
IT'S STRANGE, ISN'T IT?
I MEAN... YOU KNOW WHAT I CAN DO...WHAT I'M CAPABLE OF.
BUT YOU'RE STILL SO QUICK TO TAKE UP A WEAPON IN MY DEFENSE.
IS IT LOVE THAT DRIVES YOU TO PROTECT ME?
OR IS IT JUST OBEDIENCE?
OR IS IT SOMETHING DIFFERENT?
USING A GUN LIKE THIS...
...DOES IT MAKE YOU FEEL POWERFUL?
DOES IT MAKE YOU FEEL LIKE ME?
BEING ABLE TO END A LIFE...
...WITH THE TWITCH OF A--

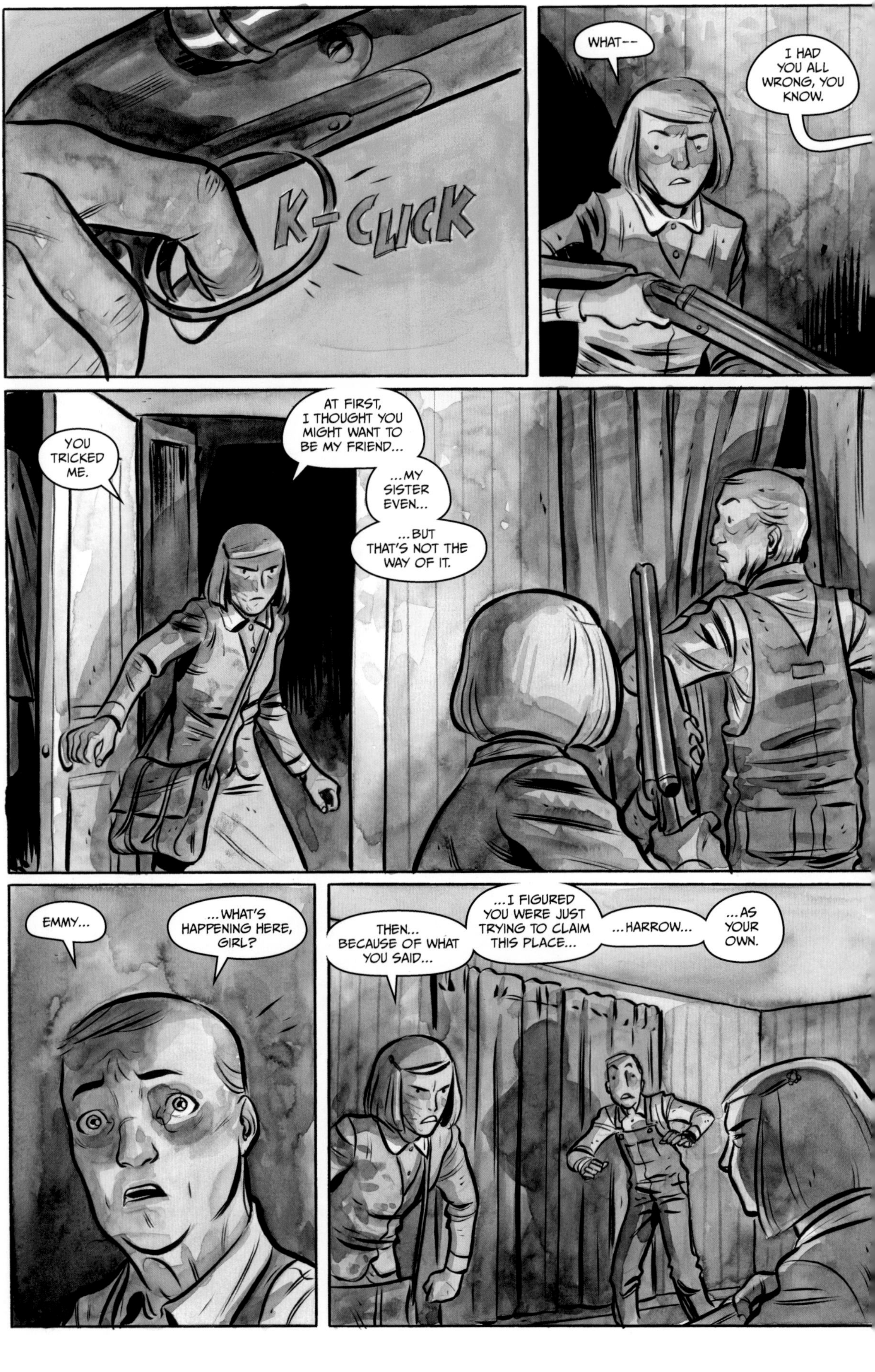
K-CLICK
WHAT--
I HAD YOU ALL WRONG, YOU KNOW.
YOU TRICKED ME.
AT FIRST, I THOUGHT YOU MIGHT WANT TO BE MY FRIEND...
...MY SISTER EVEN...
...BUT THAT'S NOT THE WAY OF IT.
EMMY...
...WHAT'S HAPPENING HERE, GIRL?
THEN... BECAUSE OF WHAT YOU SAID...
...I FIGURED YOU WERE JUST TRYING TO CLAIM THIS PLACE...
...HARROW...
...AS YOUR OWN.

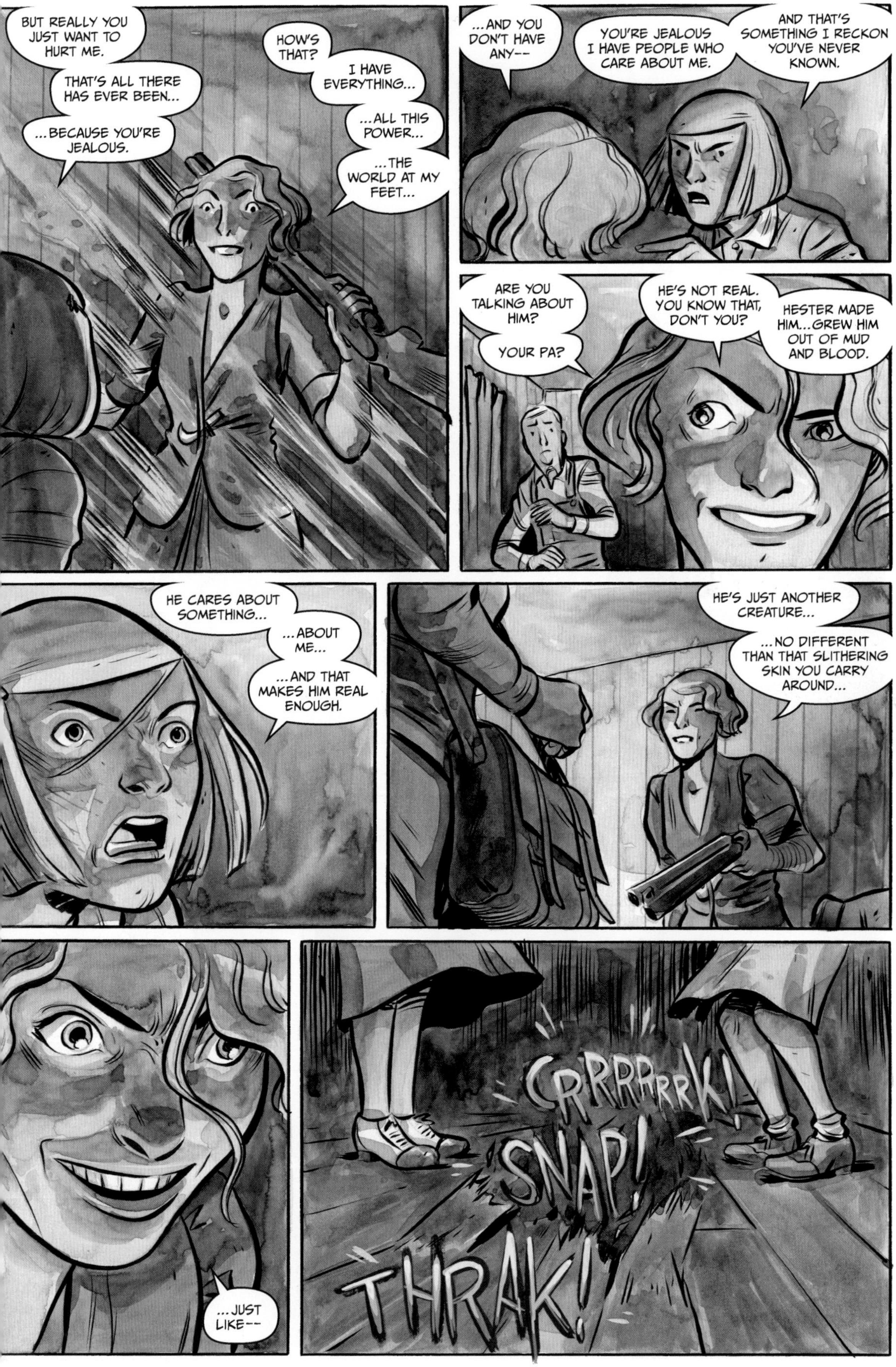
BUT REALLY YOU JUST WANT TO HURT ME.
THAT'S ALL THERE HAS EVER BEEN...
...BECAUSE YOU'RE JEALOUS.
HOW'S THAT?
I HAVE EVERYTHING...
...ALL THIS POWER...
...THE WORLD AT MY FEET...
...AND YOU DON'T HAVE ANY--
YOU'RE JEALOUS I HAVE PEOPLE WHO CARE ABOUT ME.
AND THAT'S SOMETHING I RECKON YOU'VE NEVER KNOWN.
ARE YOU TALKING ABOUT HIM?
YOUR PA?
HE'S NOT REAL. YOU KNOW THAT, DON'T YOU?
HESTER MADE HIM...GREW HIM OUT OF MUD AND BLOOD.
HE CARES ABOUT SOMETHING...
...ABOUT ME...
...AND THAT MAKES HIM REAL ENOUGH.
HE'S JUST ANOTHER CREATURE...
...NO DIFFERENT THAN THAT SLITHERING SKIN YOU CARRY AROUND...
...JUST LIKE--
CRRRRRRK!
SNAP!
THRAK!

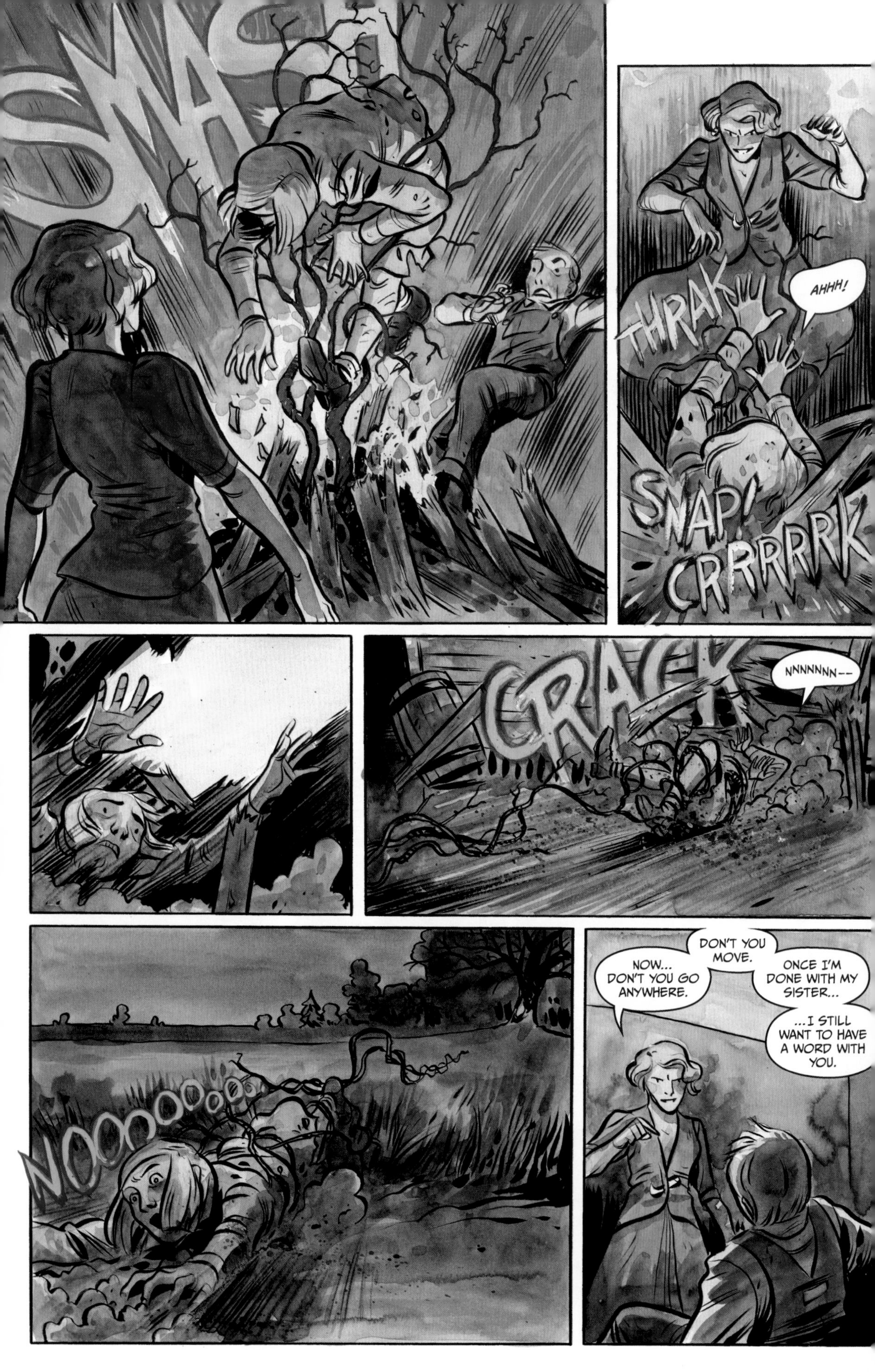
THRAK
AHHH!
SNAP!
CRRRRRK
CRACK
NNNNNNN--
NOOOOOOOOO
NOW... DON'T YOU GO ANYWHERE.
DON'T YOU MOVE.
ONCE I'M DONE WITH MY SISTER...
...I STILL WANT TO HAVE A WORD WITH YOU.

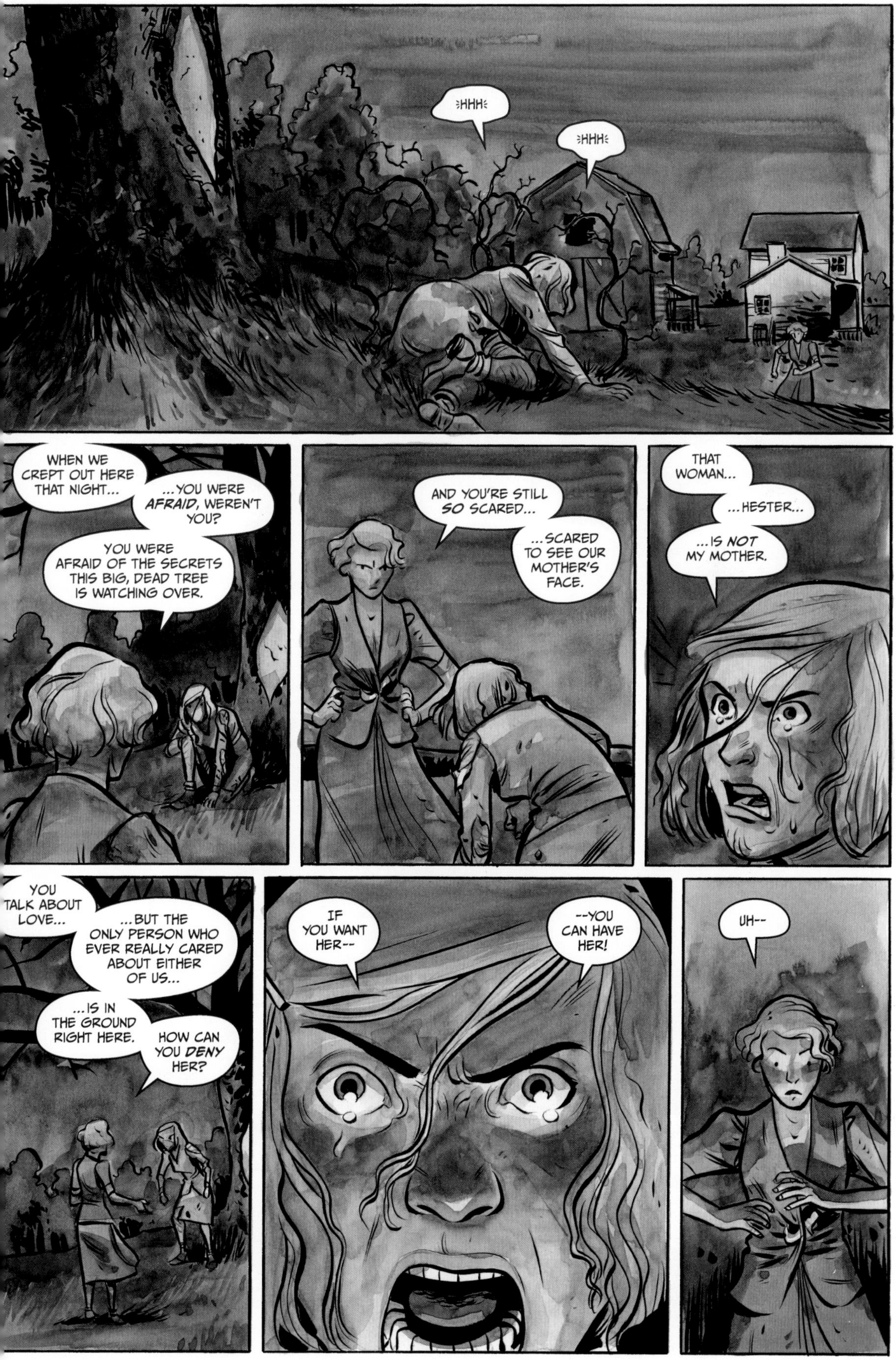
HHH
HHH
WHEN WE CREPT OUT HERE THAT NIGHT...
...YOU WERE AFRAID, WEREN'T YOU?
YOU WERE AFRAID OF THE SECRETS THIS BIG, DEAD TREE IS WATCHING OVER.
AND YOU'RE STILL SO SCARED...
...SCARED TO SEE OUR MOTHER'S FACE.
THAT WOMAN...
...HESTER...
...IS NOT MY MOTHER.
YOU TALK ABOUT LOVE...
...BUT THE ONLY PERSON WHO EVER REALLY CARED ABOUT EITHER OF US...
...IS IN THE GROUND RIGHT HERE.
HOW CAN YOU DENY HER?
IF YOU WANT HER--
--YOU CAN HAVE HER!
UH--

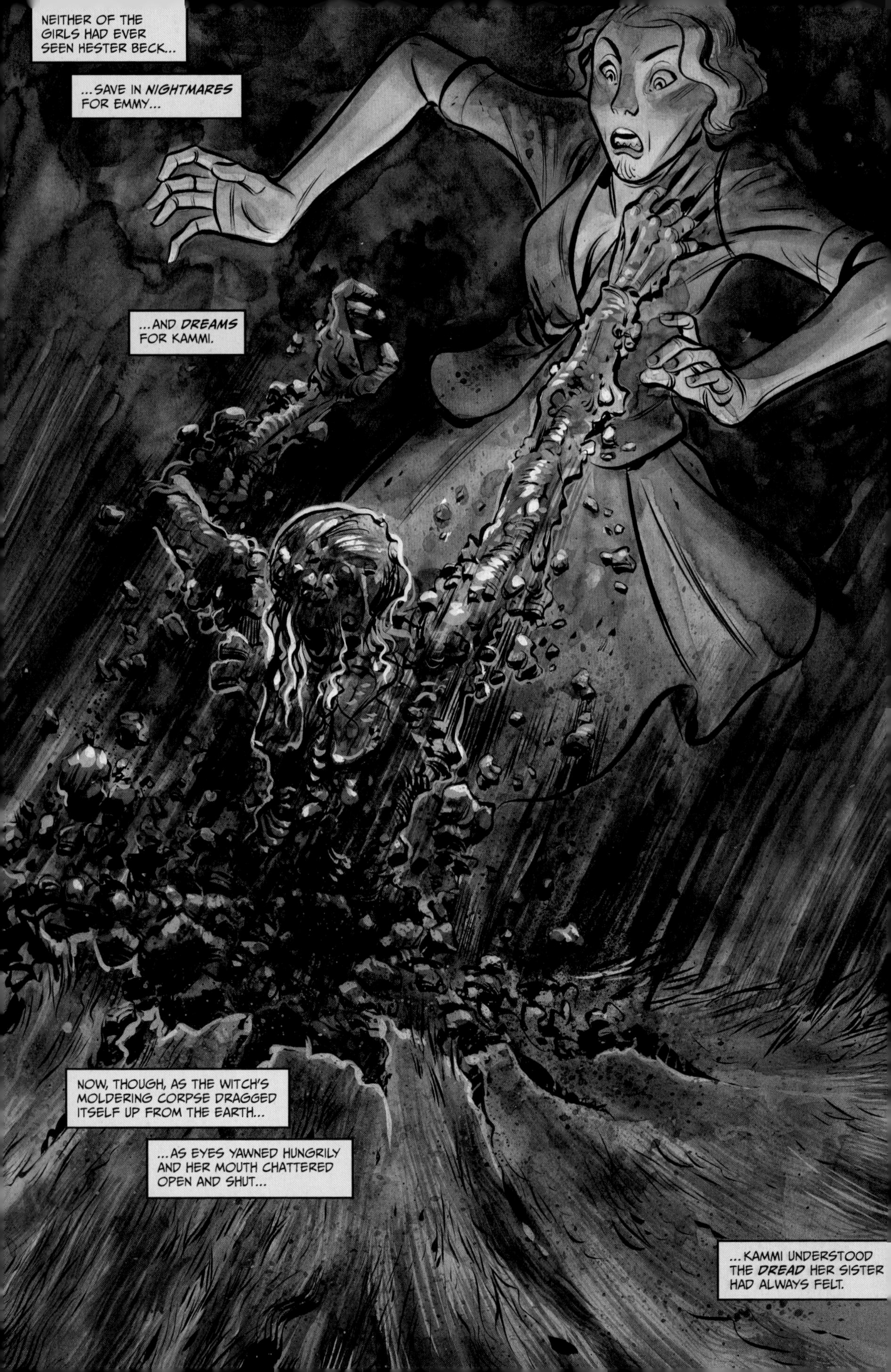
NEITHER OF THE GIRLS HAD EVER SEEN HESTER BECK...
...SAVE IN *NIGHTMARES* FOR EMMY...
...AND *DREAMS* FOR KAMMI.
NOW, THOUGH, AS THE WITCH'S MOLDERING CORPSE DRAGGED ITSELF UP FROM THE EARTH...
...AS EYES YAWNED HUNGRILY AND HER MOUTH CHATTERED OPEN AND SHUT...
...KAMMI UNDERSTOOD THE *DREAD* HER SISTER HAD ALWAYS FELT.

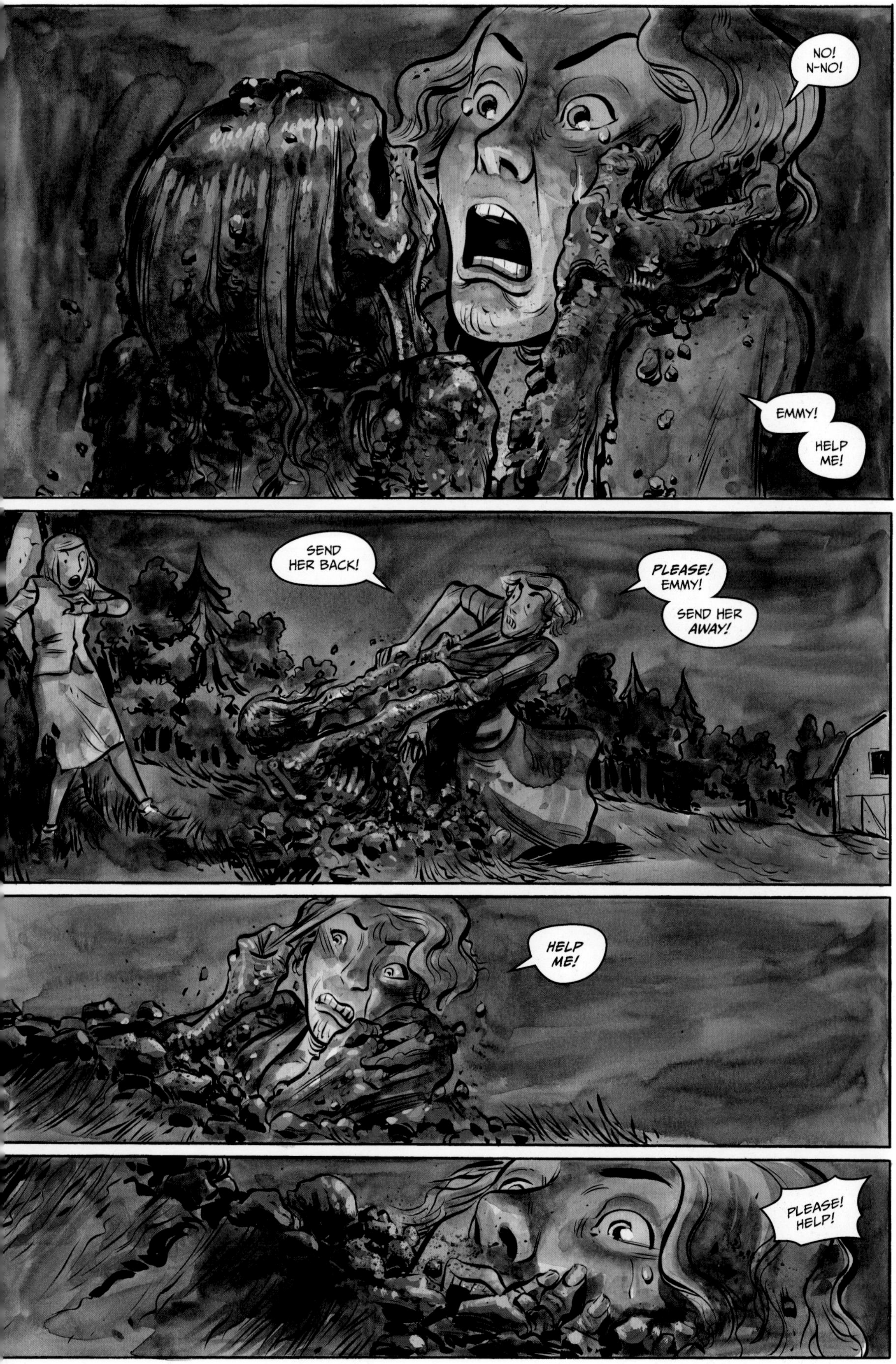
NO! N-NO!
EMMY!
HELP ME!
SEND HER BACK!
PLEASE! EMMY!
SEND HER AWAY!
HELP ME!
PLEASE! HELP!

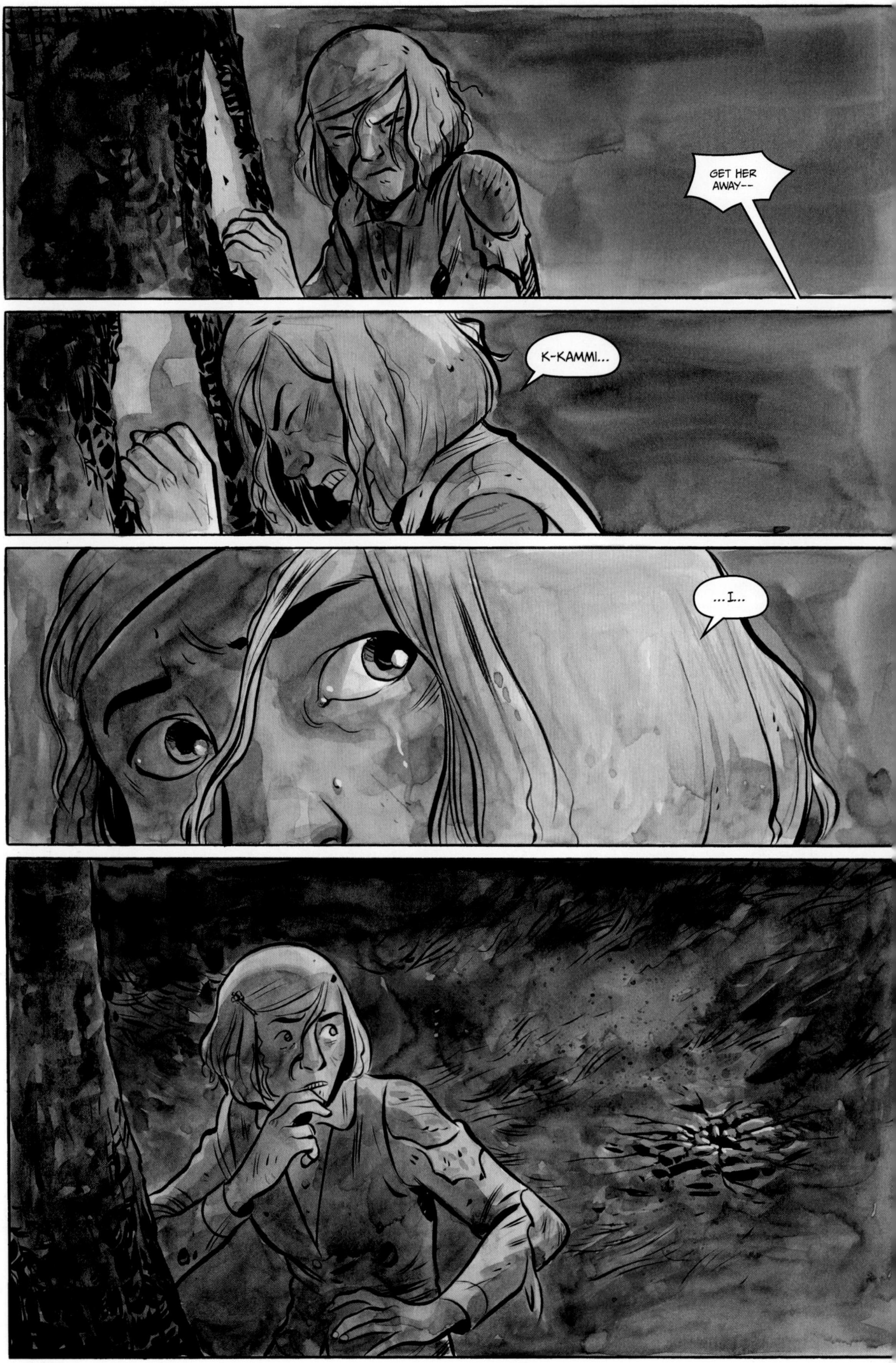
GET HER AWAY--
K-KAMMI...
...I...

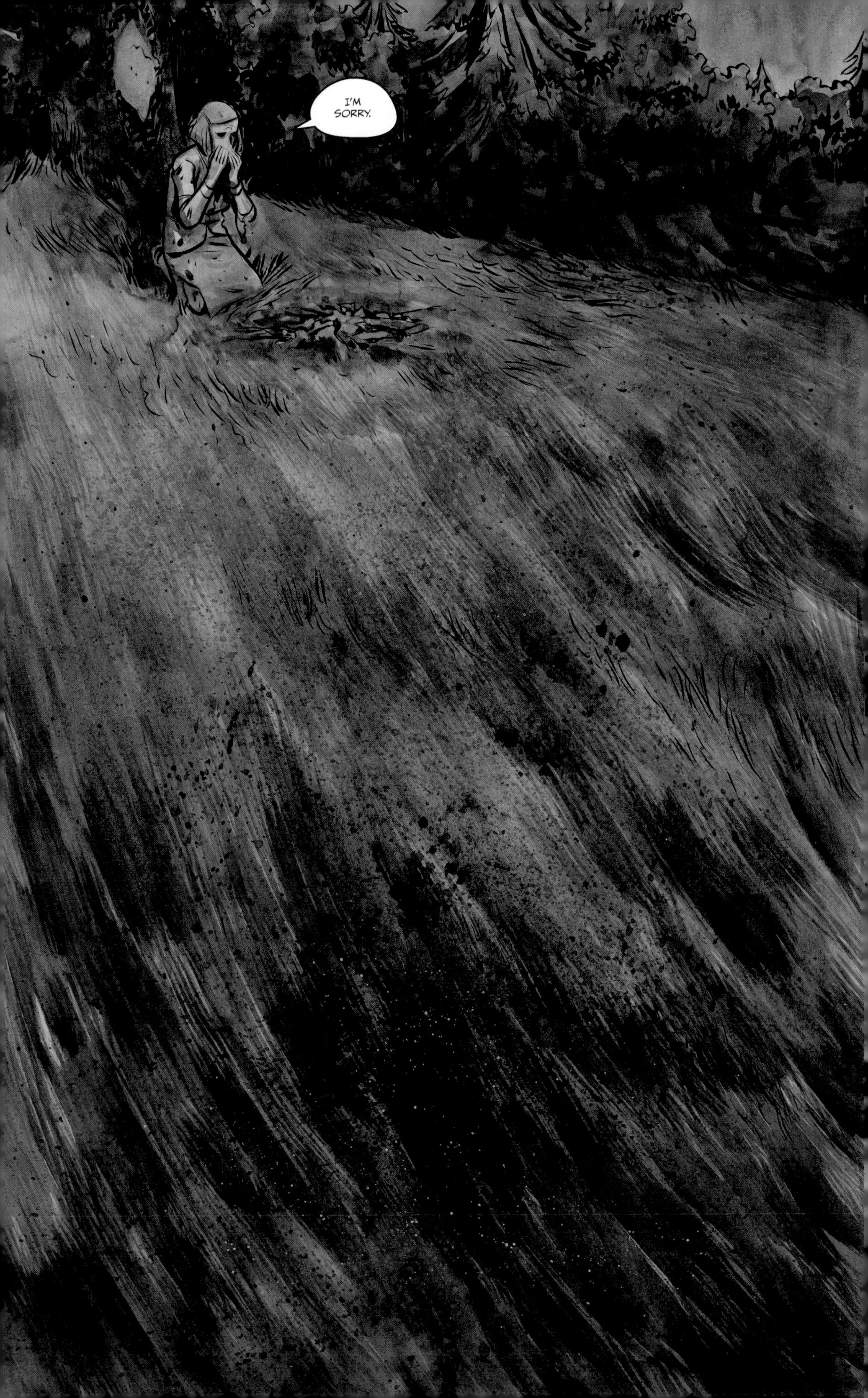
I'M SORRY.

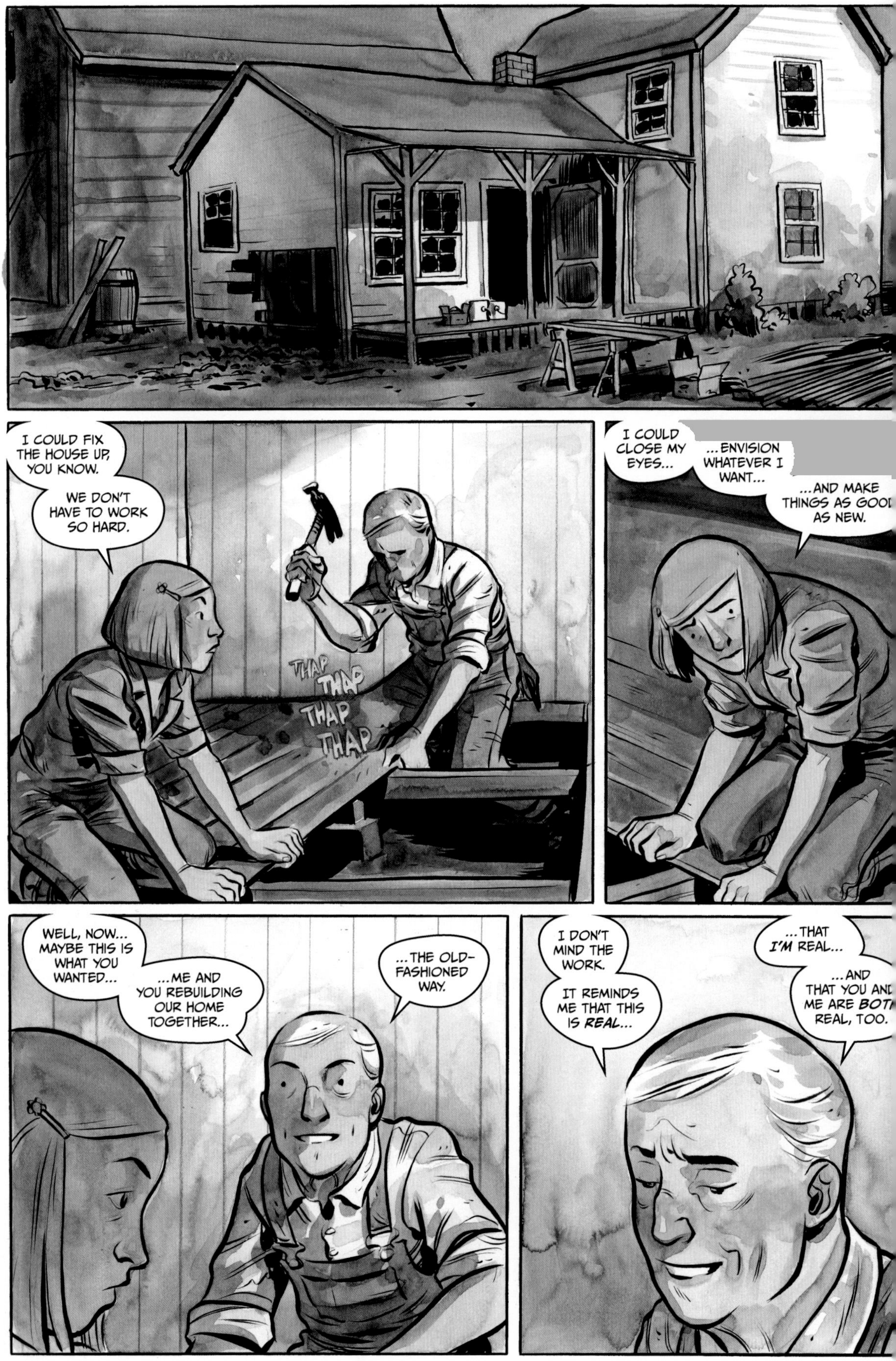
I COULD FIX THE HOUSE UP, YOU KNOW.
WE DON'T HAVE TO WORK SO HARD.
THAP THAP THAP THAP
I COULD CLOSE MY EYES...
...ENVISION WHATEVER I WANT...
...AND MAKE THINGS AS GOOD AS NEW.
WELL, NOW... MAYBE THIS IS WHAT YOU WANTED...
...ME AND YOU REBUILDING OUR HOME TOGETHER...
...THE OLD-FASHIONED WAY.
I DON'T MIND THE WORK.
IT REMINDS ME THAT THIS IS *REAL*...
...THAT *I'M* REAL...
...AND THAT YOU AND ME ARE *BOTH* REAL, TOO.

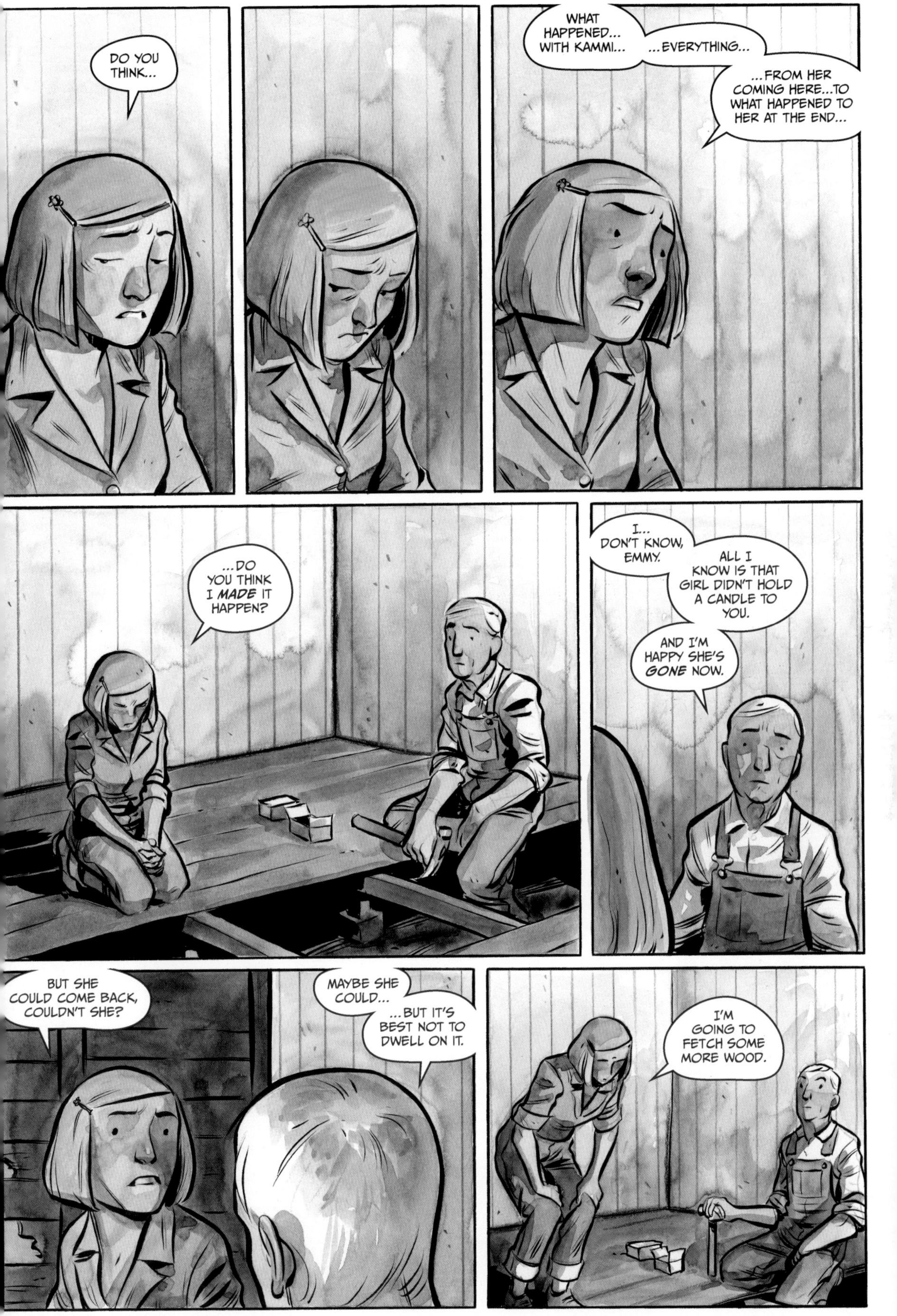
DO YOU THINK...
WHAT HAPPENED... WITH KAMMI...
...EVERYTHING...
...FROM HER COMING HERE...TO WHAT HAPPENED TO HER AT THE END...
...DO YOU THINK I *MADE* IT HAPPEN?
I... DON'T KNOW, EMMY.
ALL I KNOW IS THAT GIRL DIDN'T HOLD A CANDLE TO YOU.
AND I'M HAPPY SHE'S *GONE* NOW.
BUT SHE COULD COME BACK, COULDN'T SHE?
MAYBE SHE COULD...
...BUT IT'S BEST NOT TO DWELL ON IT.
I'M GOING TO FETCH SOME MORE WOOD.

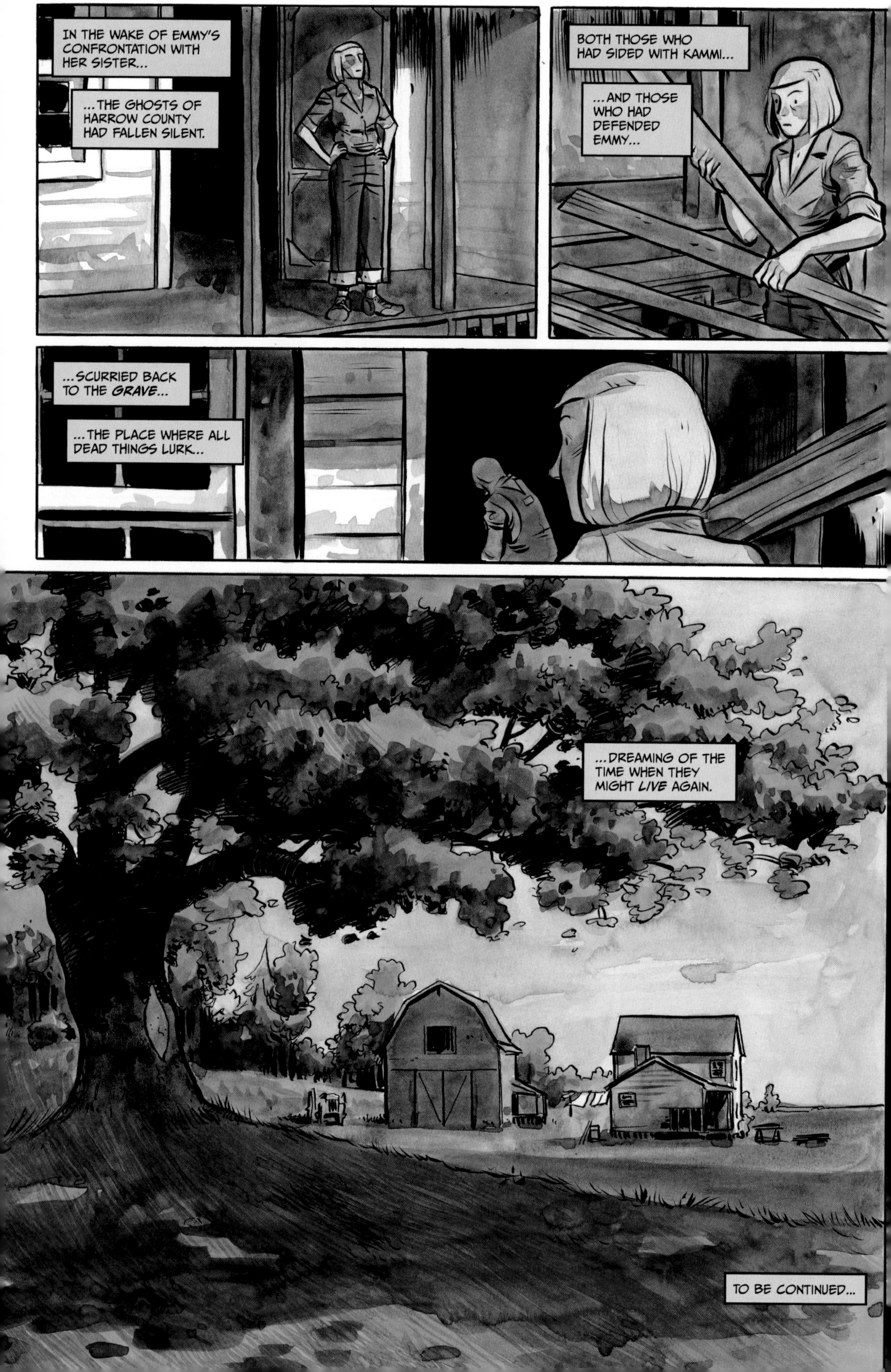
IN THE WAKE OF EMMY'S CONFRONTATION WITH HER SISTER...
...THE GHOSTS OF HARROW COUNTY HAD FALLEN SILENT.
BOTH THOSE WHO HAD SIDED WITH KAMMI...
...AND THOSE WHO HAD DEFENDED EMMY...
...SCURRIED BACK TO THE *GRAVE*...
...THE PLACE WHERE ALL DEAD THINGS LURK...
...DREAMING OF THE TIME WHEN THEY MIGHT *LIVE* AGAIN.
TO BE CONTINUED...

HARROW
– SKETCHBOOK –
COUNTY

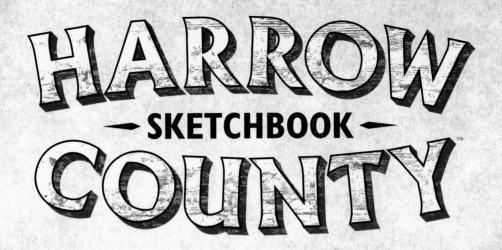

**NOTES BY
TYLER CROOK**

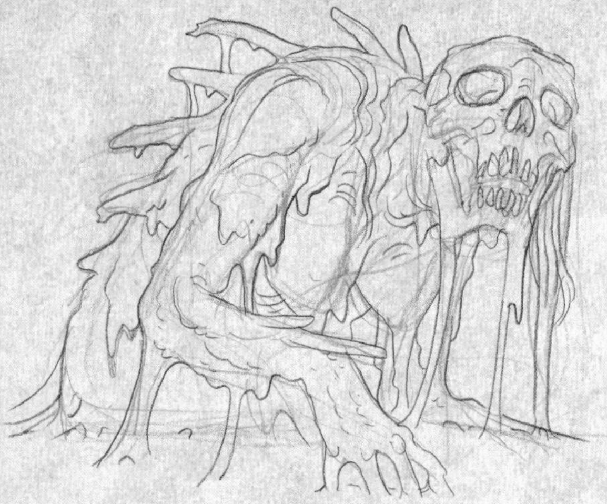

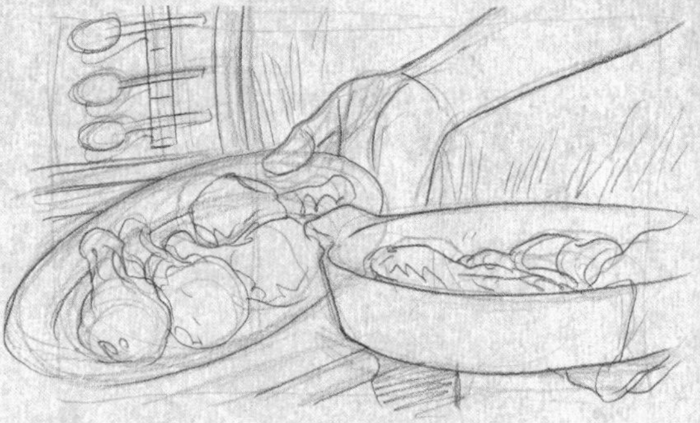

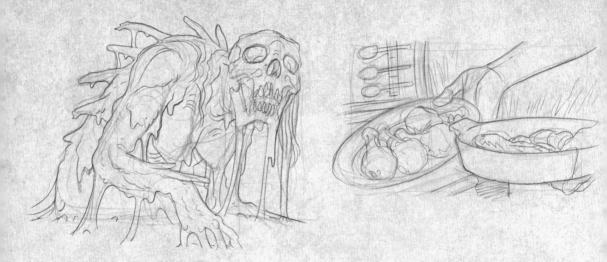

Sometimes when I'm having a hard time penciling a panel, I'll whip out a blank sheet of printer paper and do the first pass at the pencils on that. Somehow isolating a panel like that takes a lot of the pressure off and I can focus on the needs of the individual panel. Once I get something that I like, I can use a light box and trace it onto the page with all the other panels. Usually when I'm done with an issue, I have a giant stack of all the panels I had to draw this way. Here's just a couple of them.

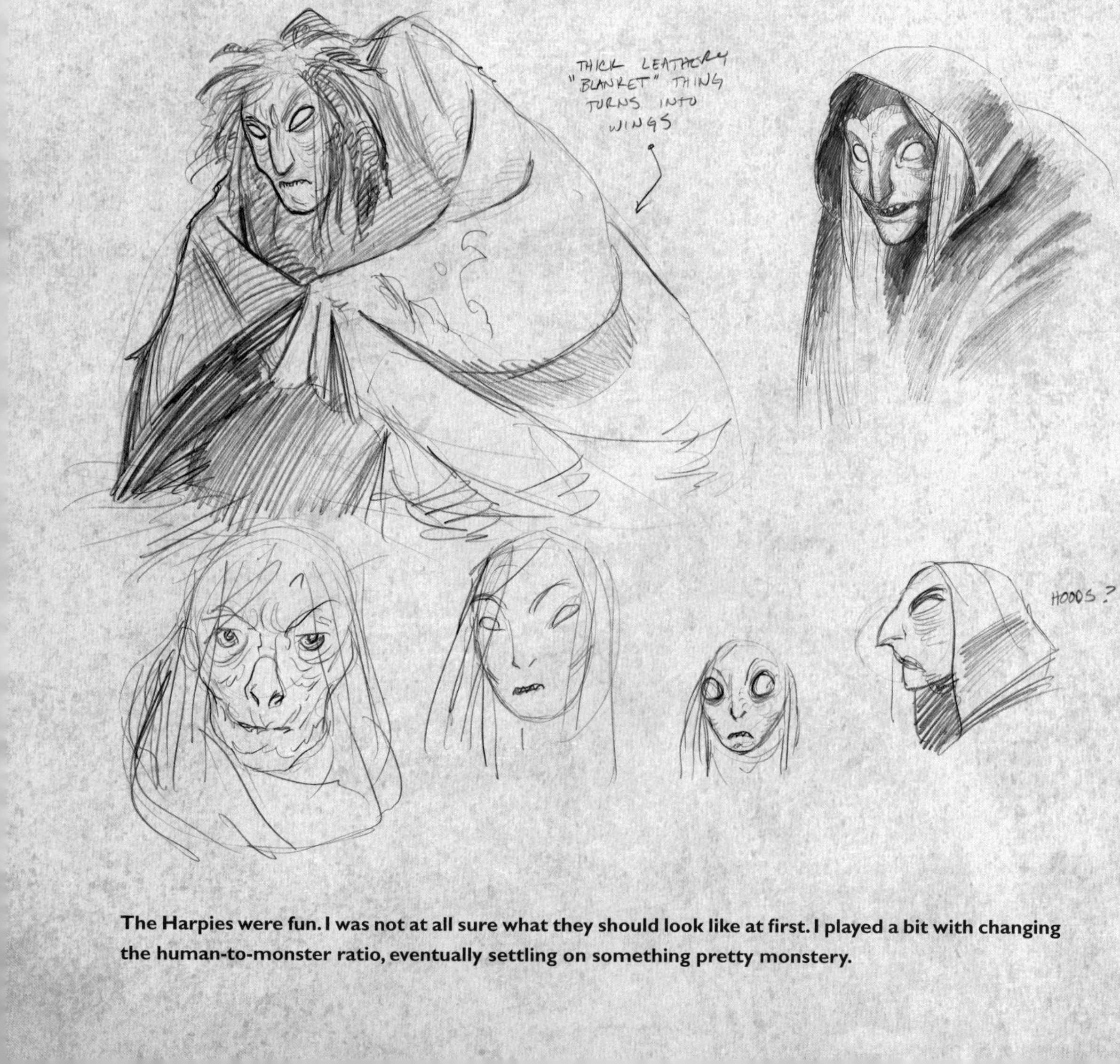
THICK LEATHERY "BLANKET" THING TURNS INTO WINGS
HOODS?

The Harpies were fun. I was not at all sure what they should look like at first. I played a bit with changing the human-to-monster ratio, eventually settling on something pretty monstery.

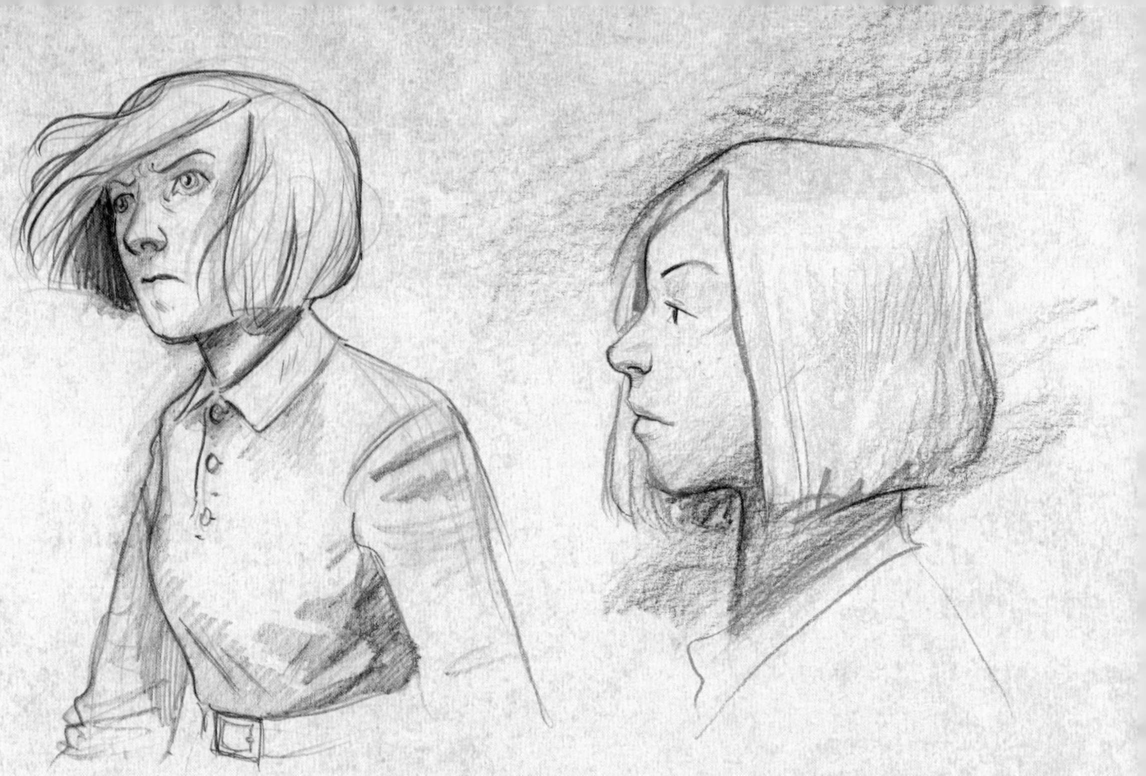

I drew these Emmys as quick warm-ups. I kind of liked how these turned out, so they stuck around. I feel like Emmy is a much more complex character than she appears on the surface, and I'm still finding new ways of drawing her so those deeper levels can be expressed.

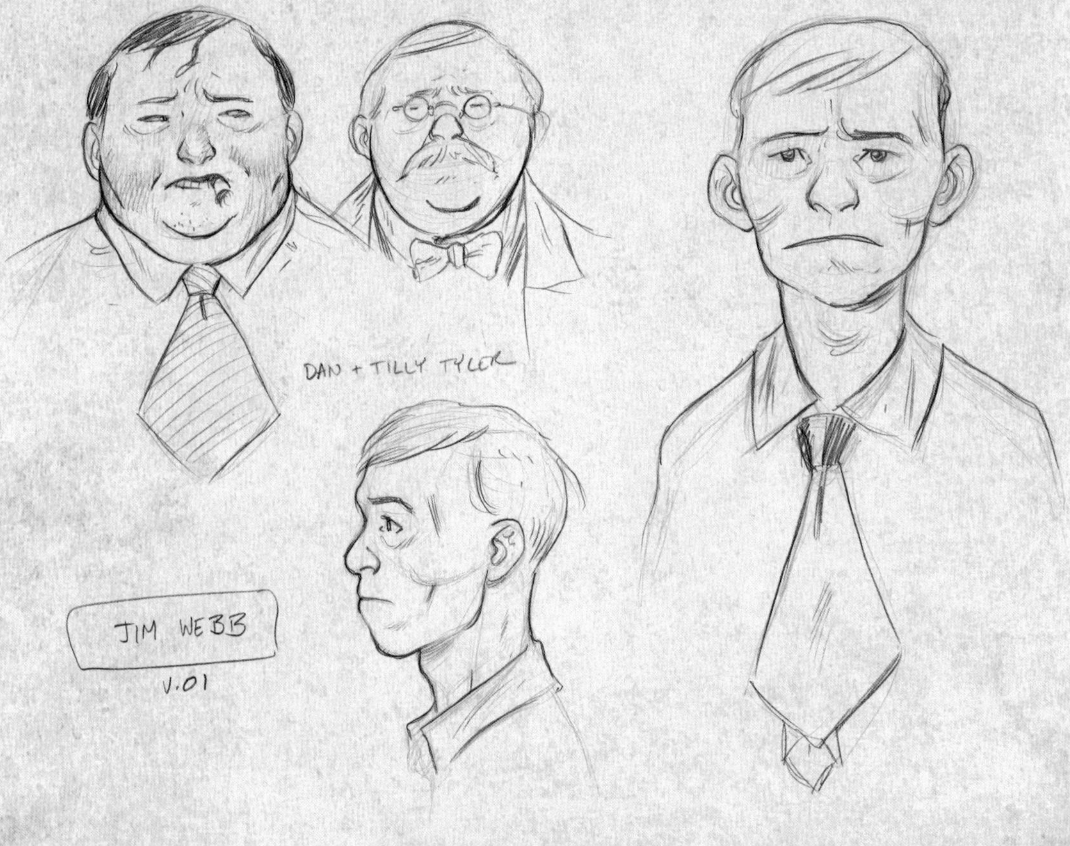
DAN + TILLY TYLOR
JIM WEBB
V.01

These were some of the initial character designs for this story arc. I liked these two big brothers. It's kind of interesting how Jim Webb changed once he was on the page—he became a bit more menacing, I think.

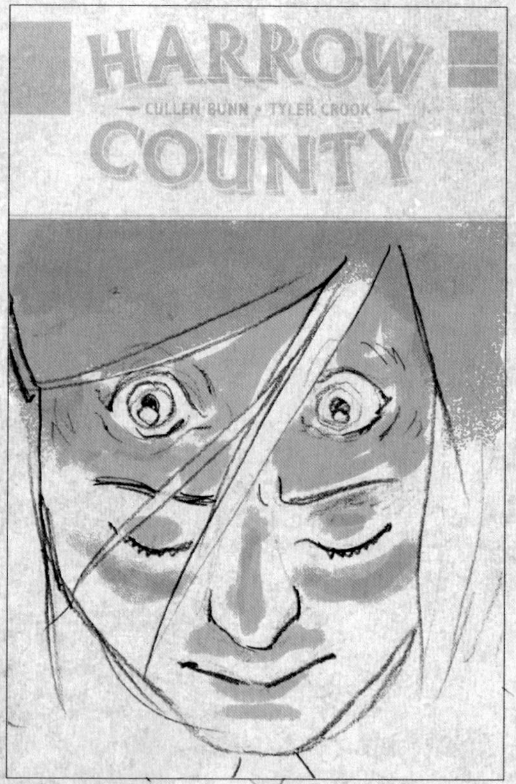
HARROW
CULLEN BUNN • TYLER CROOK
COUNTY

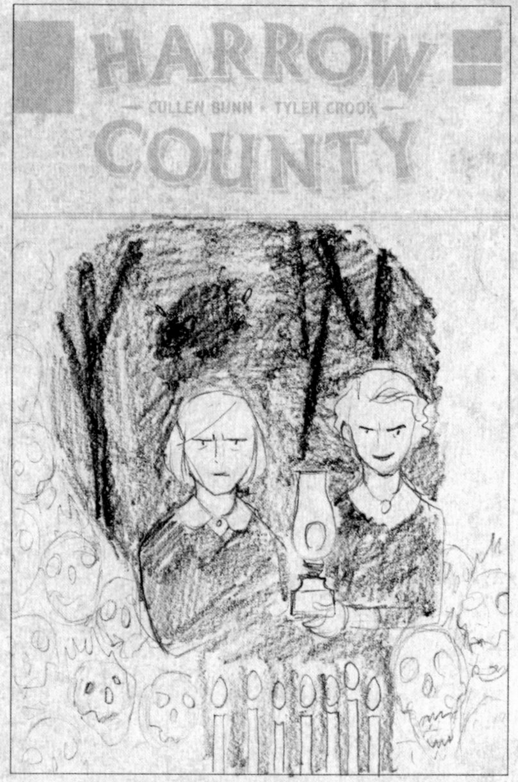
HARROW
CULLEN BUNN • TYLER CROOK
COUNTY

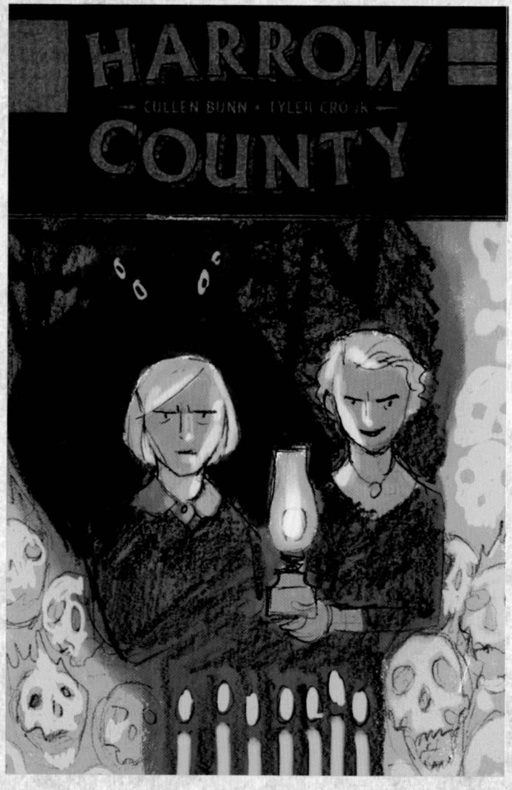
HARROW
CULLEN BUNN • TYLER CROOK
COUNTY

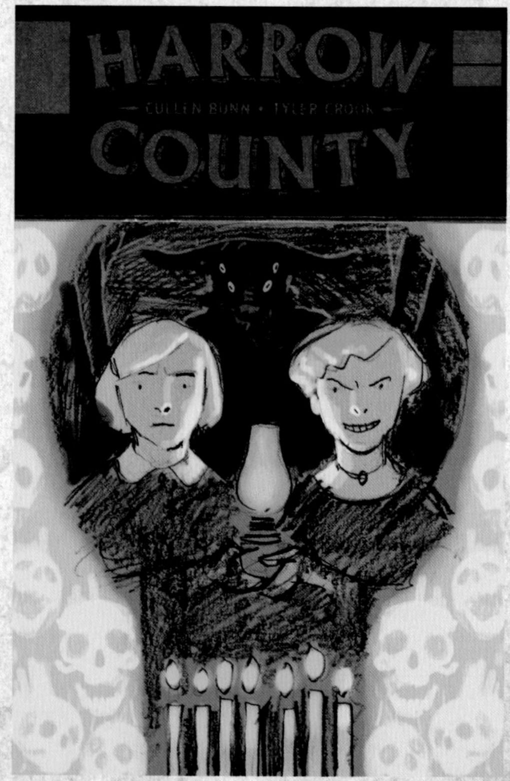
HARROW
CULLEN BUNN • TYLER CROOK
COUNTY

Covers are a real challenge for me. I feel like my process is starting to develop, but at the time I did these covers, I was struggling. I liked the sketch of Emmy with the extra set of eyes coming out of her forehead, but a few days before I turned that in, another Dark Horse creator submitted a very similar design for his book! Curse you, David Mack!

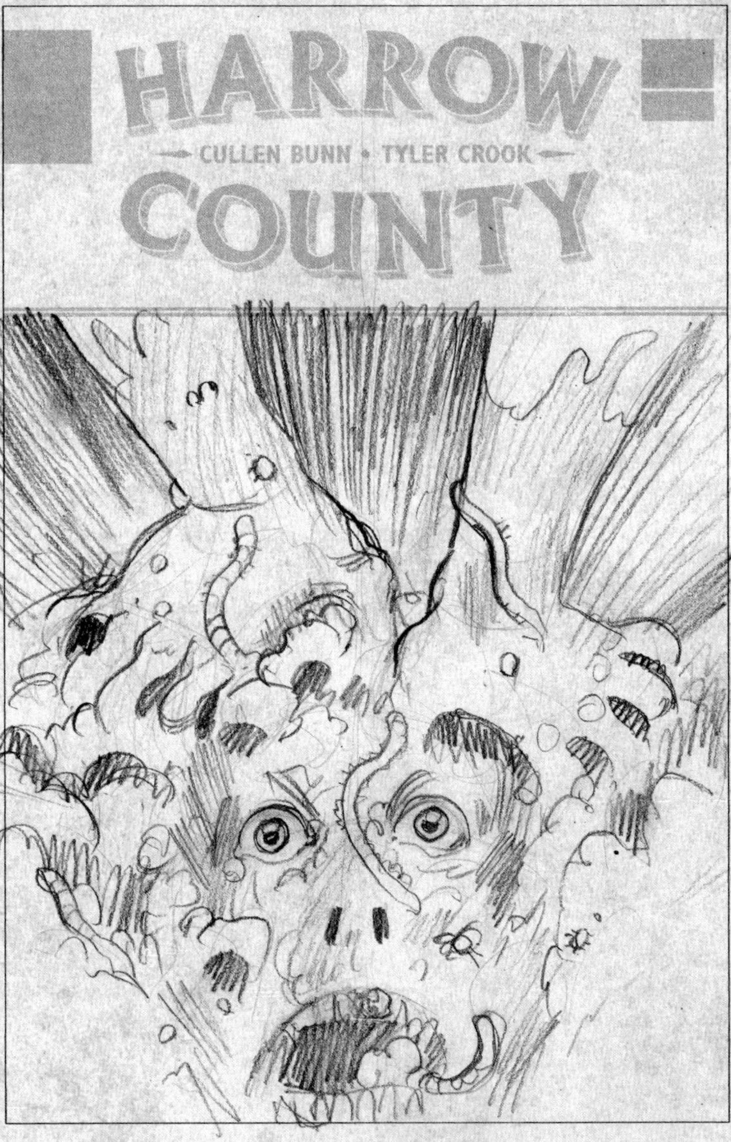
HARROW
CULLEN BUNN • TYLER CROOK
COUNTY

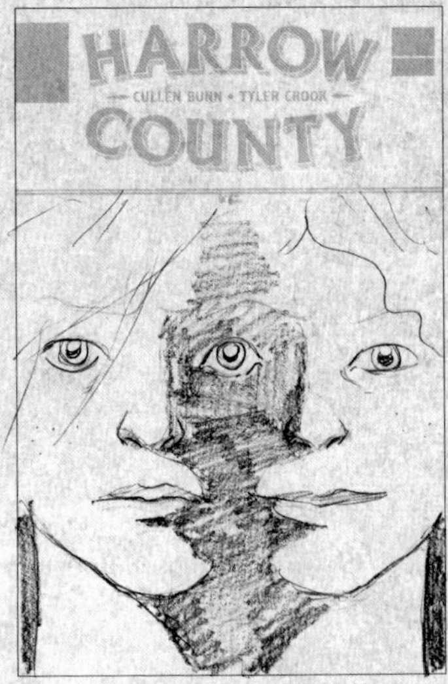
HARROW
CULLEN BUNN • TYLER CROOK
COUNTY

One of the things I've been learning is that simple and direct images usually work best for covers. Out of this batch of cover sketches for issue #6, the hands digging in the dirt were the most impactful. We added the rotting face in the dirt to make it more clear what those evil little hands were up to.

Ⓐ

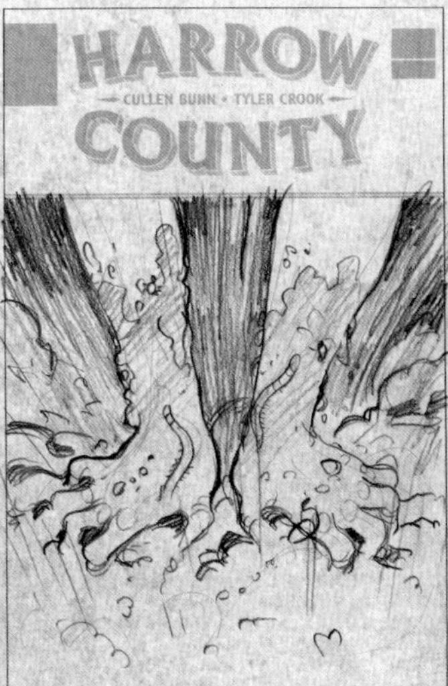
HARROW
CULLEN BUNN • TYLER CROOK
COUNTY

MUDDY HANDS DIGGING IN DIRT
BUGS + SLUGS CRAWLING AROUND

Ⓑ

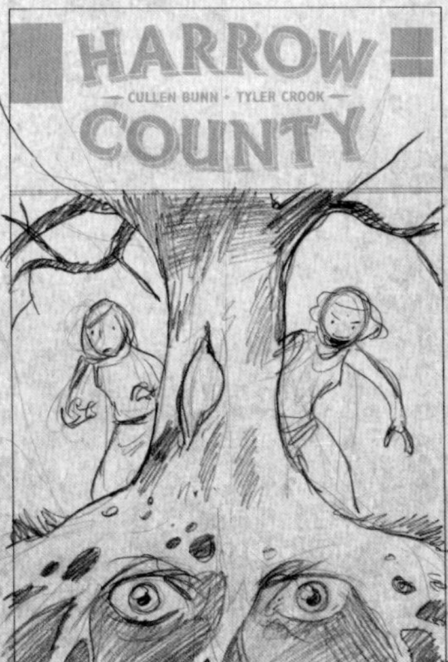
HARROW
CULLEN BUNN • TYLER CROOK
COUNTY

HESTER'S WILD EYES!!

Ⓒ

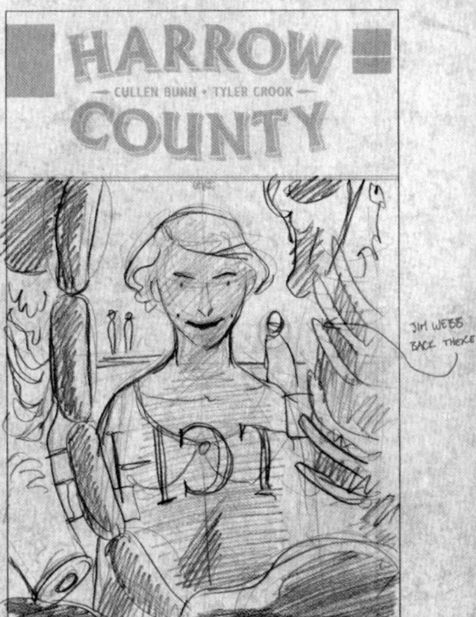
HARROW
CULLEN BUNN • TYLER CROOK
COUNTY
JIM WEBB BACK THERE

KAMMI CREEPING ON THE BUTCHER SHOP
IMAGINE SUPER DETAILED, GLISTENING MEAT
A FEW FLYS HERE + THERE.

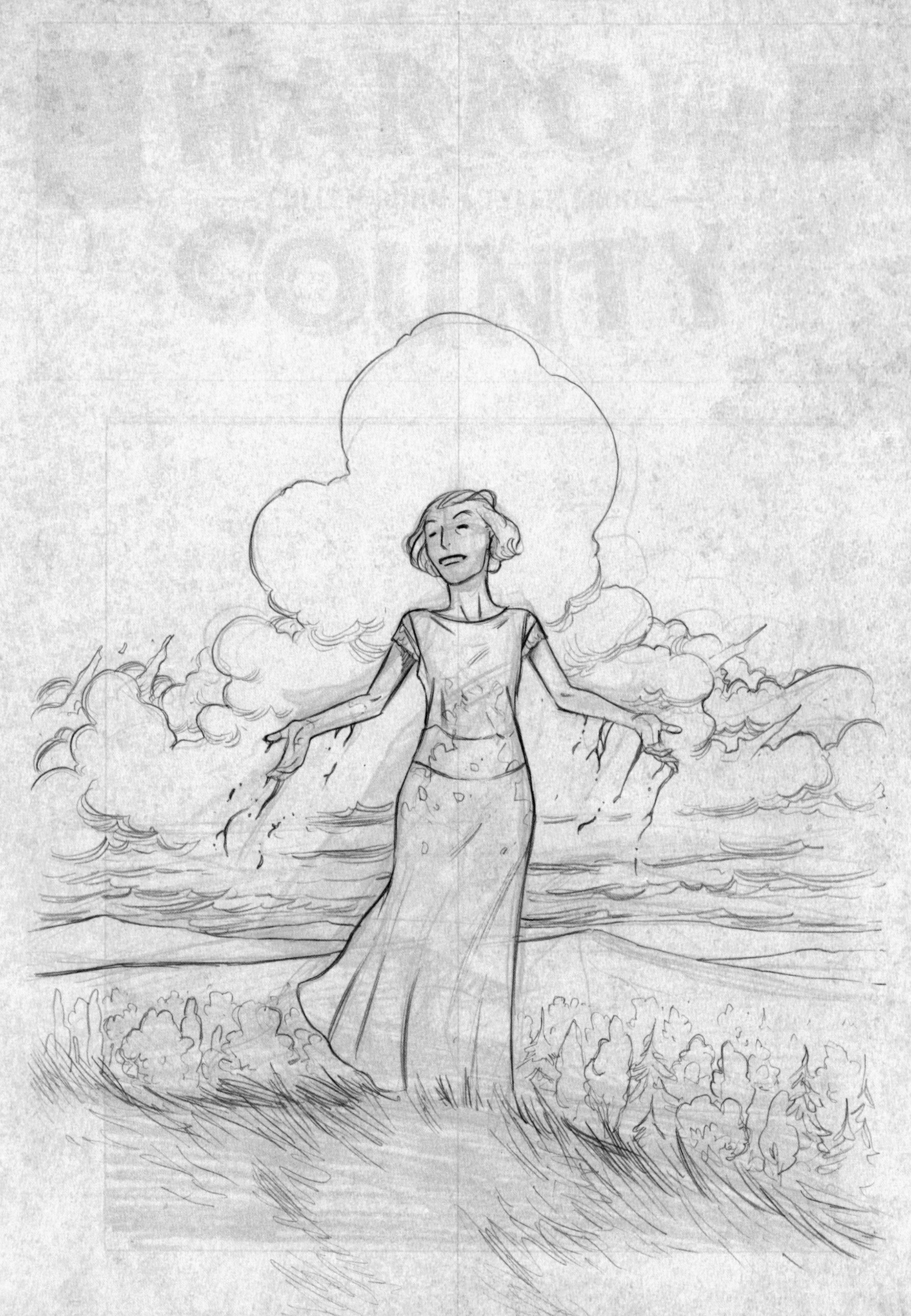

These are the pencils for the cover of issue #7. For this I've printed out my rough sketch in light red on 11 x 17–inch drawing paper. Then I use red colored pencil to tighten up the sketch and finish it with a regular graphite pencil. Once the pencils are finished, I scan the drawing into my computer and remove all the red lines, leaving me with a clean pencil drawing. After I've cleaned it all up, I can print the drawing as a light brown line on my nice watercolor paper. Then I can ink and paint the page.

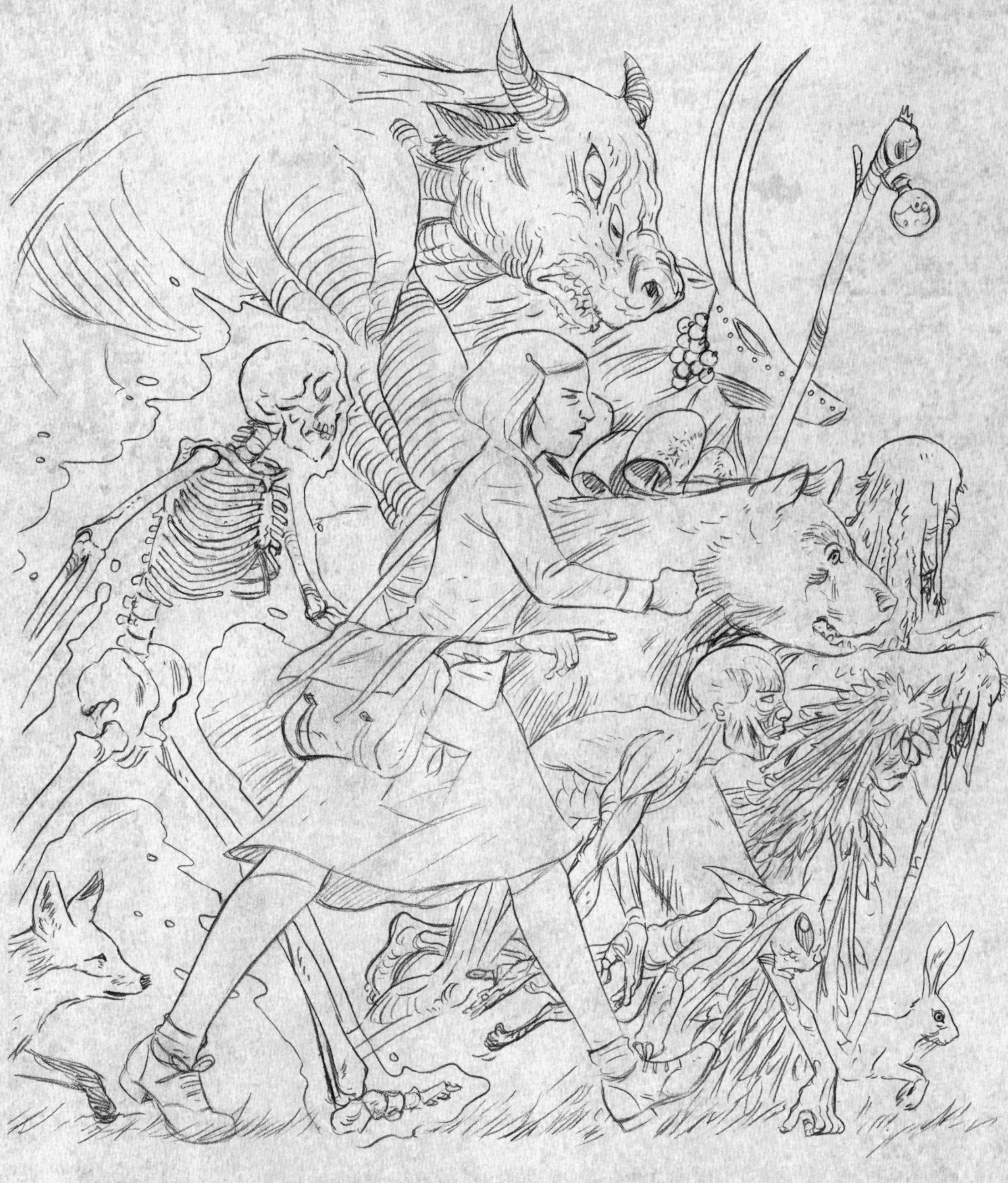

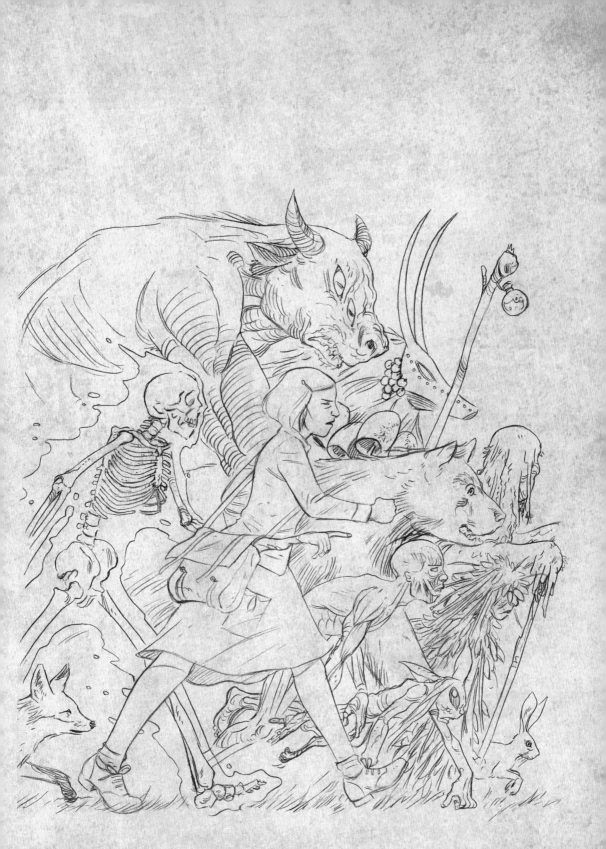

I was reading a lot of *Prince Valiant* by Hal Foster while I was working on this story arc. His work is amazing. Every single panel that dude drew was amazing, but occasionally he would draw a panel that was perfect. This drawing is an homage to (swipe from) a panel that first appeared on March 12, 1938. It's awesome how Emmy even has a haircut similar to Prince Valiant's.

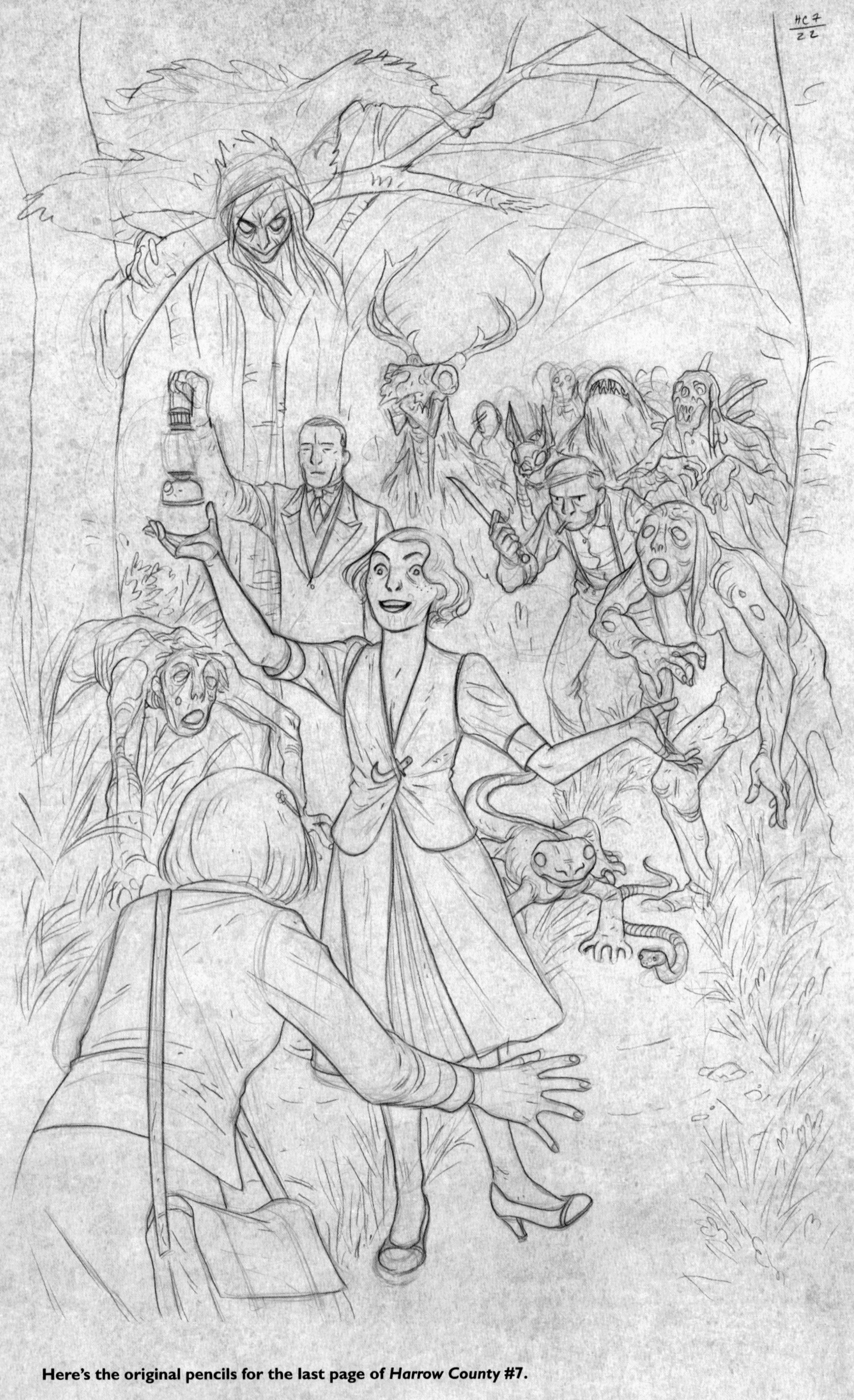
HC7
22

Here's the original pencils for the last page of *Harrow County* #7.

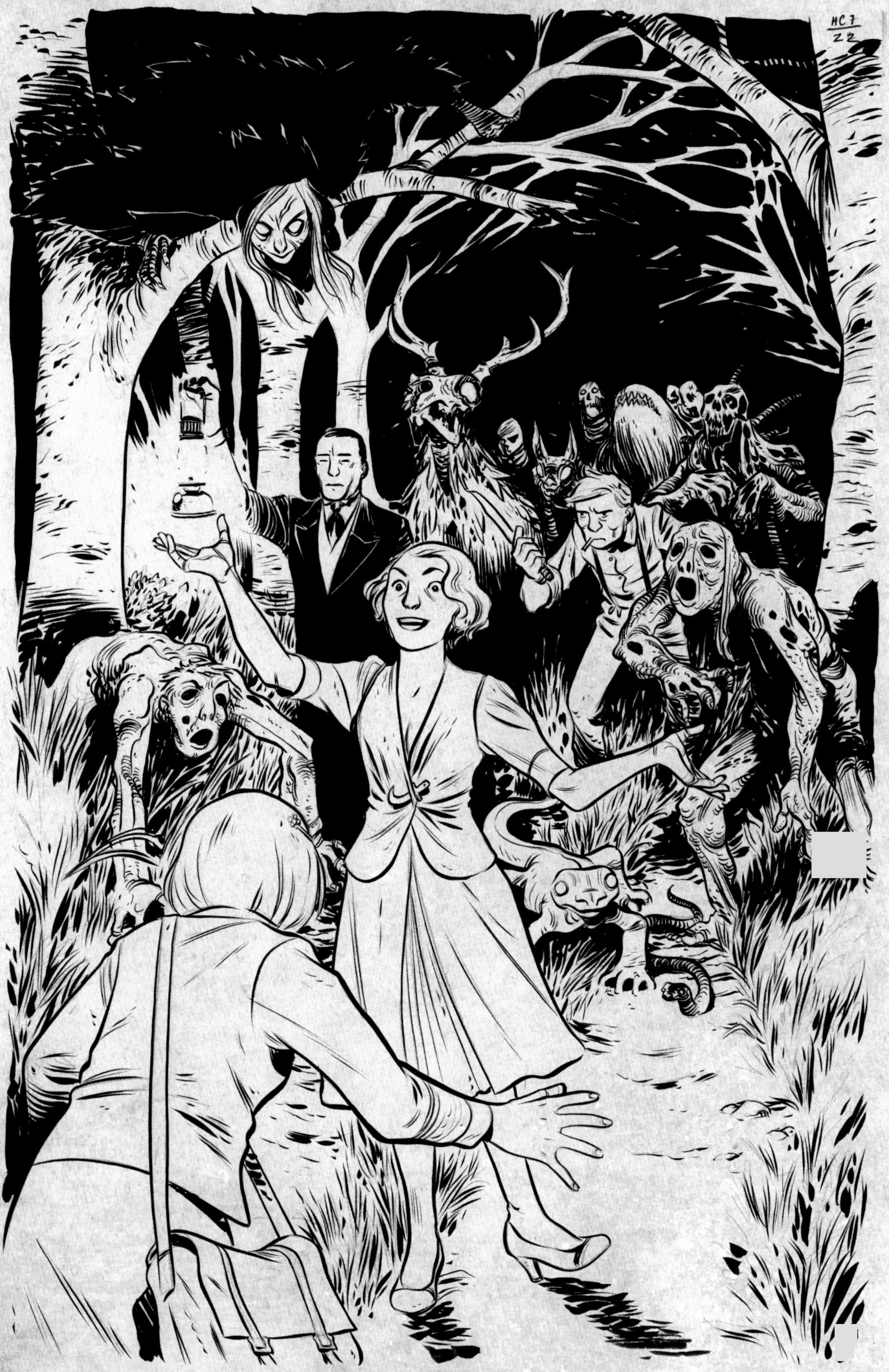

And here's a rare look at what an inked page looks like before I color it. I actually ink my pages almost as if they were going to be colored digitally in Photoshop. But instead I use watercolor and gouache.

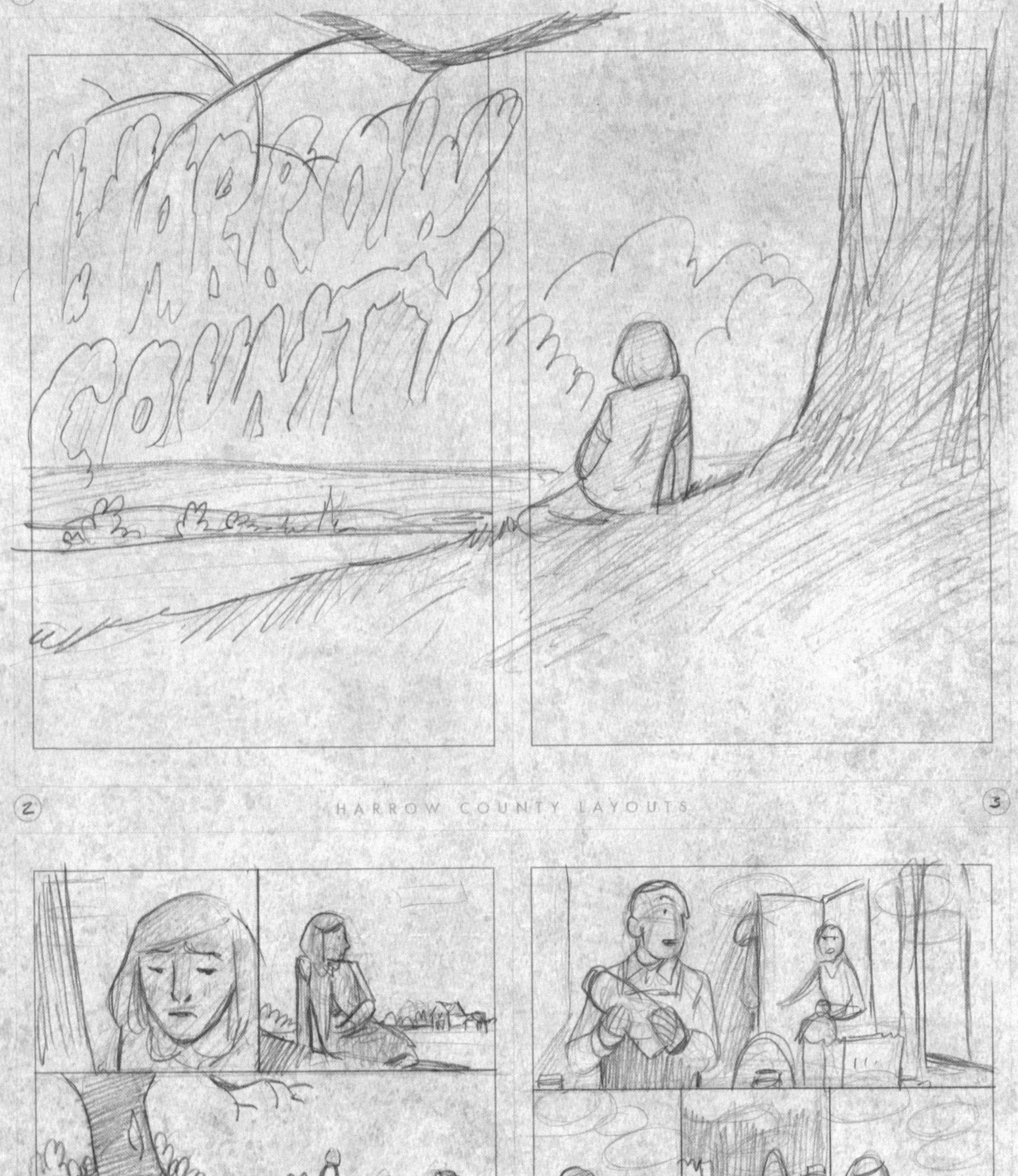
HARROW COUNTY LAYOUTS
1

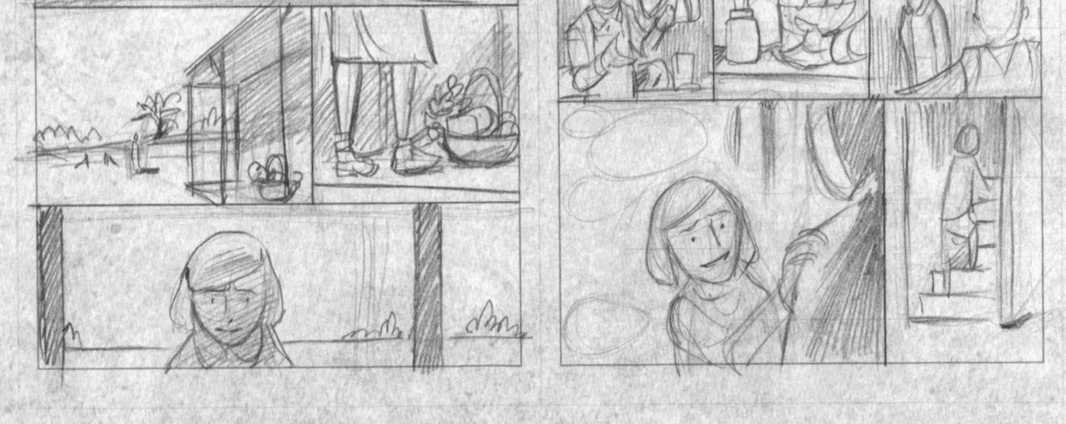
2
HARROW COUNTY LAYOUTS
3

A lot of comic artists will tell you that layouts are the heart of comics making, and I'm no different. This is where all the storytelling, staging, emotional beats, panel sizes, etc., get worked out.

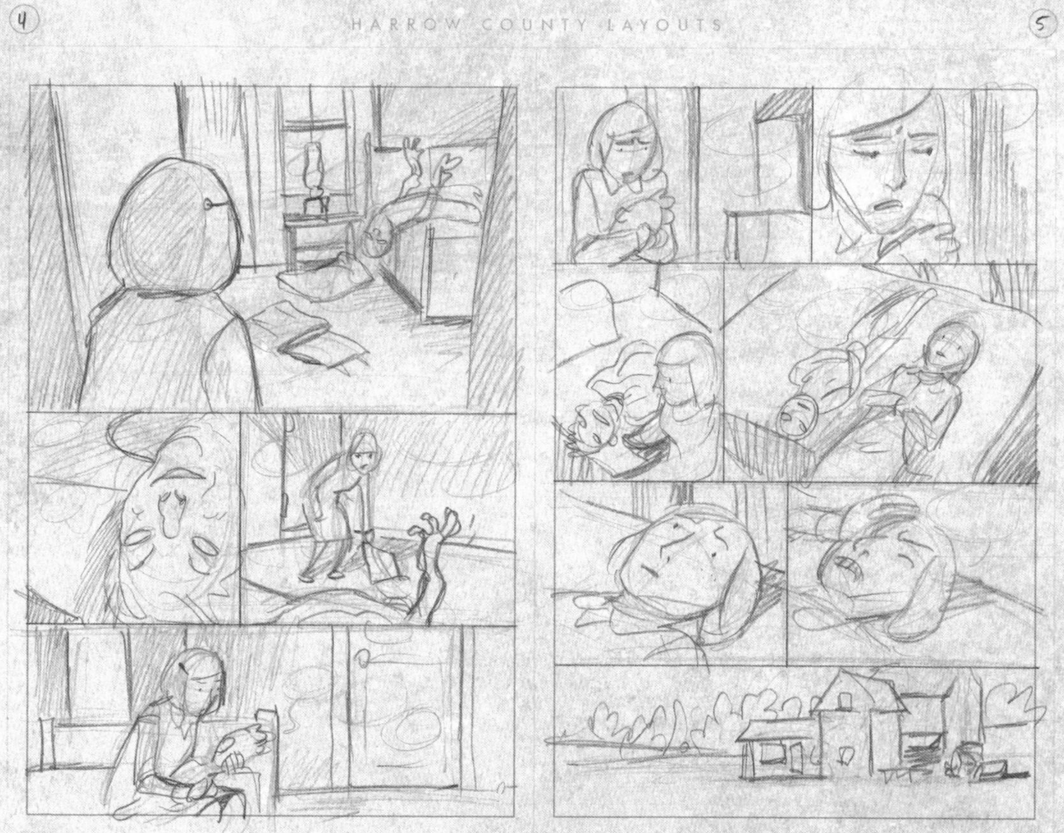
4
HARROW COUNTY LAYOUTS
5

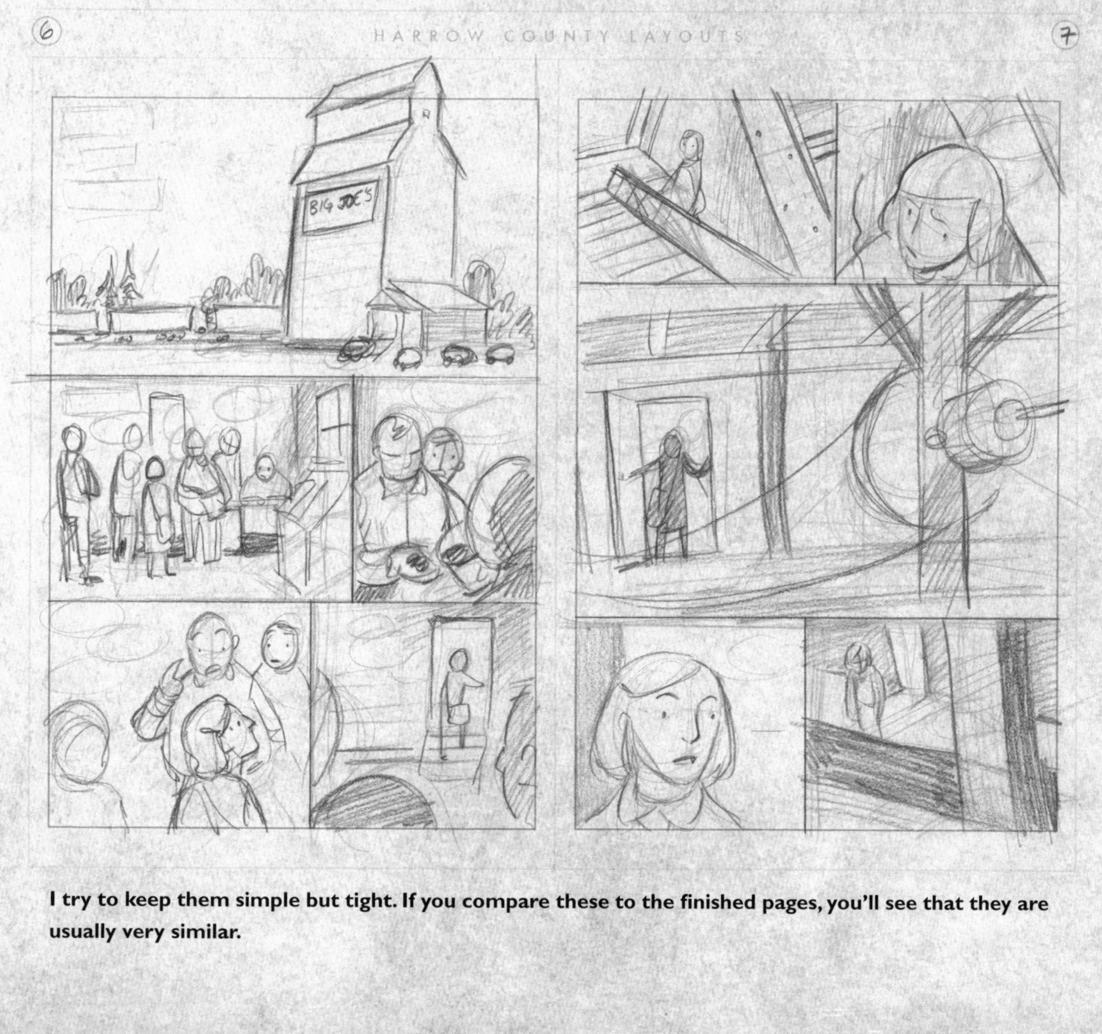
6
HARROW COUNTY LAYOUTS
7
BIG JOE'S

I try to keep them simple but tight. If you compare these to the finished pages, you'll see that they are usually very similar.

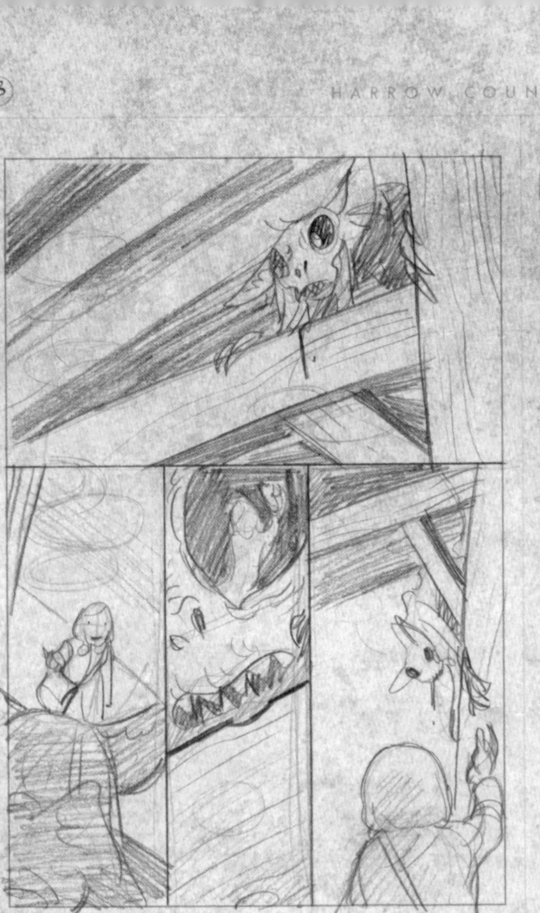

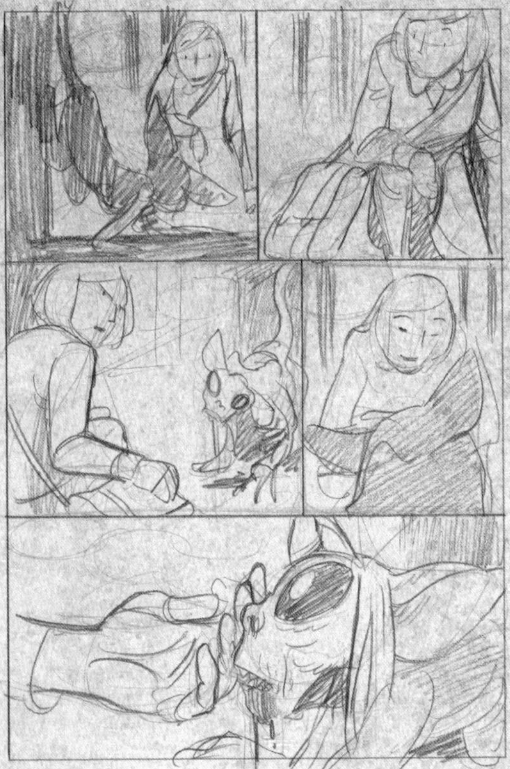

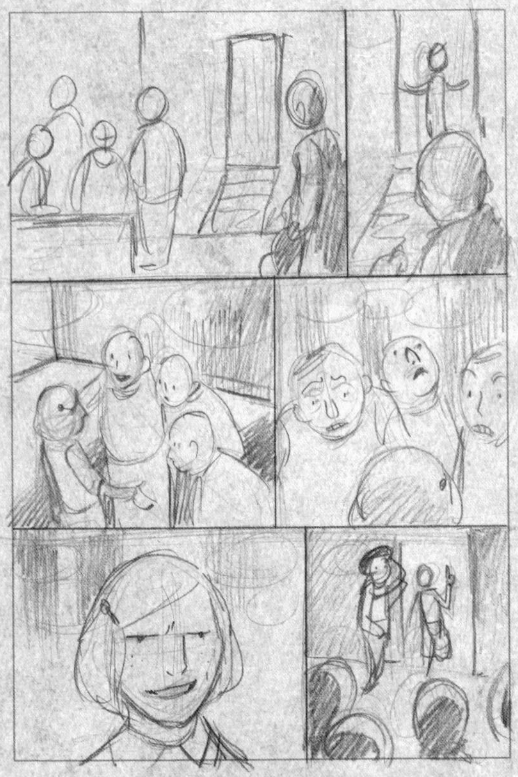

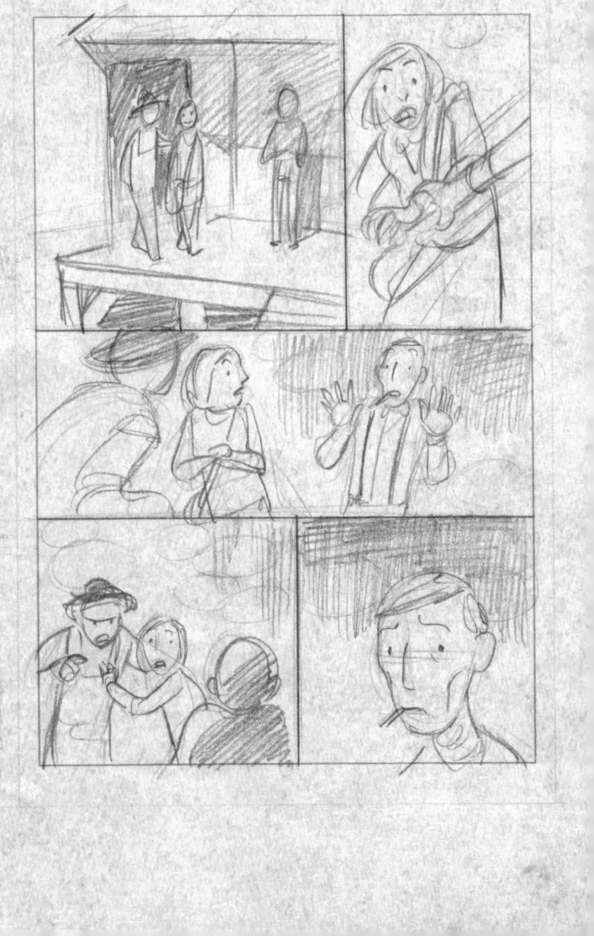

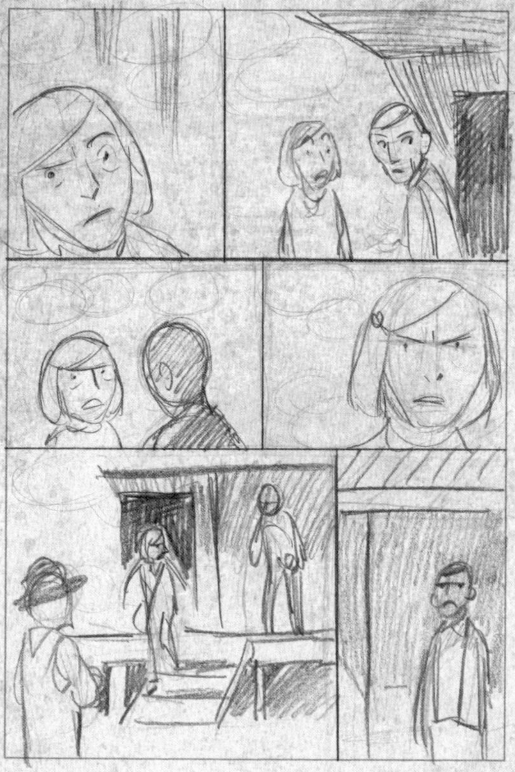

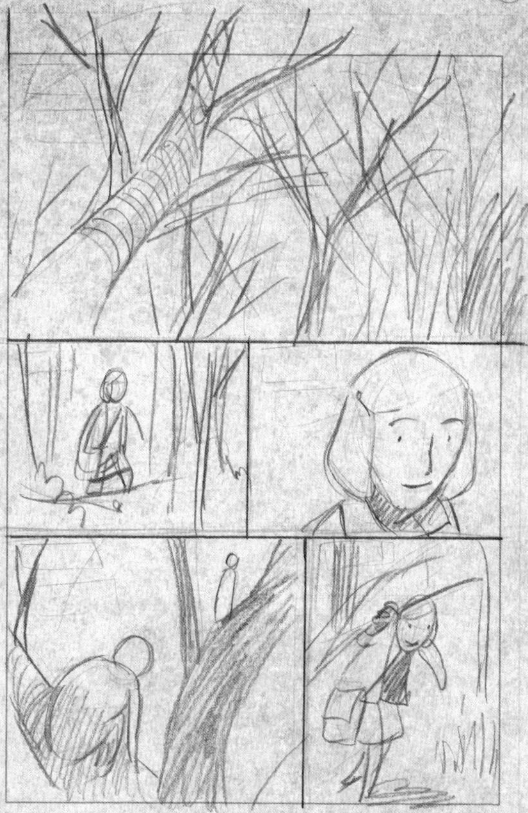

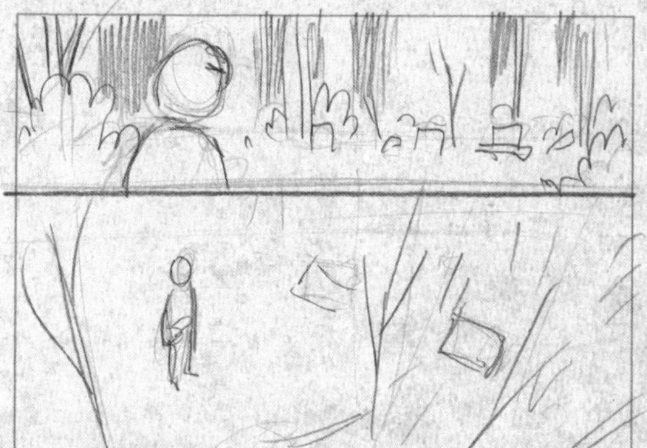

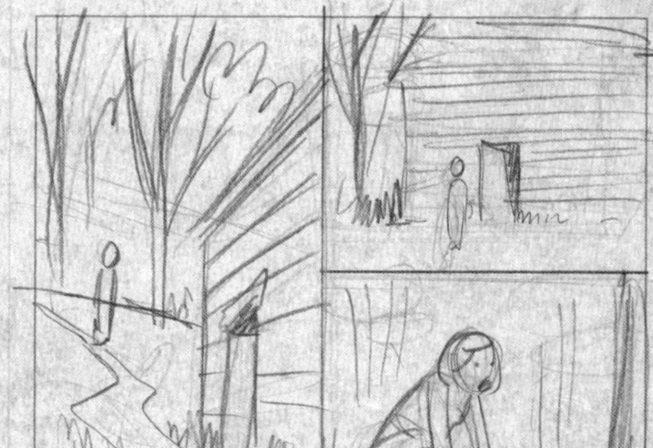

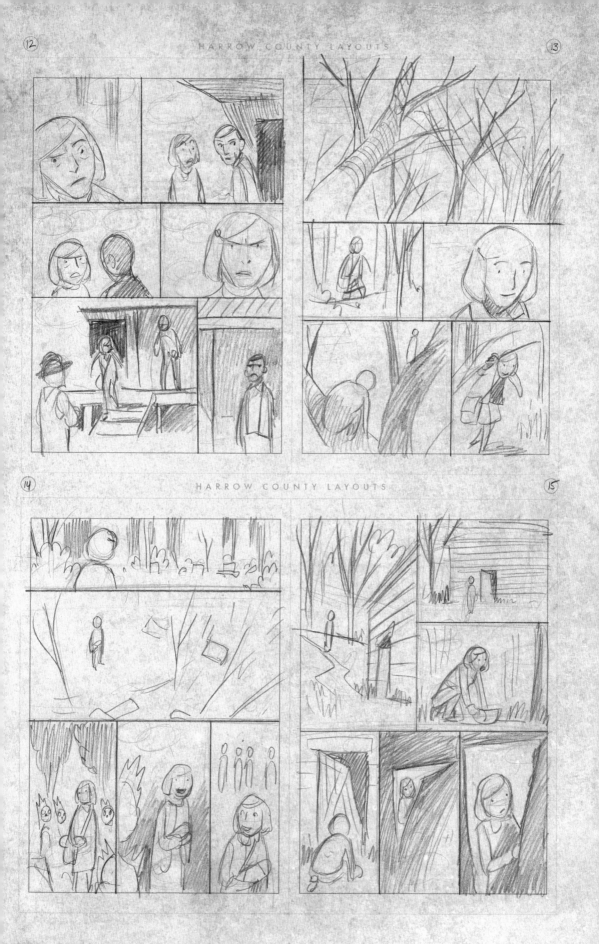

16 HARROW COUNTY LAYOUTS 17

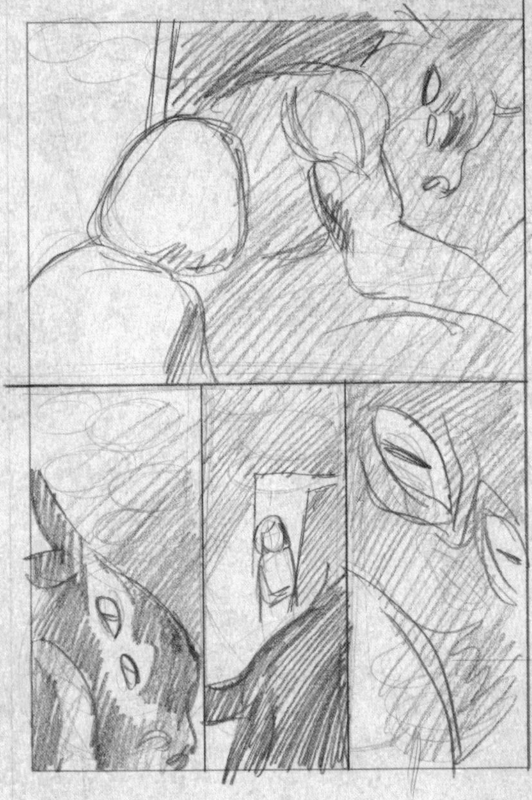

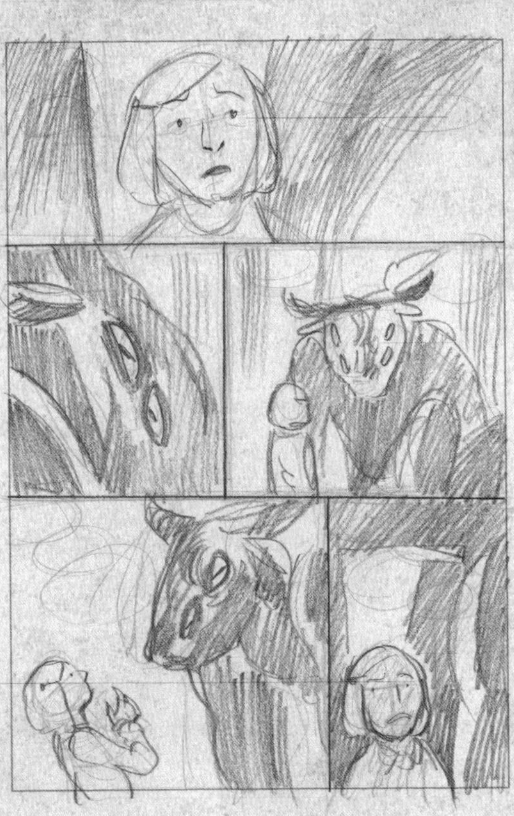

18 HARROW COUNTY LAYOUTS 19

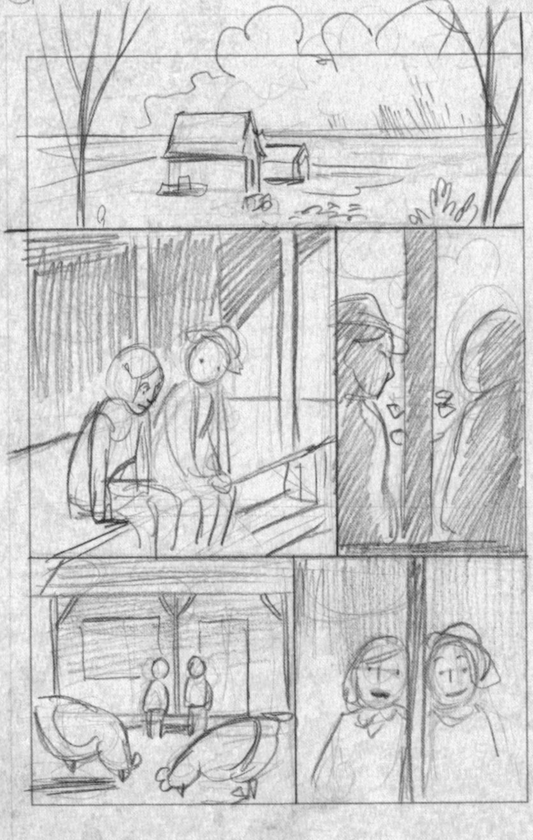

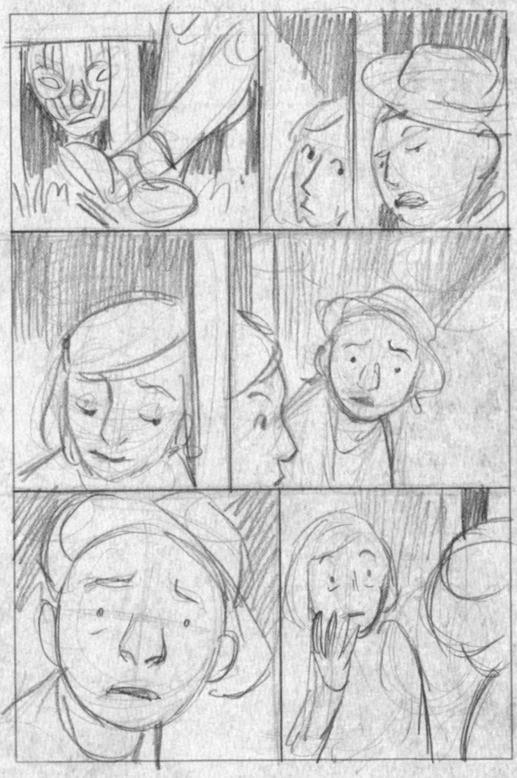

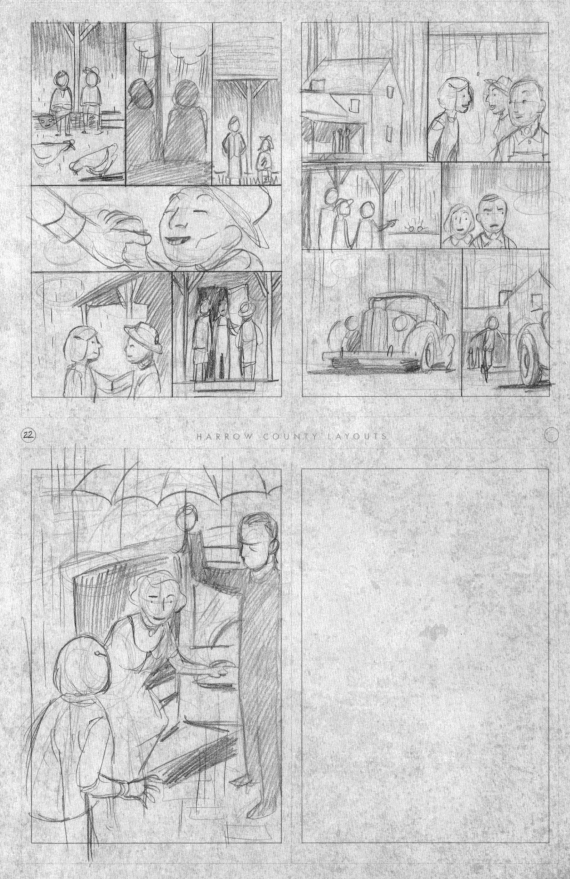

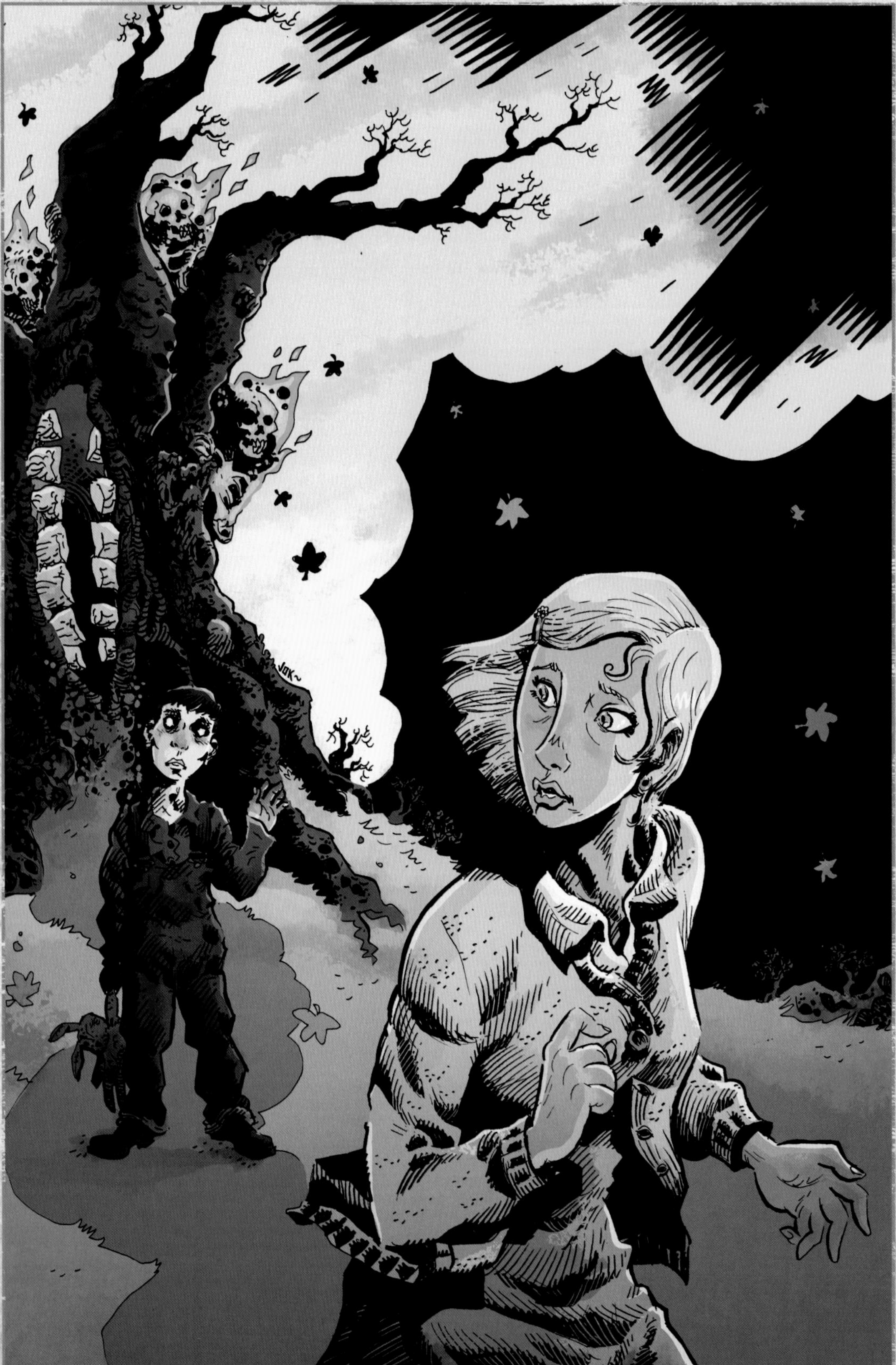
JOK

ARTWORK BY
JOK

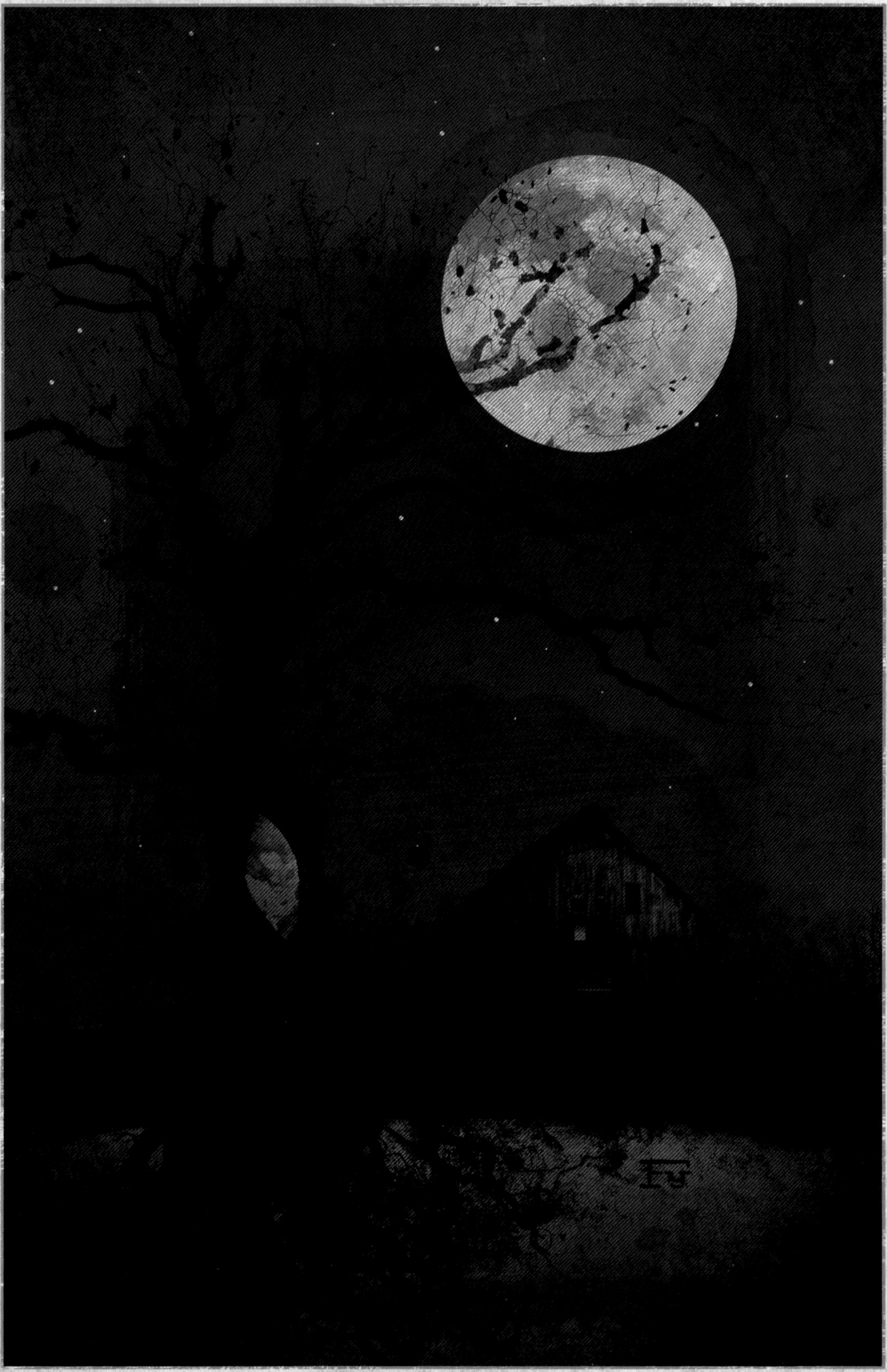

ARTWORK BY
BRYAN FYFFE

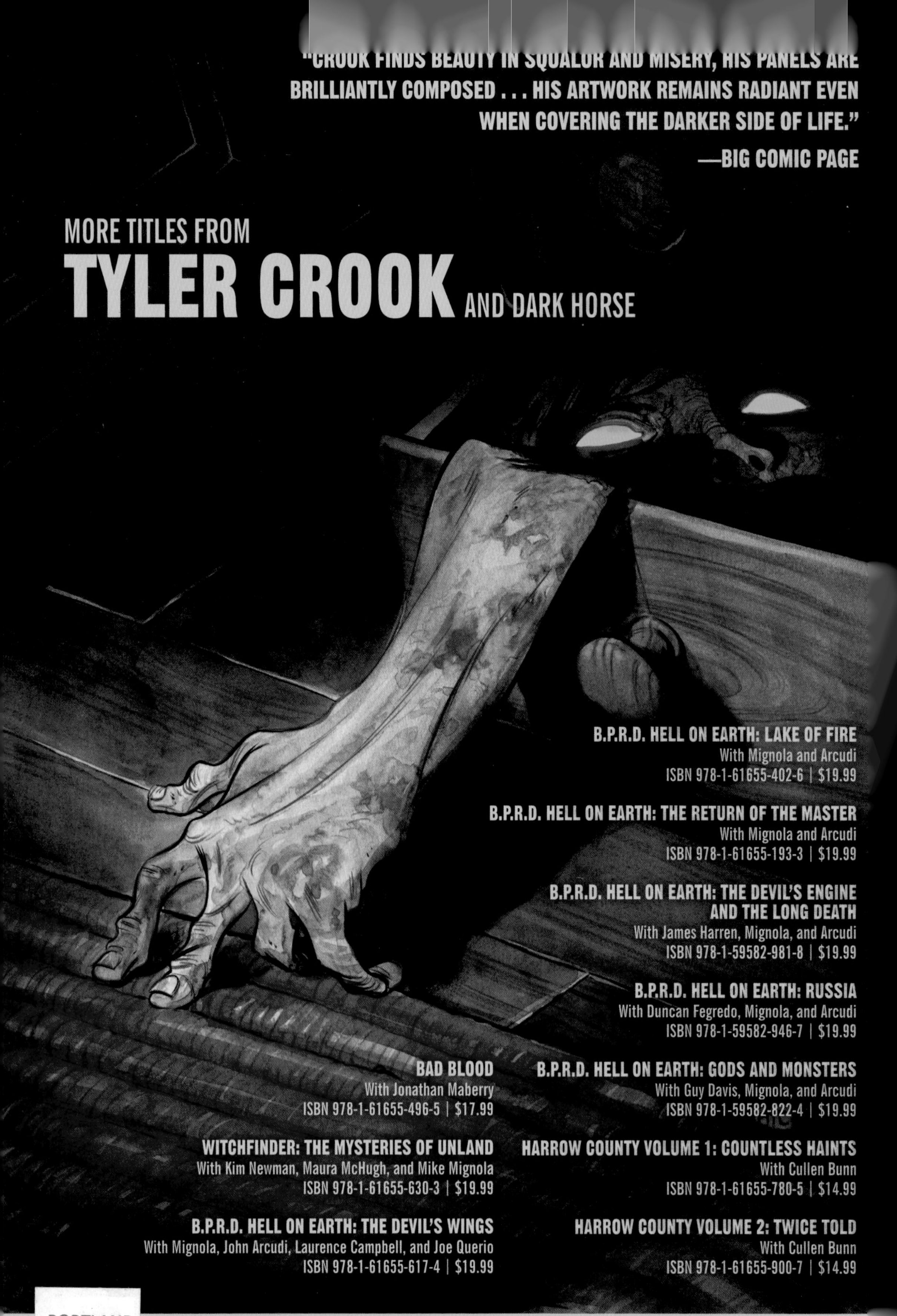

"CROOK FINDS BEAUTY IN SQUALOR AND MISERY, HIS PANELS ARE BRILLIANTLY COMPOSED . . . HIS ARTWORK REMAINS RADIANT EVEN WHEN COVERING THE DARKER SIDE OF LIFE."

—BIG COMIC PAGE

MORE TITLES FROM

TYLER CROOK AND DARK HORSE

B.P.R.D. HELL ON EARTH: LAKE OF FIRE
With Mignola and Arcudi
ISBN 978-1-61655-402-6 | $19.99

B.P.R.D. HELL ON EARTH: THE RETURN OF THE MASTER
With Mignola and Arcudi
ISBN 978-1-61655-193-3 | $19.99

B.P.R.D. HELL ON EARTH: THE DEVIL'S ENGINE AND THE LONG DEATH
With James Harren, Mignola, and Arcudi
ISBN 978-1-59582-981-8 | $19.99

B.P.R.D. HELL ON EARTH: RUSSIA
With Duncan Fegredo, Mignola, and Arcudi
ISBN 978-1-59582-946-7 | $19.99

BAD BLOOD
With Jonathan Maberry
ISBN 978-1-61655-496-5 | $17.99

WITCHFINDER: THE MYSTERIES OF UNLAND
With Kim Newman, Maura McHugh, and Mike Mignola
ISBN 978-1-61655-630-3 | $19.99

B.P.R.D. HELL ON EARTH: THE DEVIL'S WINGS
With Mignola, John Arcudi, Laurence Campbell, and Joe Querio
ISBN 978-1-61655-617-4 | $19.99

B.P.R.D. HELL ON EARTH: GODS AND MONSTERS
With Guy Davis, Mignola, and Arcudi
ISBN 978-1-59582-822-4 | $19.99

HARROW COUNTY VOLUME 1: COUNTLESS HAINTS
With Cullen Bunn
ISBN 978-1-61655-780-5 | $14.99

HARROW COUNTY VOLUME 2: TWICE TOLD
With Cullen Bunn
ISBN 978-1-61655-900-7 | $14.99

AVAILABLE AT YOUR LOCAL COMICS SHOP OR BOOKSTORE! • To find a comics shop in your area, call 1-888-266-4226.
For more information or to order direct visit DarkHorse.com or call 1-800-862-0052 Mon.–Fri. 9 a.m. to 5 p.m. Pacific Time. Prices and availability subject to change without notice.